D0384571

AMERICANA

My life had been in creative and personal ~~chaotic~~ chaos since I'd stopped making records for Arista in the mid 1980's. My band had drifted from one album to another; from one record company to the next; I had embarked on my storyteller shows as a springboard from my book 4 Ray. Blah Blah Blah — I suddenly realized that my life had no plot. NO substance. Also, by simply telling my story I found myself dealing with the issue that my life had been lived mainly as fact and fiction combined. There was actually a ~~blur~~ blur where one started and the other ended. One thing stayed in my thoughts, & all that had happened to me had to mean something; teach me a lesson; I had to learn something about myself before I could reveal it to the world. Perhaps the key to what happened to me was not what actually happened but why I let it happen.

RAY DAVIES

AMERICANA

THE KINKS, THE RIFF, THE ROAD: THE STORY

STERLING
New York

This book is based upon the author's memories and recollection of events. However, the names and identifying characteristics of certain individuals have been changed to protect their privacy, dialogue has been reconstructed to the best of the author's recollection, and some time frames have been compressed.

STERLING
New York

An Imprint of Sterling Publishing
387 Park Avenue South
New York, NY 10016

ISBN 978-1-4027-7891-9

See page 311 for lyric credits and picture credits.

Distributed in Canada by Sterling Publishing
c/o Canadian Manda Group, 165 Dufferin Street
Toronto, Ontario, Canada M6K 3H6

For information about custom editions, special sales, and premium and corporate purchases, please contact Sterling Special Sales at 800-805-5489 or specialsales@sterlingpublishing.com.

Manufactured in the United States of America

2 4 6 8 10 9 7 5 3 1

www.sterlingpublishing.com

FRONTISPIECE: Diary entry, January 9, 2004, while in New Orleans hospital.

For Eva and Natalie
Oliver, Jack and Lily-Rose

Special thanks to
Alma Karen Eyo, Linda McBride, Sarah Lockwood and all at
Konk Studios, Barbara Berger and all the loyal Kinks fans.

CONTENTS

PREFACE

AMERICANA. IT STARTED AS A FLICKERING LIGHT sending black-and-white images through an old movie projector. Faces of cowboys and Indians, superheroes, the good guys victorious over the emissaries of evil. Then as I grew the music took over. Rock, jazz, skiffle . . . the blues . . . and country songs came to liberate me, a north Londoner, growing in up in the austerity of post-war Britain. The music gave me hope and a feeling that I could express myself in song through this new art form called rock and roll. Then, as I toured America with my band, I saw the place first hand and up close—from the roadside of a dreary bus stop in the middle of nowhere to the Hollywood Bowl—as we experienced both good times and bad times. My first impressions were full of romanticized images from childhood recaptured from the relative safety of a tour bus or hotel room. However the real world soon arrived like an uninvited guest and the flickering light of fantasy turned into the cold light of day.

NEW ORLEANS

"You danced and partied at the Mardi Gras
Threw back all the beads at the parade
Fake worlds and logos in the shopping malls
where you came from
Everything looks the same the whole world now

So you headed down south
Left your old hometown
Relocated so far away from the real world
But where is the real world?"

At 8:30 a.m. one morning in the fall of 2002, a husband and wife walked out the door of their detached house, which was neatly placed on the corner of a tree-lined street in New Orleans. As they were getting into their car, two men in an old red sedan approached. One got out, walked over, and began to ask the husband, Brad, for directions before pulling out a shotgun. In a few seconds, the couple had lost control of their liberty and were at the mercy of their captors, who savoured the control the guns had given them. Brad—who worked in the computer industry and was respected by the local community—did as he was told and stayed silent as the thief pushed him firmly but gently into the living room with the pistol pointed into the side of his face.

Meanwhile, an accomplice forced Brad's wife, Peggy, into the car and made her drive to the bank to withdraw as much money as she could from the ATM. Then he brought her back to the home, where she was ordered to lie on the floor next to Brad.

The gunman aimed the shotgun at Brad, pulled the trigger, and shot him in the chest at point-blank range. He then lifted the shotgun toward Peggy's face. The gun jammed, the shooter started to panic, and both the robbers did a runner.

THE REPORT OF THIS BRUTAL KILLING in the *Times-Picayune* made chilling reading. It was horrific and tragic, but apart from the fact that I had been going to and from New Orleans myself at the time it happened, and apart from the fact that I was staying just a few blocks away from the murder, it was still the sort of thing that I thought happened to "other people." Despite the almost blasé claim that New Orleans was the murder capital of America, that one incident stayed in my mind longer than I cared to think about it.

But now I was a shooting victim myself, lying on a gurney in the trauma room at Charity Hospital—a sad, derelict building in New Orleans—with plenty of time to think. Now I was pondering over my own nightmare situation, but at least I was alive, and even though some things had started to make sense, I did wonder how I—a north London fellow—had ended up in this place. It was an uncomfortable predicament to be in, but almost a fitting way to reach this point in what had been a pretty random life to date. The past seemed to come back with relentless clarity—the names, dates, and places flooding back as I lay in bed while the medication flowed and the life-support system did its job. Unexpected memories that jumped in and out of my head seemed to chastise and taunt me as I lay there. "You stupid bastard, what the hell are you doing here?" I asked myself. I had no answer to that question, but I hoped one would eventually emerge before I died.

They were looking for the guy who shot me. A policeman with the unlikely name of Officer Derringer had brought in some smudgy photocopies of suspects, and without seeming disrespectful in any way, I told him that all the suspects looked to me like grubby smudges on the paper. Who was to blame for what happened to me? Was it just a random incident? I wouldn't know for a while. More to the point—why was I here in the first place? Derringer said they had a fix on who the shooter was and had even arrested the driver of the car, but the question kept going around in my mind: "What made this happen?" All sorts of conspiracy theories raced through my head while my system was still in shock.

A few days earlier, a drunk, angry person at a bar had threateningly said to me, "I'll kill you." A common turn of phrase from an irate and emotionally out of control person, but in my present situation the words had taken a new significance. Perhaps I was simply in the wrong place at the wrong time; if anyone had hired a hit man to kill me I'd already be dead—but the thought did cross my mind. Maybe it was my work as a songwriter that drove me to be in this situation. I was looking for a new creative lease on life, and I'd literally lost my way and ended up in this exotic but confusing place. I'd finally finished recording my album in London and was in New Orleans to conclude a writing project and resolve issues in my personal life before returning to mix the record. Then I got shot. My life was in danger; for all I know I was already dead. Now the songs I'd been trying to put together kept going around in my head as if to torment me, and they took me back to where this mess began.

It had all happened in what seemed like a flicker of a moment, and suddenly here I was, just stuck here with drip feeds and wires sticking out of me. I was safe—for the time being, at least. And the morphine was good. . . .

1

THE EMPTY ROOM

"In a room called desolation that resembles a tomb
It's here we find our hero, the subject of this tune
He gets up from the table he walks across the room
He looks out of the window at the clouds of gloom
He turns and sees a mirror reflecting someone he once knew
He feels his nose and mouth and whispers who are you?

No memories to haunt him no ghost to exorcise
No pictures on the table to bring sentimental tears to his eyes
The past belongs to those possessions obligations and the ties
Forced on him so long ago
Now he's wavin' them good-bye
And now he doesn't feel pathetic
Now he's not such a loser after all
That empty room can't torture him because he's dispossessed it all.

Everybody needs an empty room
Those nostalgic memories, they'll drive you to doom
Lose all of those old attachments, start again, and very soon
You'll find yourself just thinking about the life in front of you
You'll be happy and contented in that empty room."

Rumour has it that the first jazz was played on Perdido Street in New Orleans; Louis Armstrong himself was born on a street nearby. The honky-tonk saloons there were the places where he and others like him honed their trade and practiced their art. These horn players developed their hooks and riffs while watching whores pick up customers and then fight one another to decide who was the pimp's favourite. Legend has it that no good music comes about from just good things; that good and evil exist side by side; that music can exist in between the cracks of the real world because music has its own set of rules. The honky-tonks are gone for the most part (except for where the tourists hang out, and those clubs are usually simulated versions of the honky-tonks of the old days), but why is it that blues and jazz are so inseparable from dark places and dubious characters? Dingy clubs, pimps, and whores. It's just a step away from gospel and religious fervour, the uplifting spirit of the soul. Soul; what's that all about? Maybe soul is a good spirit that has journeyed through the dark places and come out happier and wiser on the other side. When I'd played in R&B clubs as a student in London, all these elements surrounded me, but I did not think about it; I just played the music. The music wasn't all about darkness, whores, danger, and bitterness. It was also a celebration of the human spirit, but when I was a teenager the dark danger seemed exciting.

So why was I here? Perhaps I wanted to write about something I could touch and feel. Something about my actual life experience, tangible and in the present. I may have conned myself into thinking that I was going down to New Orleans for a number of artistic reasons, one of which was to find what I thought to be the true essence of American musical culture. This discovery would, according to my thinking, put my own work back on track so that I could either confront or escape my own untidy life. In recent years I had become a transient observer, never settling anywhere and, after a life on the road, never committing to a place or a person.

On the last few Kinks albums I had been writing music for large corporate record labels, which had been hard work. Even though eventually it was creatively rewarding, it had drained my enthusiasm, and the music sounded like the band had tried too hard. I wanted to rediscover what absolute fun it is to write songs. Some of the characters I used to channel the songs from were familiar "friends," but the ideas themselves could still be fresh and exhilarating when written in a new environment. Down-to-earth statements made by real people, not imaginary characters. But in New Orleans, it was the characters I saw on the streets who resonated with me. I might be walking down a street in the French Quarter when something I saw or heard would trigger off a musical idea or catchy lyric that would make me smile and sometimes break out in laughter.

Some people say I write songs about Englishness, but there are great characters all over the world, and in New Orleans they seem to stare you in the face. I felt so at home that I could have been in London talking to a barrow boy in the Petticoat Lane market instead of to a street vendor in New Orleans. That's what makes music universal. It's not the getup or the strut or the pose. It's not a slurry faux accent; it's the people—true characters who can be translated into any culture. I was in my creative "Empty Room," and I was only going to fill it with things I actually needed, not things that were there just to be collected. There would be no more surplus in my life. I felt confident I had found the place that could be my spiritual home.

It was a feeling that I hadn't experienced since the last time I saw my dad sing and dance "Minnie the Moocher" by Cab Calloway. My father had never been out of the United Kingdom, and yet he sang songs about the Missouri and Mississippi. Cab Calloway tunes and Hoagy Carmichael ballads that he must have heard on the radio. He must have heard Paul Robeson sing "Ol' Man River," because his impersonation was eerily close to the original. When I discovered Lead Belly and Big Bill Broonzy, Dad gave his approval. He also loved old movies, but he mispronounced names—including "Humpty Gocart" and "Marion Brand." He had a very basic education; he was self-taught in most things, and as far as I knew he never had a bank account. He carried bundles of cash around and always had a knife in his side pocket so he could peel an apple or skin a rabbit. I saw him do both. He danced in an uncoordinated way, yet with the natural rhythmic elegance of a Watusi warrior. He never held the hand of his partner and swivelled his hips in an un–politically correct way, yet he could charm a woman. Dad was definitely tribal. He had all the moves and gesticulations of a lady-killer but was a devoted family man. With his shirt strategically sticking out through his braces and over his trousers, and with the way he shimmied across the front room when he danced, he was more rock and roll than I was or could ever be.

When I started writing songs I always played them for my dad, and his influences stayed with me. As a result, I would write stuff that could be played on harmonica, guitar or banjo, and washboard and sung by semi-drunk audiences. In New Orleans there would be plenty of those in bars and clubs, as there were at many a Kinks concert. My dad had passed away years earlier, but he was the emotional fabric that held my musical world together. I realised that since my parents had died, part of old London also died in me. It rendered me spiritually homeless. My physical homelessness also reflected a sense that my songs were looking for a new direction. People tell me, "Ray, if the songs are coming good and fast, you are happy."

ONE TOUR HAD BEEN FOLLOWING ANOTHER since I was nineteen. Now decades had passed, and I felt as though I were running out of time. You could say that in song terms, my life was in its climactic part—a very critical second bridge before the final chorus—and it needed to be set up right so that the ending would come in a dazzling flourish of harmony and rhythm and climax in a satisfying cavalcade of dazzling notes. More than anything else, I wanted to end my tune with a sense of satisfaction that it was finally a perfectly structured song. This was far from the reality. Since touring with my band had taken over my life it had been a haphazard quest for a sense of being and belonging. Now I had embarked on an ambitious solo journey that required more virtuoso qualities than my common sense could deliver, and as a result, my personal life started losing its sense of direction. It was like I had started playing a solo and had run out of notes and my backing musicians had cut their losses and gone home. Everyone around me argued otherwise, but that's the way it felt. Still, I continued my solo efforts.

Maybe I had run out of things to say about England, and at the time the whole Britpop phenomenon—without sounding too simplistic and disingenuous—was the last breath of hope for European beat music. To a certain extent, all new contemporary music was regurgitating itself in the mid-1990s. Britpop had been a celebration of the British sensibility that didn't say or add anything new except techno sounds and multicultural rhythms. The England I wrote about had either vanished or only ever existed in my head. The buildings were the same, but the people had gone.

"Mr. Jones my next-door neighbour
I feel I've known you all my life
I haven't seen you for a while now
How's the family? How's that beautiful wife?

I hope your dreams were not forgotten
And you've become downtrodden

Get your health together
Get your wealth together
Get yourself together
Jones, you were my next-door neighbour."

WHEN I WAS GROWING UP IN NORTH LONDON, Britain had a good old-fashioned three-tier political party system of upper, middle, and working classes, exemplified by a Churchillian, bulldog-spirited conservatism on the right and a blue-collar, old-school, labour-defined socialism on the left. The middle classes all seemed to live in suburbia and waffle around in comfortable little corners of the community. When I went to art school I encountered a few "Communists," but they were all affluent and all about the style rather than the politics. They wore long sweaters, smoked dope. I had one college friend whose father had been a famous spy, but when my friend returned to England after visiting his father in Moscow, he would often find himself being followed to the local pub by what he described as British secret service agents. Perhaps this was to ensure that he was not preaching communism to the other students. From what I could glean from him, the Soviet Union was not a very pleasant place to live.

The girls at my art school seemed either long-haired, bohemian Juliette Gréco types or butch with no makeup. Some cut their hair short and claimed to be lesbians mainly so that most of the boys would be afraid to ask them out on dates. The school was full of predominantly middle-class students, but it was clear both by the way I spoke and behaved that I came from a working-class home. It was a relief for me to know that fact. I knew that the posh kids at junior school were middle class, and the upper classes were not seen or heard of because it was rumoured that they rode around on horses at weekends and had chauffeurs to drive them to their schools. When I reached my teens I began to realise that it wasn't as simple as all that, but it was close. Strangely, it did instil a kind of balanced version of England in my head. My dad had brought me up to know that trade unions fought for the rights of the common man against the mean ruling classes. Socialism was to be revered and, on occasions, feared, as it took up the cause of the downtrodden.

Harold Wilson's Labour government had just taken power when my group, the Kinks, became successful, and it remained in power through most of our early career. Taxes were heavy during the late 1960s, so I really had cause to sing "the taxman's taken all my dough" in "Sunny Afternoon." When some money did eventually come after lengthy law suits with my music publishers, I was offered tax-relief plans. My advisers even tried to persuade me to live abroad, but stubbornly and perhaps stupidly I opted to stay put in England and in return get taxed to the hilt. In a strange way I thought I was doing it all for "the revolution" and that it would end up a better, more equal society, but I soon discovered that some people were more equal than others—meaning that there is always someone somewhere who gets to be on top. Even so, I regret not trying to become a tax exile, as many other performers of the time did. That was not my style, in any event, these were the days before global television sport, so I wouldn't have been able to go to Arsenal home football games if I were stuck in the Cayman Islands or Monte Carlo.

In the 1970s, I even left my working-class roots in London to live in the commuter-belt comfort of semirural Surrey, among Tories and upper-class toffs. I never owned a horse, but I had a stable and a barn if ever I needed one. Why not? I was finally earning a few bob and chose to find a place where my kids could have some space when they came to visit. My parents could share in some of my success by staying with me at weekends. However, I was never swayed to become conservative or Tory. I might have lived in a country cottage surrounded by rolling hills, but in my head it was still a small tene-ment in Holloway. My dilemma was that I valued many traditional aspects of the past that are associated with conservatism, but that is often the case with working-class people. Still I remained a staunch Labour supporter even in the mid-1990s, when the Labour party I had been brought up to believe in had become an outdated and somewhat ineffective force. As Margaret Thatcher gradually eroded any clout the unions had, it was becoming clear that the socialism of my father was becoming a spent force. After the well-respected thespian Glenda Jackson announced she was cutting back on acting to become a member of the Labour Party, I thought to myself, "Which

Labour Party is that, then? The New or Old?" When the Berlin Wall came down, even the old-style Russian communism started to fade. The trendy "lefties" I once knew referred to themselves as Marxists. While the dreaded Iron Curtain had been lifted, for some reason I mourned it, because now the division between left and right would be even more blurred.

The last connection with my perception of "Old Labour" died with a man called John Smith. For a while he was leader of the Labour Party when they were in opposition. I'd met him briefly at the airport in Copenhagen when we were both in transit. He spoke and looked the way a good old-fashioned Labour leader should. He even downed a pint of lager while he ate breakfast, but I put that down to him wanting to appear to be one of the chaps.

One morning in May of 1994, I was driving through the tastefully land-scaped Surrey countryside when the radio news broke that John Smith had died. For some reason I was so deeply moved that I stopped at a picture-postcard church in Ockham to go inside and say a prayer for the deceased Socialist. It was then that I realised that I was in effect saying a prayer mourning the loss of the Labour movement that my father had brought me up to believe in. That in a way I had been suckered into aspiring to the "good life" in the sedate Surrey countryside. The political world in the UK was about to be treated to a dose of "New Labour"—a seamless blend of polite socialism meshed into conservative policies and a dreaded political correctness that the seemingly benign Tony Blair and his followers would gradually finesse to an Orwellian level. The telegenic, smiling face of Mr. Blair was every-where. We, the British, were also about to become one of the most scruti-nised CCTV nations on the planet; Big Brother had actually arrived, and it was only a matter of time before the world would become a TV reality show.

On May 2, 1997, the day Tony Blair was elected and his "New" Labour swept to power, I was in New York. I watched his "coronation" on TV; he enraptured his adoring audience with a presidential, winning style. The reality was that years of Thatcherism had helped reduce a country's morale to such an extent that it helped make this possible.

A pompous-sounding political commentator berated every fallen Tory politician. "That's Heseltine. . . . Well, his political career is over. . . . Back to the Home Counties for him and Thatcher; what fate awaits her?" It was as though the commentator, who was live from London, was ready to announce the guillotine for the vanquished politicians. I found myself speaking to the TV screen: "Nice one, Tone . . . enjoy today before you find out what kind of mess awaits you." My sense of political balance had been shifted. To me, Tony Blair looked, preached, and behaved like a Tory. The New Labour Party didn't speak for working people anymore, but I felt a little like a phony for not doing anything more political than to just refer to politics in my songs. At least Glenda Jackson was getting stuck into what she was allowed to do from the back benches as an MP, which was more than I was doing. There was in fact nothing I could do. New Labour was bound to happen.

I walked out to a coffee shop on Columbus Avenue and was relieved to hear that nobody had heard of Tony Blair and, for that matter, some people hadn't even known that an election was happening at all. It was a few months before Lady Diana died tragically in Paris; when Tone took centre stage he helped sow the seeds of celebrity culture. I had to face the fact that it was Mr. Blair's time: this could not be denied. Old Labour had become as redundant as an old scratchy 78-rpm record in the digital age. The only way to survive was not to be around to witness the self-congratulatory hubris. On the other hand, perhaps I felt dated myself because my version of Britain belonged to another time. The Industrial Revolution was finally over, as was the Empire, the Commonwealth, and the working-class hero. A new class was emerging that was more educated; well-mannered, but more conspiratorial, ruthless, and a tad insincere.

This all coincided with the arrival of the Britpop music movement. The Kinks and I were cited as being the inspiration for the new "scene," which included bands like Blur, with their professional suburban Cockney attitude, and Pulp, who, aside from making fine pop records and playing for the "common people," looked as though they could fit in at a fox hunt ball rather than a working-class dance hall. The Kinks had worn pretentious, aristocratic red hunting jackets when we first started, but we only had to open our mouths and the world knew that we were baseborn. It was the beginning of a new political and musical order, only it was more corporate and "posher." Supergrass had become the new Small Faces; Oasis, the new Beatles. Blur and Pulp cited the Kinks as being inspirational to them. Enfants terribles and agents provocateurs both, with witty, cleverly crafted songs that would appeal to the emerging, educated, style-savvy middle-class, laddish culture, but they were to the point of almost being too politically correct.

There was a "fancy-Dan" element to Britpop's beat that claimed to be inspired by but was slightly condescending toward the 1960s. The only problem was that at that time I felt that all the music seemed to have been crafted by the same PR people as Tony Blair's spin doctors. I was invited to a party that celebrated my contribution to the musical new "wave"; I felt truly honoured to be associated with it, but my RSVP wasn't sent. I was on a different journey.

"Now all the lies are beginning to show,
And you're not the country that I used to know.
I loved you once from my head to my toes,
But now my belief is shaken.

And all your ways are so untrue,
No one breaks promises the way that you do.
You guided me, I trusted you,
But now my illusion's shaken
Thought this empire would be here
At least a thousand years.
But all my expectations and aspirations,
Slowly disappeared.

Now all the lies have gone on too long,
And a million apologies can't right the wrong.
Soldiers die but the lies go on,
But soon we will awaken.

In our expectations for the future,
We were not to know.
We had expectations, now we've reached
As far as we can go.

And all your manners are too, too polite,
Just to prove that your conscious is white and bright.
You had your day so get ready for the night,
For another dawn is breaking.

We had expectations, now we've reached
As far as we can go."

I WAS TO DISCOVER THAT AMERICA is made up of many cultures and nationalities. Since the late 1990s, I had became acquainted with a girl from the Midwest named Rory.*

I met Rory during a meet and greet after a show. She and her then-boyfriend lived in a small town in Minnesota and claimed to have hung out at Prince's studio when he was at the height of his fame in the 1980s. My band made jokes about her, referring to her as Miss Minnesota whenever we did a date in that vicinity. She was the epitome of rock chic. Long slim frame, she must have been five foot ten, even without the high heels. She had flowing natural blonde hair that came down to her waist and piercing blue eyes that gave away what must have been Scandinavian origins. It figured when she explained that she'd grown up in St. Paul, which was well known for its Scandinavian heritage. She flicked her hair out of her eyes as she described how the Scandinavians had originally come to America to pop-ulate the Midwest probably because of the climate, which resembled their own. The winters could be icy cold and the summers crisp and hot, just like Rory's personality. Rory spoke seven languages. She used to drive me around in her beaten-up Chevy and played me traditional northern European folk music, which I found full of monumental brooding chords and weird rhythm shifts that had to have had an impact on American folk music. (When we played country music in the car though she would sometimes sing lyrics in what Swedish she knew, occasionally adding a few duck noises. She claimed that her mother had been a flight attendant on Republic, which I sometimes referred to as "Duck Airlines" because of the duck painted on the fuselage.)

Being around Rory made me acutely aware of the diverse cultural influences that had been absorbed into the American continent—how other cultures had impacted onto and influenced American folk music. The blues had supposedly come from Africa and then the South, whereas North American folk music was influenced by northern European immigrants who'd come to build new lives in the land of opportunity. The Scottish, Irish, and Scandinavian culture had all influenced and contributed to the phenomenon I knew as Americana.

Rory was much younger than me, but she had an Old World wisdom that impressed me. To be truthful I was more than a little flattered to have her around. She was the "chick" that every rock and roller should have on the arm. I was astounded to see that while she had the tall, slim figure of a fashion model she could eat like a horse. I could only attribute her leanness to the fact that she burned off the calories by keeping out the cold, which was a necessity in Midwest winters.

However, the thing that clinched it for me was that Rory said that she originally came from St. Paul. When I was kid and played guitar with my brother Dave we often sang a song called "Big River" by one of our heroes, Johnny Cash, who claimed in the song to have met a woman accidently in a bar in St. Paul. That coincidence settled it for me; even though in Mr. Cash's song "Big River" he ended up crying floods of tears for "that" woman, I was still not deterred. I hoped that I would survive. But who was I kidding? I didn't need anyone to cause my downfall—I was more than capable of causing it myself.

Rory was well-educated and smart. Despite her dazzling good looks, she appeared to have a lot of soul attached to a natural wisdom that made it easy for me to confide in her. More to the point, she was not a groupie, even though she would have been top of her league if she had decided to be so.

She seemed like me in some ways. We had both reached a watershed in our lives and felt the need to move on to pastures new but did not know how.

IN 2000, I TOOK MY FIRST TRIP TO NEW ORLEANS. The day before I left, Rory called me and asked me why I felt the need to go there. I simply replied that I thought that I might find some interesting subjects and better musical riffs down there. Maybe it—whatever "it" is—was a chance to explore parts of my creativity that had been lying dormant and trying to escape. The Kinks had played New Orleans several times on tours, but we always left as soon as the gigs were over. Maybe it was the years on the road and disillusionment with my homeland that attracted me to this city—the search for one elusive place similar to the one I had seen as a kid in a Belgian documentary about Big Bill Broonzy.

My idea of musical surrealist nirvana existed in a twilight world where music can be played deep into the night in a mysterious subterranean setting. This imaginary nirvana, the Riff Club, had existed for me since I first played in Soho as a teenage guitar player. I had lived the dream once and wanted to recapture it. Now I felt the need to find the elusive "Riff" again in order to tie up all the loose ends in my life, so I could finally say to myself that at least I tried to discover the reason I went on this weird journey. I'd created my own big riff—my band's first success—with "You Really Got Me." Whenever I created a subsequent riff, an image of the Riff Club came into my head.

I thought again about Rory's question: Why go to New Orleans? Because a riff was there, waiting to be discovered. I thought, why not give it a try? After much persuasion, she'd agreed to come with me, so we met up where I was staying in New York and then headed out to Kennedy Airport. It would not take more than a few hours before we would find ourselves in New Orleans, which was like nowhere else in America. A mixture of France and Spain, with the Caribbean—especially Cuba—thrown in for good measure.

Heading down south would be quintessential to my American experience so I took home-movie footage out the car window on the way to the airport. The Twin Towers of the World Trade Center were in the distance, drifting in and out of autofocus as we drove across the Triborough Bridge. Thinking back, it would be the last shot I would ever take of them. That camera stayed with me on all my trips to the South and on all my visits back and forth to London and to Ireland, where my infant daughter was living. I was hardly ever in any shot because I was putting a version of my life together and writing a soundtrack to go with it. Later, as I watched the images play back through the camera, I wondered what version of reality I was actually living in. It was unclear what was the real world and what was fake.

The cab passed the old TWA terminal, which was like a derelict reminder of the glory days of Howard Hughes–style air travel. When it opened in the 1960s, the terminal was a state-of-the-art, futuristic example of what passenger-driven aviation should represent—an architectural dream with large arches, extravagant stairways, and spacious check-in areas. In 1996, TWA flight 800 came down over Long Island, killing all on board. The company declared bankruptcy in spring 2001, and ceased to operate independently. The only thing missing from the otherwise immaculate but empty building was the odd dinosaur wandering around to give the place an authentically prehistoric feel.

We had left the apartment in New York in such haste that I forgot to pack my passport, and there was a new policy about identification at check-in for domestic flights. Missing the flight because of identification issues was not an option. I happened to have a copy of a book I'd written with a picture of me on the back, so after much persuasion the check-in clerk allowed me to get a ticket. A year or so later, after 9/11, this would have been an impossibility.

There was open seating on the plane, so we managed to get into aisle and middle seats only to discover that the woman in the aisle seat across from us was already vomiting over her Mardi Gras beads. We had seen her earlier in the bar in the airport lounge—where some people were already stumbling around drunk and talking to themselves—and compared to everyone else she actually had seemed quite sensible. Now we were only halfway through the two-and-a-half-hour flight, trapped on a full plane, and sitting in a "vomit corner."

When we finally arrived, the woman was still drinking, but somehow she got it together in time to be the first to collect her baggage. She was out of the airport before anyone else was—probably headed straight for a bar on Bourbon Street.

They call New Orleans the Crescent City; if you look at it from high above as you fly in across Lake Pontchartrain you see the Mississippi River snaking through it. Louis Armstrong Airport seems small when you get off the plane, and a party atmosphere continued through to the baggage claim area as tourists ready to revel were already celebrating. We were picked up by J.J.*, a local club manager who a friend from a record company had asked to show me around. J.J. was a vivacious brunette at first glance, but she became more world-weary the longer you looked at her. Her knowledge of retro blues and little-known R&B was at times overwhelming, and she gave the impression she had sat on a bar stool in every music club in America. She had great teeth, but a dark gaze that could kill from a mile away. She looked people up and down and spoke in a way that implied a subtext—that she wanted more from them emotionally than they were prepared to give. There was no small talk with J.J.; she went straight into you. She looked Rory up and down as she spoke to me.

"You'd be welcome to stay at my place, only it's full already. I didn't expect two of you."

She drove us to the hotel, which was slap in the middle of the French Quarter, near Bourbon Street, full of more partying tourists and, yes, more vomit. People wandered aimlessly around with frozen daiquiris and hurricane cocktails in plastic containers clutched in their hands. A tall, black, athletic-looking porter carried our bags to our room and started eyeballing me when he heard my English accent. He casually explained that the room he was taking us to was haunted, as was most of the French Quarter.

It turned out that the room we were in was an old slave quarters, and I lay awake wondering how they could've packed fifty slaves into such a small room. The porter had spooked me out and left a very strange impression on me. His eyes rarely blinked; they stared out from the sockets so that all that could be seen were the whites of his eyes. In a bad black-and-white B movie, this would have been a sure sign that the porter was a member of the undead. His "hex" had worked on me—he must do it to every tourist who visited the hotel—and the frozen daiquiris I drank afterward didn't help.

The next day we moved to a B&B in the Marigny district, a quieter area away from the hustle and bustle of the French Quarter. I was booked in for approximately two weeks, but was going to look for someplace more permanent if I decided to come back in the future. I chilled out for a couple of days and took an instant liking to the city, although I was still undecided about living in New Orleans, and needed to explore the place first.

---

* Composite character   17

I went to the Circle Bar for a drink, where I met a local journalist who asked me why I liked New Orleans. I said that even though I had only been in town for a few days, it felt like there was no musical snobbery in the city; you didn't have to be a jazz musician, a rock musician, or a folk musician— you could be anything you wanted; it was all music, that's what appealed to me. He later wrote a very complimentary piece in the local paper, welcoming me to the musical "community." No one else had ever said that to me, let alone put it in print—not even in London—so that made me feel at home.

I borrowed a four-track recorder from a musician friend and a keyboard from a local studio and started writing in the spare room at the front of the B&B. The sounds of the freight trains were the first thing to strike me, as though the trains were accompanying me on the journey. They were a constant reminder that I was not committed to or settled in any place. This was a testing ground for me rather than a definite relocation. The songs were coming, but it was the haunted quality of the place itself that affected me most. It was a friendly place but there were a lot of lost souls down there, and perhaps I was just another one of them. Songs about lost souls in haunted places summed up my predicament perfectly. Who was I, and where was I going? I bought a Big Chief notepad at Winn-Dixie and took a streetcar called Desire. Walked to Elysian Fields and fell in love with the place. It fascinated me but disturbed me.

THE TOURIST

"I'm just another tourist
Walking around the slums
With my plastic Visa
Out drinking with my chums.
I dance and sway while Abba play and I flash my platinum
To the sound of 'Livin' la Vida Loca'
While in the heat of the street
The native beats his drum

Take the money 'cause it's just another tourist
Having lots of fun."

E verybody is entitled to their own opinion, and some people who are supposed to be in the know say that without a doubt New Orleans is the place
that spawned the origins of rock and roll. My impression is that even though
rock music is represented in the city by clubs like the House of Blues, the
Howlin' Wolf, and various other venues around town, rock doesn't exist
much there, or even strike me as being more popular than any other kind of
music. I had the feeling that in the Big Easy music is considered good as long
as it swings and you can dance to it.

A lot of my songs try to tell a story; most songs I write have an intro
and then a verse that sets the landscape; then a chorus that reminds the
listener what the song is about; and a middle eight, which is the relief, or
the breakout, or the "journey-back" section. Life is like a song that can be
performed in many styles using different techniques, but basically it pans
out the same shape whether we like it or not. The end can be a fade-out or a
fulfilling climax, depending on how the interpretation of the song evolves.
Some songs just stop dead, without being fulfilled, and all that work done
in the buildup amounts to zero. I didn't want that to be my fate; so I wrote.

My first mornings in New Orleans were spent in the B&B listening
to traditional jazz on WWOZ, the local community radio station sponsored by the New Orleans Jazz and Heritage Festival and Foundation. "The
Darktown Strutters' Ball" wafted in from the next room while I wrote down
some rough lyrics to a new song. Soul and blues classics punctuated my days
while I tried to instil myself with some fresh musical energy. I hoped these
new songs wouldn't be too Anglophile or, worse still, an attempt to mimic
the regional soundscape. Announcements about upcoming concerts at the
Funky Butt, Tipitina's, and Snug Harbor would play on the radio while I
drank my morning coffee and ate a cake from the bakery on the corner. I
stopped trying to write "blues" when my first hit, "You Really Got Me," made
the charts. When I'd written the song as a teenager, I thought I was writing
something that John Lee Hooker or Howlin' Wolf could record, but I was
just a "honky" from North London, so what did I know? I always sought out

a great riff, but would put my own spin on it thereafter in order to retain some originality. I sang in my London accent, which in many ways separated my band from the rest of the Brit Blues–influenced rock bands: Cream, Led Zeppelin, and others, who also used riffs similar to "You Really Got Me." That signature "riff" was also later credited with laying the groundwork for the heavy-metal movement, even though I still claim that it was a naive attempt on my part to write a legitimate blues-jazz track. When "You Really Got Me" came out, there was nothing like it on the radio in the UK or America, so it catapulted our career. Now I was in New Orleans—not to copy, but be inspired by the music of the region.

The nights were spent trying to avoid going out to clubs with friends; I knew these clubs would involve drinking and the obligatory "hang" with other club-goers, but after the live music stopped playing, I soon got bored, made my excuses, and left. When I arrived "home" I would spend the night refining new ideas whilst trying to write down the clustered notes of the trains and riverboat siren as it passed along the Mississippi; dissonant yet reassuring at the same time. The ghostlike freight trains were still heading into town, appearing as old friends during my sleepless nights. There was a voice starting to emerge that came from within me rather than from the characters I'd been watching.

"*Every time I hear that lonesome train roll down the track*
Going away to unknown destinations
I believe there's someone out there making the great escape . . ."

These fragments were setting the scene; a setup for a big story that I hadn't worked out yet. There seemed no reason to go anywhere, so I just kept the thoughts happening. Maybe my subconscious knew that I was in the right place but for the wrong reason; perhaps these thoughts were articulating the dreams of someone else who was fast asleep in the next room. I started a song called "The Art of Moving On." Maybe I knew there was a significant message in there for me that I was afraid to confront. I still hadn't moved on emotionally from my marriage, from my country, and, more significantly, from my old band—the Kinks. I knew I had to find a new band because before now, there was always the band to convey my ideas to the world; now I was in the process of trying to record without them. The first line of "The Art of Moving On" is:

"I must remember never to say I remember."

My problem was that I kept remembering—and it wasn't all good.

I stared up at the fan in the ceiling going around and around like a wheel, which put me in a hypnotic state. Time and place didn't seem to matter.

2

WINGS OF FANTASY

"When I'm far away in some godforsaken place
That I'm driving through
When my emotions turn to blue I think of you . . .
Living day to day, building up the debt
Living in excess, getting in over your head, not caring less
Wish I could set you free over the insanity
Imagining you and me flying on the wings of fantasy."

SURREY, ENGLAND, SEPTEMBER 2001

My demo CD of new songs played on my car stereo as I drove and skidded at high speed on a dark country road. The headlights flashed on looming trees with branches thrusting tentacles out like terrified phantoms. My private life had exploded, and I didn't care. Bits of me were scattered everywhere. It was like a bad film noir, but this was really happening. My suitcases were in storage, I was afraid to move on and throw away the past, yet at the same time I was scared to live in the moment and uncertain about the future. One thing was for sure: I knew I couldn't die. That would be too corny. I had to live through this. My own song played on the car stereo and seemed to add a soundtrack of foreboding that summed up my predicament:

"So high in the sky while down here I just wonder why
Am I part of nature's scheme or just a man in a machine?
Burning oil and turning wheels
Living in denial chasing the dream
Running faster and faster but running out of steam
Living the illusion accelerating past

The world in a blur but we're finishing fast so
I fly on the wings of fantasy . . ."

I sneezed. The car swerved over. I blacked out for a second and lost control. The sneeze had diverted my attention for that crucial moment as my body went into an involuntary spasm. I blinked as I sneezed, and that was it. I slammed on the brakes instinctively and skidded to a stop. The Mercedes was much too powerful and sophisticated for a mechanical incompetent like myself. There were some headlamps facing me. There was an eerie silence on the road, and for a moment I thought the mechanical monster glaring at me with its lights full on had no one at the wheel. I took stock of the situation and saw that I'd glanced the side of a passing Land Rover. Luckily, it was a quiet English country road. If it had been in town there would have been a pileup. I exchanged numbers and insurance details with the other driver, a horsey lady with a Lady Di hairdo and two aristocratic-looking pedigreed dogs sneering down their noses at me from the backseat. No damage done, but the Lady Di look-alike double-checked for scratches anyway.

She blamed me. I tried to blame my allergies. I always hated cars in any event; don't understand them; just point them and go. Once I had a flat tire and called the Automobile Association and hid behind a tree in shame while my girlfriend at the time asked the mechanic to put on the spare. The AC does my sinuses in, and the gas fumes, too; there is no way I can get used to the damn effects. They make me sneeze. During certain physical actions— sneezing, coughing, going to the bathroom—we are so focused and in the moment that we lose touch with everything around us. I tried to explain all this to the woman driver, but it was pitch-black and she didn't give a damn anyway. We exchanged details and then drove off. As I continued to drive I thought about my near miss.

It's like when song ideas come. I plan/contrive all sorts of clever-dick musical moves, but then out of the blue good things happen. Can't remember the exact time or place. A chemical clicks into place, and the idea occurs.

I had earned my chops as a London lad playing in my band, the Kinks, but then after a few hits I had become a transplant from the city to this refined country location, and for a while it had left my creativity blocked. I'd

love and lust beneath those layers of petticoats. Pioneers with Scandinavian features and ladies with Max Factor complexions, chiselled noses, trim waists, and piercing blue eyes. Or the Katy Jurado look: dark, half villainous, seductive, knowing full well that she'll get the bad deal in the end and maybe even a bullet as payment for her devotion. Shooting from those beautiful hips—eyes ablaze with passion. And then the bandy-legged hero. Always a Scott or a Brett someone or a Brad or Dexter somebody. Lance, maybe. Square-jawed, steely eyes, and a smile just like Kennedy, that president from past lost hope. Clean-cut Bostonian pin-striped collar, as aristocratic as his missus—she full of southern connections, sassy, slightly snobbish, as if there were a bad smell under her nose to keep that aloof look. Slow-mo eyes on pink-tinted blowups of Mr. Zapruder's 8mm show vulnerability in the eyes. The fear and realisation of the horror. Caught in an indelible freeze-frame. All these fragmented images of my youth. I wanted to see the real thing; be there; experience firsthand that Americana. And the cars. The bloody auto-mobiles: the distance, full of possibilities and mystique. The movies. Heroes with suntans and perfect teeth riding into the sunset on the trail to the West.

"I had this dream America was always a very special place
Heroes of the old Wild West
Wild Bill Hickok and the rest
Now I see it fall from grace
'Cause reality has hit me in the face
Hey, hey, hey, I am riding on the interstate
All across America
Along the great highway."

The great highway was still out there, but now, because of the new "terror," the road to freedom seemed blocked. My phone interviews with Boston, Philadelphia, and New York didn't happen that day because everything seemed to have shut down. The first few shows had to be moved because of the chaotic state of affairs and airline disruptions. Concert tours by other artists had been cancelled, even though I was adamant that my tour would go ahead.

Now I was without my band, my creative unit, which was almost a substitute for my family unit. My marriage was also at an end. I thought about saving it—which meant virtually retiring and going to live in Ireland—but America was starting to beckon.

The year 2001 was the year the world changed forever. The buildings' collapse was more than just an act of terror; it symbolised the world as we knew it coming to an end. The bombers believed that virgins would be waiting in heaven to greet them. I wrote songs to try to understand why the world had finally gone mad.

In the months prior to the event, I had spent most of my time alone in a secluded house in the country, and that's where my extreme insomnia began. I had the feeling that if I stayed there alone for too long it would drive me over the edge, so I felt the need to move out in order to start my album. I had more or less split from my band in 1996 and toured with my solo show *Storyteller*, which, while it had many "new" songs, had been predominately made up of my old Kinks material. Great as the old songs are, as much as I loved them and still do, my new songs were telling me "Things must change."

Everything had a new meaning. I needed to leave England.

I WAS BECOMING politically estranged from my homeland. I'm not saying that the eastern bloc was a good thing—in fact it was, by all accounts, an evil place—but I actually missed the Cold War, because then we knew who the bad guys were. In 1989, when President George H. W. Bush heard that the Berlin Wall was coming down and that the Cold War was apparently over, he did not seem happy. Maybe he knew this would be the type of war America could not win. In 2001, his son reacted the same way when he was told about the terrorist attacks. The European Union was starting to erode what was left of the UK. Now the U. S. was under attack. My youngest daughter was safe in Ireland, at least, but gradually I was losing contact with my own culture and becoming cut off from reality. The world was entering a dark place and taking me with it. I felt as though I'd imploded personally and professionally. The only way through it, to justify my existence, would be to finish my solo record.

I tried hard to put some musicians together, but I couldn't find the right combination. I made lots of demos, knowing they would never be released. In

August 2000 I did a concert at the Jane Street Theatre in New York, where I performed new material—"Otis Riffs" and "Stand-Up Comic," among others. I had done the concert with an assortment of New York musician friends led by the band Yo La Tengo. Although my record company wanted to record the songs straightaway, I delayed starting the record until I had the right band.

Travelling back and forth from Surrey to London to try to find a new band, and the ping-pong travel from London to Ireland to New York to play material for record companies, was becoming arduous. The shuttling back and forth started to take its toll after a while, and I have never been a good traveller. It was like I was living in a permanent state of jet lag. In between, there would be *Storyteller* shows to keep me occupied. I tried an assortment of players, but while they were good as individuals they didn't seem to gel as a band. The original Kinks band was never renowned for its great individual players. My brother, Dave, was an innovative and powerful guitar player, while I was a fair-to-middling pianist, guitar player, and singer. Drummer Mick Avory seemed to slot into Pete Quaife, who had a certain flair on the bass, but none of us were what could be considered virtuoso musicians. When we came together though, we were a great band. The players on my new demo songs played professionally, but they seemed too perfect. I was longing for those happy mistakes, those errors that make a band unique. John Lee Hooker and Howlin' Wolf were not what anyone could describe as great technical players, but it was their feel that had inspired Dave and me—that almost clumsy attitude on guitar that made them appealing and gave the music that magical word, "soul."

For a while I stopped going up to our Konk Studios in North London to make demos and used Paul Weller's Black Barn studio in Ripley, Surrey, near where I was staying. I even dragged my old drummer, Mick Avory, off the golf course to play on a couple of demo recordings. The sessions down at Black Barn produced a few songs I was really proud of. "Cover Band" was about a band trying to present new work, but after they got a gig in a bar, the owner insisted they play cover songs that all the drunks could sing along to. It was meant to be a sad song full of pathos, but it started to get sniggers from the musicians once the lyrics set in. In the same session we laid down "The Fields are on Fire," a song about a recent outbreak of foot-and-mouth disease that resulted in thousands of cattle being slaughtered, which led to fields full of burning cattle carcasses all over the UK. If the song had been set in Colorado or Montana, it might have resonated in a profound way, but I chose to set it in Devon, England—the most provincial of places—and when it was played back, it got a mixed reaction. Then there was a tune called "Poetry," about someone lost in a shopping mall in middle America, buying clothes from retail chains, eating at fast food restaurants, only to have the singer deliver the venomous line, *"And in a shopping mall somewhere you'll fall down on your knees crying out loud, 'Where is the Poetry?'"*

I realised that the other vital ingredients in a band were sensibility and, most important, a sense of humour.

All these songs showed promise, but I needed a focus. My songs are important to me—I have known for a long time that I am a lousy communicator except for my songs, and more than anything else my songs define me as a person—but this seemed irrelevant as I began my tour after 9/11.

BURNING BRIDGES, AMERICAN TOUR
SEPTEMBER 2001

"It was a really beautiful day
Not a cloud up in the sky
But nighttime falls and trouble's brewing
Say to myself, 'What are you doing?
What are you proving?
You can't keep living a lie.'"

It was September 21, 2001, and I'd never flown on such an empty aeroplane. The cabin staff seemed particularly on edge and focused on anyone going near an exit or to a toilet, particularly if that person was in the area near the pilot's cabin. There was a feeling of unease all around. Logan Airport in Boston was normally one of the friendliest airports to arrive in, but on this occasion we were confronted with unusually stern-faced customs officials.

The next day, at the sound check at Harvard's Sanders Theatre in Cambridge, I launched into an improvised instrumental as Pete Mathison played along. It was a drifting song with no apparent structure, and as I played it I considered the possibility that words are not enough or too trivial to express an emotion and that an instrumental sometimes has much more power to connect. I was unusually nervous before the show, which had sold out. I was concerned about doing my best and being respectful, but I was basically there to entertain—to take people's minds off the world, which was impossible to do in America at that time.

When I walked onstage that evening, I received an ovation that seemed to go on forever. It was as though people were appreciative simply of the fact that we risked coming to America at this time and that we had turned up at all. Many other artists had postponed tours and even used the attacks as an excuse not to fly, but in some strange way the situation gave me a reason to play in order to bring some sense of normalcy back to a world that had gone crazy.

We were scheduled to do the *Late Night with Conan O'Brien* TV show on September 25, and on the solemn flight down to New York, the aircraft seemed to glide in an uncertain directionless manner as if the pilot was trying to protect us from seeing what was below. There was a collective sigh from all the passengers as we passed over the Ground Zero site, still smouldering beneath us. We took a gradual turn across Long Island toward Kennedy Airport and saw the smoke cloud spiralling up into the sky. The trip into the city by car was equally sombre.

We arrived at the NBC studio still not sure of what song we were going to perform. Every song lyric seemed to have a new meaning. At this time, certain songs were banned from the radio by Clear Channel, which was, understandably, particularly sensitive about their programming. Backstage we discussed with the music department which song to perform, and after a long debate we opted for the song "Days," almost as a song of remembrance. Max Weinberg, the show's bandleader, said that he lived in New Jersey and knew some people who were in the buildings. Jimmy, the band's guitar player, was unusually quiet. It was not even two weeks since the incident, and everybody was coming up with their own remembrances of that day. Someone with the NBC backstage staff told us that somebody he knew in the fire department had said they'd found a stewardess's arm in another building close to the impact building, and the hands were still tied together at the back. I found this particularly gruesome. He also said that several people who lived in his town had been killed in the disaster.

The show itself went off without a hitch, and the house band gave a professional and moving performance.

We didn't hang around in New York after the show; we drove out from the NBC building to Somerset, New Jersey, where we were to stay overnight before driving on to the next gig in Falls Church, Virginia. As we left New York City and entered the tunnel to New Jersey at night, the tall skyscrapers looked unusually ominous; I thought back to the artwork for the Kinks' album *Phobia*, which had depicted New York as a city in flames and corporate society descending into Armageddon. It was a relief to get across into New Jersey. The gaping floodlit hole downtown made it look like a giant concrete tooth had been extracted from the mouth of New York City. We played lots of music in the car, particularly the Stanley Brothers, Lucinda Williams, and some old Cajun music. We left Somerset the next morning and headed for the next venue along the great highway.

The band travelled mainly by van, which was driven by my tour manager, a tough Liverpudlian who insisted we fly the British Union Jack on the side of our van as a show of support for America. Flights were very rare, because there was no guarantee they would even leave, let alone get to their destinations, and we couldn't risk missing a date. So we played it safe and went by road overnight where possible.

After Falls Church, we headed to Cleveland. The hotel in Cleveland was one of those spacious turn-of–the-century buildings that must have gone up at the time when horse-drawn coaches drove up to the elegant entrance and deposited passengers arriving for a ball. I imagined the ghosts of these people still walking in and out, a strange parade checking in. I pondered over how many people had stayed in the room I was staying in and about the anonymity of living in hotels.

The TV in my room was broadcasting scenes of people rioting in Afghanistan, and Mayor Rudolph Giuliani seemed to be on all the time with new sound bites. CNN, as usual, played the same fifteen minutes over and over, like a recurring nightmare. I suddenly realised I had a fear of heights; was there any wonder?

The Cleveland show was at a smaller venue, befitting my more intimate *Storyteller* show. Afterward, local promoter Jules Belkin came backstage and congratulated me on the performance. We discussed the old days of touring with the Kinks, and we tried to work out how many shows we'd done together. The talk turned, inevitably, to the impact of the disaster on business; Jules reassured me that the turnout had been good, considering the circumstances.

We arrived in Kansas City on October 7, the day the coalition forces started bombing Afghanistan, and there were fans outside the venue with banners saying: "Welcome to our British allies." All along the trip, houses were flying the Stars and Stripes in a moving display of patriotism.

Eventually we got on a flight from Denver to San Francisco, and then we took the coast road down to Los Angeles, which had its own take on the situation; the hotel where we stayed had a neon sign displaying an electronic Stars and Stripes. Only in La La Land could this happen.

All through the tour, I was playing the local radio and listening out for new American music to inspire me, but it was the old blues and Cajun CDs we played in the car that drew me in. By the time we arrived back on the East Coast to play the last concert at the Westbury Music Fair on October 30, the World Series was in full swing. During the last song of my concert, someone shouted up from the audience something about the baseball game that was being played that night. I just said that I hoped they (the audience) would win their battle, because I had just won mine by simply getting through this difficult tour. The drive into New York was edgy, and there were roadblocks into the city. The police stopped our van because I had been videotaping the Empire State Building from the van window, and for a moment they threatened to confiscate my camera if I didn't erase the footage I had just shot. The New York City marathon was scheduled to take place during the upcoming weekend, and I was shocked to discover that the race was allowed to go ahead. The city seemed so vulnerable and exposed after the attacks a month earlier, but on reflection it was sending a clear signal that the American way of life would go on regardless.

We got through the 2001 U.S. tour, but somehow I had still not found the real musical America that had inspired me as a young musician. America had symbolized adventure, possibilities, and fulfilment of ambition, not the wounded and tormented giant I had just been travelling through. I wanted to remember the good times as they were.

BACK IN THE DAY

"Back in the day when we were little kids
We used to imitate the latest hit parade
And sang the good old songs.
The radio would play
And all those movie stars
Would live a fantasy
With all those pretty chicks
And all those handsome dudes
With all those way-out moves.
Back in the day."

As a child, I was fascinated with most things American. The members of my large family were all movie fans and loved watching American films. Like other boys my age, I'd sit in the cinema all Saturday morning, watching westerns and gangster movies. The images up on the screen were so glamorous and exciting compared to the dreary struggle to rebuild Europe after the destruction of the 1940s. If I didn't exactly want to be American, I at least wanted to experience part of that world.

Toward the end of the Second World War, my parents moved away from the inner city to escape the war-torn London slums and bombed-out buildings. During the Blitz, when Germany bombed London, approximately 43,000 Londoners were killed and 50,000 injured; more than one million dwellings were destroyed.

A few years before I was born they say my mother took a day off from looking after her daughters in rented rooms in Holloway, Islington, in Inner

London, and in a gesture of prefeminist defiance took a bus a few miles up the road to the London suburb of East Finchley, where she got off to walk around the green parklands dotted around North London. It was not far to travel in miles, but for a working-class woman of that time it was a brave and seemingly foolhardy venture. There were tree-lined streets, and it was more gentrified than the back-to-back terraces of Blundell Street and Pentonville, which still bore the mark of the Industrial Revolution. Mum wasn't ambitious for herself, but she was determined to find a better life for her family while her husband, Fred, was busy trying to make a living in the markets of Smithfield and Holloway alongside my Uncle Sonny, who worked on the railroad at King's Cross.

That is how the inspiration for my record *Muswell Hillbillies* was created. East Finchley was a few stops on the bus from Holloway, but in its own way it was a major migration from the inner-city "projects" to the more leafy suburbs. It was a critical move, and while in many ways it helped define me as a person, it also had the effect of making me feel as if my family had been cut off from its roots.

My early visions of Americana came from cinema and an assortment of A- and B-movie cowboys. Randolph Scott, John Wayne, Dale Robertson, Clint Walker, and Tom Mix at Saturday-morning pictures. Even the science fiction of Flash Gordon and his weird mix of futurism and the camp medieval costumes epitomized American culture for me. Dale Evans exemplified the ideal female: devoted companion to the clean-cut Roy Rogers. Gene Autry embodied all that was clean and fair and downright good, while the Lone Ranger in his domino mask, along with his devoted Indian sidekick, Tonto, were bold, adventurous, and from all accounts not at all as camp in real life as they appeared on the screen. Then there were the guns. Deliverers of truth, justice, and the American way. Superman could catch a speeding bullet with his bare hand. Run faster than a locomotive. The Cisco Kid and Pancho, in their sombreros, flickered through my black-and-white-TV childhood. In what was a then-perfect male-dominated fantasy, the women stayed at home and made cookies to tempt the sweet tooths of their hardworking pioneer husbands, who were busy building their way westward. I was dizzy with the sheer spectacle and enormity of the American dream.

I wondered at its scale—the vastness of its seemingly endless panorama. I was inspired by its optimism, as opposed to the comparative drabness of postwar suburban London, where I grew up. I'd go to the pictures two or three times a week—sometimes I was taken to the same film twice by my film-crazy older sisters. This obsession was followed by Italian neorealism and French New Wave—Vittorio De Sica, François Truffaut, Jean-Luc Godard—then the British cinema and writings of the angry young men: John Osborne, Alan Sillitoe, Stan Barstow, Tony Richardson, and the like. Suddenly, when I hit my teens, being working-class, suburban, and white meant something. Cowboys and Indians took a backseat while I honed my style to fit my kitchen-sink accent and grew my hair long. One thing didn't change—my love of the music inspired by blues, country, and rock. I had both the New Wave working-class attitude and those American musical influences. Once a week as a teenager, I would go to a jazz club in Highgate that was located in a church hall near where I lived. "Trad jazz," as it was known, was almost as popular as rock and roll, but the dances were more sophisticated and more sedate than the sexier movements of rock, even though both were based on jive. I loved the songs, but knew nothing about their origins except that I associated them with the American South. "The Darktown Strutters' Ball," "Ain't Misbehavin'," and "Frankie and Johnny" were all considered to be traditional Dixieland because they were performed in that style at the local jazz club.

On TV we had *The Amos 'n' Andy Show* from America, and Jack Benny had a black valet called Rochester, but apart from that, my only exposure to black culture was through blues and folk music. I had a mixed-race niece, but she was family, and we never thought about race in a negative sense. I never associated music with race—it was just music. The traditional jazz scene was not all hoochie-coochie, jitterbug, and jive. There was a sultry, shuffling blues in which a boy and girl would dance close together, with their eyes closed, as the words drifted on the singer's breath and muted horns played a soft counterpoint.

"You'll find yourself just thinking about the life in front of you
You'll be happy and contented in that empty room."

3

THE FAKE WORLD

"So you headed down south
Left your old hometown
Relocated so far away from the real world
But where is the real world?"

I started going down to New Orleans more often after the 2001 tour. The tree-lined streets like Esplanade and Chartres reminded me of North London, where I grew up. The community seemed liberal and friendly, unlike the America that had frightened me when I first started touring there with the Kinks in the '60s. On a later trip I watched the Mardi Gras parade, with its superb marching bands, and the floats, with their outrageous costumes and dazzling choreography. On one occasion, Nicholas Cage was on the float that led the parade because, like many of his Hollywood compatriots, he had invested in property in the city and was a frequent visitor.

I originally went to New Orleans partly for songwriting inspiration and partly for a holiday. An old girlfriend once said to me, "You have a career as a songwriter, you can live anywhere. The world is in your head anyhow," because she wanted me to make New Orleans my base. Yet I could not commit to living with her in the way she wanted. Touring relationships are fine when the hotels take care of the housekeeping, but once you check back into the reality motel the dust appears on the furniture, the laundry piles up, and there is no room service to clear away the dirty dishes.

When Rory had once driven me around small-town America in her beaten-up Chevy, she gave the impression that she was a "travel anywhere" wild romantic with a spirit of adventure, but deep down she was the normal American girl; I got the impression that she needed the pension plan, health plan, and, more than anything else, needed to pay off her student loan—something that looms over most American college graduates. I was beginning to wonder where I fit in as part of that package.

"Hoping I can find my dream
In New Hampshire or New Orleans
Find a place where I can stay
And once I'm there I'm never going away so

Hey hey hey
From Portland, Maine, to San Francisco Bay
All across America
Along the Great Highway."

Rory was bright with looks to match, but like so many others she had become attracted to the fake world of nightclubs away from reality. J.J. was a seasoned clublander, and was fortunate to have landed a good gig working in a decent club. Rory, on the other hand, might not endure the club scene so well. She personified the blind innocence of the American dreams I'd always had. She was optimistic and forward-looking, the opposite of the pessimism I felt in the UK at that time.

"And even if the dream goes wrong
Still stay for the last song, another night another day
One more chance to throw it all away still."

Whenever I had a day off on the road before going down to New Orleans, we would sometimes drive around the particular city we found ourselves in, and I would fantasize about moving there. Maybe my life was being dictated by my songs and I didn't know it. In my head we were the two characters riding along "The Great Highway" that was taking us somewhere—we didn't care where.

"Bright eyes like wishing wells, Instamatic kiss and tell
Optimistic self-belief, college girls with perfect teeth
Technicolor realism in 20/20 vision
Animated multiraced and always out there in your face
Ooh la she can be cruel if you upset her

And life is not a road movie so wake up to reality.

Hey hey hey I'm driving on the interstate
All across America, along the Great Highway . . .

The great illusion it may be
But always something else to see
Always some little hick town
To pick you up when you are down
Another day another shake
Melted with a slice of cake.
At a jukebox in a smoky bar
A girl stands looking at the stars
She's dressed in denim wearing shades
And outside is the Great Highway
She sips a Coke walks away
It's just a second in a day
But all her culture's on display
She might be a dreamer
But maybe I'm a dreamer too
Hey still searching for America
Living the dream in America
Along the Great Highway."

That was the dream. Now I was living in a fake world, driving down a dead-end street, and if it continued this way I would be on a collision course with the real world.

THERE ARE ALWAYS TEMPTATIONS ON THE ROAD. When you're in the spotlight onstage it makes you seem special and invincible, which can attract people to you, but it's not until they find out that you are an ordinary person with the same problems as everybody else that the lustre starts to fade. The concept of the road is freedom, and that very word implies a certain amount of cavalier behaviour, but being on the road in America is governed by one overriding factor: the distance. The sheer size of the landmass, the networks of freeways and interstate highways make it seem that there is no way home. Certainly in the pre–mobile phone era, the distance was an irresistible, unmovable reality. In England, traffic jams aside, there is no place that's more than four or five hours' drive away, but in the United States you are looking at up to days.

My own father travelled in the course of his work and had an eye for the ladies on occasion, particularly after he had a few beers. Once, when my brother and I were infants, my mother knew my dad was having a beer with a certain woman; she put me and my baby brother into a pram, wheeled us into the pub, plonked the pram right between the buxom floozy and my dad, and exclaimed, "'Ere you are, darling, you take over and get on with it." Reprisals on cheaters are easy when you live a block or two away from the offence, but they're much more difficult when you are on another continent and subject to a time change. After a while, relationships that were once precious and cherished seem to lose their focus. Some guys on the road spend all day looking at family snaps and talking about their loved ones, to the ever-increasing boredom of their compatriots. Other tour members deliberately shy away from the family guys just to get a break from their own thoughts of the loved ones they miss back home.

Certainly in the generation I came from you would be considered sexually suspect if you never paid any attention to women. I am by no stretch of the imagination a pretty guy. I might write pretty songs, and I hope some of it rubs off on me as a person, but generally speaking, women don't clamour to be with me. Met a girl once who stayed with me on the road for a week just to "see how you do it," only to discover that the "it" she wanted to know about was writing songs. I had to disappoint her, because writing songs is much too personal.

So that's the way it happened. It was not a case of me saying, "I am married: stay away." In the modern age, with Google and other search engines, it is relatively easy to find out whether someone is married or not. Everybody has the ability to find out anything they want about whomever. The biggest handicap on the road is loneliness.

As Oscar Wilde once said, "Each man kills the thing he loves." We all destroy; and I did but it had nothing to do with any woman. It was more to do with my accumulative errors. Mostly though, it was because of overwork.

I KNEW MY MARRIAGE BREAKUP IN 1998 was a mistake; the truth is that I never thought I would bond so much with my daughter Eva while my marriage was falling apart. The day her mother left with her to live in Ireland, something fell apart inside me, even though I tried to keep on working as if it had never happened. I decided not to lose touch with my infant daughter and flew to Ireland to see her as often as I could. This went on for nearly three years and added to the work stress, but I tried to stay buoyant and remain an upbeat dad. When I returned to my empty house, my work gave me little or no consolation. I wrote a song called "Messages from the Republic" about my daughter trying to leave messages from the Republic of Ireland on my answering machine.

Now, my daughter was reaching preschool age, and I was as determined as ever to stay in contact with her. More than anything else I wanted her to remember me as being a good dad. When possible, I would fly over to Ireland, pick her up at the airport, and then bring her straight back to England on the next flight. We would stay in Surrey, where I would work, keep her entertained with DVDs, cook her food, and then read her bedtime stories. She was developing a slight Irish brogue, so I found myself putting on an exaggerated Cockney accent, which she would start to pick up after a few days. I was playing Professor Henry Higgins in reverse. This prompted Eva's mum to complain that our daughter had returned to Ireland with a pronounced Cockney accent. I would drive Eva around the countryside while playing early rock and roll on the stereo, particularly Chuck Berry, whom Eva referred to as "Mr. Chuck." As she bopped around in the back of the car, she screamed with delight, "Mr. Chuck is so funny, Dad; would I like him if I met him?" I thought about the great man's reputation and pointed out that while his music is great and was inspirational to me, it would be best if she didn't meet such a controversial rock and roller as "Mr. Chuck." We also played Cajun classics, which Eva loved, probably because the violins and accordions resemble Irish traditional music.

Then during my next transatlantic flight I was half asleep and started to hear a voice in my head repeating over and over: "You have a career as a songwriter, you can work anywhere." Nice thought. I could work anywhere, that was true, but I also needed to live somewhere. I needed to settle down. It wouldn't be New York—the city was still in shock from 9/11. The Upper West Side of Manhattan was becoming less blue-collar, and corporate people were moving in. My next-door neighbour had been a window cleaner when I first stayed there; now his apartment was occupied by an investment banker.

Now I was literally living my life like a sightseeing tourist with a video camera, taking handheld shots of pretty local curios and sites of interest, while out of view there was a murder or a bank robbery or a police car chase in progress. I was oblivious to the big picture, only focused on what I wanted to see. I was carrying a small video camera at this time and filming everything I saw. I did shoot my shadow as I walked down the street with some friends one day, a sequence that turned out to be quite symbolic when I played it back. My shadow was there, but I was not. It was as though my whole life was in limbo without any sense of time or space, putting me almost in a fugue state. Nevertheless, I continued on my mission to discover the Crescent City. The streets of New Orleans bore names that evoked colour, romance, and musical history—the very things that attracted my band when we first toured America. The country that symbolised freedom and opportunity. How wrong we were.

4

THE INVADERS

"The world as we knew it
Would never be the same
The day the Invaders came."

AMERICA, JULY 1965

In the early 1950s, West Germany and Japan were, albeit reluctantly, British and American allies, but the Cold War was still at its height. Most of battle-torn Europe had to be rebuilt, and in Britain it was also a time of social upheaval. Communism was still the scourge of the so-called free world, but the USA was firmly in control of the "red menace." Years before, Orson Welles had briefly terrorized the American population with the radio broadcasts of *The War of the Worlds* by H. G. Wells. People listening were convinced that Welles's program, about creatures from outer space landing in America, was a documentary and therefore was actually happening. This radio program proved that manipulation by the media could have a devastating effect on an unsuspecting public. They say that people actually jumped out windows to their deaths during the broadcast for fear of being attacked by Martians (although these accounts were exaggerated).

UFOs had been sighted across America, and films such as *Invaders from Mars, The Blob, Creature from the Black Lagoon*, and Don Siegel's brilliant *Invasion of the Body Snatchers* served as a warning that there were still forces of evil waiting if ever Americans dropped their guard. However, the possibility of Martians landing in Manhattan was strictly consigned to the bin marked SCIENCE FICTION. America was secure. Its borders were safe. Its population was protected from dark forces.

The Japanese assault on Pearl Harbor and the brutal and cowardly attack on the American military base there had been enough to take America into the Second World War. Later, the postwar communist threat was stifled in Korea, and while the paranoia of McCarthyism had abated, the Cuban Missile Crisis proved that the bad guys were still out there. President Kennedy and his "court of Camelot" offered a liberating age of enlightenment.

It was against such a backdrop that the unbelievable happened. The "Invaders" landed. In actual fact, the American mainland had never been invaded. Until the Brits came along, that is.

The Beatles were the first wave of British beat bands to come to America. Apart from having great songs, the Beatles were accessible and cute, and American audiences could understand them. They were a mixture of the Three Stooges and the clean-cut all-American boy next door. But apart from having a few big hits, the Kinks, who followed a year later, were another proposition altogether and were considered an unwelcome threat. We were, by comparison, a disorganised rabble and out of our depth culturally. We had an attitude from the London suburbs, which was totally alien to most Americans and, for that matter, anyone outside North London. Anyway, how could an American audience be expected to understand the Kinks when we could barely understand ourselves? The Beatles and the Rolling Stones were well-oiled publicity machines. Nothing was left to chance. America understood them and accepted their carefully nurtured shenanigans with understanding. The Kinks, on the other hand, were difficult to cast in any role except that of outsiders.

"You Really Got Me" had gone to number one in the UK and charted in the top 10 in America. It was the complete antithesis to the normal pop songs of the time, including those by the Beatles. "You Really Got Me" and its follow-up, "All Day and All of the Night," were aggressive, working-class attitude put onto record. There were no American accents, and our band went to great lengths to ensure that the recordings were raw, without any echo, the way the songs sounded live in a club. The lyrics were written in the style of the kitchen-sink dramas of British writers like David Storey and Alan Sillitoe. Songs that could have been spoken by characters like Frank Machin from *This Sporting Life* and Arthur Seaton from *Saturday Night and Sunday Morning*. The third hit single, which was a massive American hit, was called "Tired of Waiting for You." This was contrived to be a more accessible-sounding pop song; it still retained the angry growl of "You Really Got Me": while the lead vocal followed a conventional pop melody, the "growl" hung around menacingly in the background. On the surface America was there to be conquered, and the Kinks were seemingly ready to embark on this challenge. Commercially we seemed ready, but personally we were in complete disarray.

In 1965, anyone who knew and cared about the Kinks would have said this was a bad time to go anywhere. The band had broken up briefly, in an unceremonious way. After more than a little provocation from my brother Dave, Mick Avory, our drummer, had tried to knock Dave's head off with part of his drum kit in front of five thousand screaming fans in Cardiff, Wales. The general consensus in the music industry as well as in the press was that this event was the final death nail in the career of the Kinks and it was only a matter of time before we would finally implode. We had auditioned drummer Mitch Mitchell (later of the Jimi Hendrix Experience) to replace Mick, who had gone into hiding after being wanted by the police for causing grievous bodily harm (charges that Dave later dropped). We had bowed to pressure from the managers and record executives and reformed to make a single for the American tour entitled "Set Me Free," backed with "I Need You" on the B side. Dave and Mick barely spoke during the recording, and the tension was so high at that time that studio staff were quaking in their shoes because the situation was always on the verge of blowing up in our faces. My wife, Rasa, had given birth to a baby daughter a few weeks prior to our starting the tour, and we were still living in a small bedsit apartment when I had rushed out the door, leaving her literally holding the baby. Our management team was on the verge of splitting, and a legal dispute over my publishing for my song catalogue was brewing. Not an ideal time to embark on our first assault on America.

By the time the Kinks did their first US tour, in the mid-'60s, it was apparent that America was a vastly different place compared to the one I imagined in my youth. Now there had been racial tension in Alabama, segregation, organised crime was becoming legit, a soon-to-be-assassinated Martin Luther King Jr., and the death of a president who promised to have a man on the moon in the seventh decade of the twentieth century. The images and illusions of my childhood visions of Americana were rapidly falling apart before my eyes, and I got the distinct feeling something bad was about to happen as I went through customs on arrival at Kennedy Airport in June of 1965. A big fat customs officer spelled it out. "Are you a Beatle or a girl?" I was about to have my first encounter with Americana. I smiled courteously at the big fat officer. "That's right. I'm a girl and so is my brother." As a result, we were nearly prevented from entering the States at all. After a few holdups, we were eventually allowed to go in, but our press conference was delayed, and this prevented us from having a Beatles-style arrival.

The first New York show, at the Academy of Music, was a complete triumph, even though there was concern from the press about our behaviour being less accommodating than that of the Beatles and the other Merseybeat lads, who were for the most part jovial all-around entertainers who very wisely "played the game," adopting the American rules of "engagement." The Kinks were to be loved or hated, and we ruffled the feathers of far too many important people. Thankfully, Mo Ostin's Reprise Records promoted our band with enthusiasm and a certain amount of pride, particularly as the Kinks were the first "young" British act to be signed to the label after a slew of middle-of-the-road Las Vegas–style singers. Although the label didn't completely understand our first two singles, the songs had connected with a young, "hip" audience.

WE WERE ACCOMPANIED AND MANAGED by the sharply dressed Larry Page, because our other two managers, Grenville Collins and Robert Wace of Boscobel Productions, decided to stay in the UK. We didn't understand this decision since the tour was so crucial to our success but it seemed they wanted to develop "other areas" of their management empire. The reality was that after the various punch-ups, conflicts within the band, and bad press, they all considered the Kinks' days to be numbered as a result of the incident in Cardiff a few months earlier. In the pre-celebrity culture of that time, controversial entertainers were considered to be bad news and would never come back once their press ratings dropped and their records fell from the charts. Nowadays our behaviour would have warranted front-page celebrity coverage, but in those more conservative times we were avoided like the plague.

In military terms it was easy for the Invaders to penetrate the larger, liberalized cities. It was the American heartland that would eventually defeat them; ironically, the heartland was also the very source of the artillery used by the musical Invaders—country, hillbilly, and blues—to penetrate the USA. The Invaders turned the culture against itself, but it imploded.

This was the basis on which the Kinks, all still not yet twenty-one years of age, were thrown into battle to confront America full on. If we had "played the game" and taken all the opportunities thrown at us things might have been different, but the lack of organisation on behalf of our management combined with the complete disarray the band was in after the incidents leading up to the fateful show in Cardiff left us not able or willing to take advantage of our success. Instead, the Kinks were prevented from touring the United States again for four years by what is believed to be a ban by the American musicians union.

The 1965 tour was filled with bad energy.

Actually things had been falling apart before we even got on the plane to New York, with Mick's unceremonious spat onstage; my worries about my wife and new baby needing a space to live while I was away; and impending lawsuits between the Kinks management teams of Boscobel/Robert Wace and Grenville Collins on one side and Denmark Productions/Larry Page and Eddie Kassner on the other.

Anyone in their right mind should have known that it was reckless for the Kinks to embark on a tour of America. Larry Page even said after the Cardiff incident that it was the end of the Kinks, but nevertheless he steamed ahead to confirm and organise the tour regardless. I believe there was something evil going around at that time. Once we were in the States, people kept on harassing us for various reasons. Our management had a falling-out with a police sheriff in Philadelphia. There was a confrontation with our local driver in Peoria, who terrified us by erratically brandishing his gun around. At Pete Quaife's instigation, we almost went to the house of infamous clown–serial killer Wayne Gacy—at the time a community organiser—who was involved with coordinating the fundraising concert we performed at in Springfield, Illinois. I remember we were doing a television spot—I think it was for Dick Clark's show—and this guy kept goading me:

"When the commies overrun Britain, you're really going to want to come here, aren't you? Your wife is Lithuanian. Is she a Commie?" I found this comment offensive and ridiculous so I just turned round to push him away. I don't know if I even made contact but he fell to the ground like a child. Then he got straight up and walked away, apparently unharmed. Somebody said he may have been an American union official but that was never confirmed. There was always someone grabbing and pulling us off to do something somewhere or another. Page and Kassner were around all the time trying to get me to sign a new publishing contract with them. Then apparently Page and our agent fell out with a promoter on the West Coast. Possibly we had been underpaid or maybe they wanted to get more money for the dates. I'll never know.

Ironically the money did not matter to the band because at this time I recall that the Kinks were on a fixed salary of forty pounds (then about a hundred dollars) a week, even though we were playing the Hollywood Bowl and headlining at mainly sold out concerts. I wasn't able to cope with all the pressures put upon me. I would lock myself away in my hotel room and just leave to fulfil my obligations. Whenever I did emerge from my room it was as though there was always trouble and bad karma waiting.

AMERICANA. It wasn't like the movies after all. It was much deeper and more diverse than I ever imagined it could be. You couldn't see the bad guys coming, after all, and they didn't wear black hats to distinguish them from the good guys. Some of the bad guys were clean-cut, with white teeth and cropped hair.

The 1965 tour that resulted in the ban gave me the impression that the Kinks were in one of the black-and-white film comedies that came from Britain's Ealing Studios in the 1950s, while the rest of America all around us was in Technicolor, CinemaScope. There was a perceived difference of opinion between what was considered good taste and what was bad taste. A classic case in point was when we had appeared on NBC's *Hullabaloo* variety show in February, a few months before the tour. At the top of the program all the artists in the cast were told by the director to "groove" away on the spot to the latest dance as each individual act was introduced during the show's opening sequence. Merseybeat band Freddie and the Dreamers, along with all the other artists, did as they were told and obeyed the director's orders. But when it came to the point where Frankie Avalon and Annette Funicello introduced the Kinks, the camera cut away to show me and Mick Avory dancing cheek to cheek. This would have possibly been acceptable on the BBC's *The Morecambe & Wise Show* or in a seaside vaudeville act, but to the mainstream American audience we must have looked like a couple of cavorting homosexuals. This was a total counterpoint to the aggressive music we played. America just didn't understand the Kinks the first time around. We got the impression that we had unknowingly offended and upset a lot of people. I'm not sure with whom or with what, but there was something strange going down on that tour.

On July 3, 1965 we played the Hollywood Bowl with a number of other groups, including the Beach Boys, the Righteous Brothers, Sonny & Cher, the Byrds, and Sam the Sham and the Pharaohs. We accounted for ourselves well in such distinguished company, particularly after Larry Page had announced that he was going back to England the following morning, as he did, and left Sam Curtis, our road manager, in charge.

The tour was in chaos but we blindly followed the advice of what was left of our management, who told us we had to go play at San Francisco's prestigious Cow Palace. However when we got there, we didn't get to play at all. When we arrived there was no equipment set up for us, nobody spoke or explained anything to us, we were just there. This was both humiliating and absurd. At one point I remember running onto the stage only to be dragged off again by security guards. No one really knew the whole story, not even the band; perhaps Page and the promoter didn't know the whole story either. The upshot was that there we were, thrown into a situation that was too scary to contemplate. Our manager had disappeared and left us to take the flak. I actually felt like an alien on what seemed like planet paranoia.

We went on to play the rest of the tour, first in Honolulu, where we played somewhat ironically—considering we were British Invaders—to American servicemen, and then back to the mainland for concerts in Spokane, Tacoma, and Seattle, where we played to sell-out shows with the likes of Jan & Dean and the Righteous Brothers. There were no further hiccups, even though we did notice a higher level of police to contain the over-enthusiastic audiences. Even though these final shows were a success, it was clear that in one way or another damage had been done due to complete differences of opinion, divergent attitudes to culture, a lack of business compatibility, and total mis-understanding on all sides. The inevitable result? An indefinite ban from working in the United States was imposed on the Kinks immediately after the tour was over.

These Invaders went home beaten and battered to lick their wounds in the musical wilderness for four years before regrouping to mount another assault. Today it is still not entirely clear to me why the Kinks were banned from America. Mick Avory, the Kinks' drummer, possibly summed it up best when he said it was a mixture of bad management, bad luck, and bad behaviour. He wasn't far off.

5

AMERICANA

"All-American eagle swoops down from the sky up above
All-American napalm blocks out the light from the sun
All-American hero, is that the way the West was won?"

They called us the Invaders the first time around, but when we came back to the U.S. in the fall of 1969, we had to start from scratch. We had continued making records and having success in the rest of the world, but America was still there to be won over. Our management had been trimmed down, and Larry Page had moved on. Grenville Collins, Robert Wace's partner in Boscobel Productions, had volunteered to accompany us on our trip back to America. Ren Gravatt did our PR, and Reprise executives—in a touching gesture to show they could change with the times—had exchanged their black cashmere suits for hippie beads and caftans. Mo Ostin was still at the helm of Reprise; he was determined to rebuild the Kinks as a major band. The album released at the time was called *Arthur (Or the Decline and Fall of the British Empire)*. I was also more confident in myself, so I didn't stay in my hotel room like a frightened shut-in, watching *Captain Kangaroo* and *Mister Rogers' Neighborhood*, as I did the first time I was in New York. However, I still watched these children's shows when I could . . . they were an antidote to the bad news of the war in Vietnam, which filled the airwaves on a daily basis. They also served as a calming influence at the beginning of the day, giving me the opportunity to be young and innocent again before turning into a rock and roller by the time evening came around.

"All-American napalm blocks out the light from the sun
All-American Cowboy, Rules with the Fist, a Smile, and a Gun."

Now, five years after the ban had started, savvy New York businessman Allen Klein—and, more notably, the astute New York attorney Marty

Machat—had somehow managed to get the ban lifted and America granted the Kinks a work permit allowing us to return. We were presented with a short document to sign—some sort of confessional that I didn't even bother to read. To this day I still don't know its contents or what we were alleged to have done. All I know is that for years after that time, I was told that whenever we put in a visa application, a red light went off somewhere, as though our file were still on record. But, happily, I've never had an application denied.

When the Kinks embarked on the assault on North America in 1969, we were each, for the most part, very happily married, with what seemed like normal family lives. I had moved back to North London from Elstree, away from the large faux manor house that I had bought in a failed attempt at aristocratic grandeur, and returned to my modest suburban semi, where I felt more comfortable. I was also near my family again. Mum and Dad lived two hundred yards down the road. Dave lived with his wife, Lisbet, in Southgate, in a beautiful old Victorian vicarage next to the local church. By now Dave had three sons and enjoyed all the trappings of happy married life in London's quiet northern suburbs. Mick Avory was in a long-term relationship with his partner, Jackie, whom he later married. John Dalton, who lived in Hertfordshire with his wife, Val, had permanently replaced Pete Quaife on the bass. Pete had returned for a while after his initial departure in the mid-'60s, but after making the album *The Kinks Are the Village Green Preservation Society* he had decided to quit the Kinks forever, which was a particularly sad blow for me, as Pete was both a friend and an original member of the band.

Grenville Collins flew with us to New York. He and Robert Wace were having disagreements over various other projects they were managing, but Grenville decided to come and look after us so the disorganised debacle of the mid-'60s tour would not be repeated. Our tour manager and equipment roadie at this time was Ken Jones. Ken had started off as the "band boy" in 1968, joining us during one of our lean years, when we were struggling to keep ourselves together during the American ban. He regretted not being around in the heady days of the swinging '60s, but had stayed loyal to the point of almost being the fifth member of our unit. His deep-set eyes, slightly turned-up nose, and protruding chin were separated by a drooping moustache. This, combined with his shoulder-length hair, gave him a tough *Easy Rider* look. It wasn't until he spoke and his soft, glum, droning, slightly Irish-accented voice came out that it became apparent he wasn't a scary biker after all. He was just "Jonesy."

Ken always wore tinted spectacles because of his poor eyesight, which he claimed was the reason he never passed his medical exam for military service. We later discovered that the real reason he was passed over was because he was deaf in one ear. He did do some maintenance for the Royal Air Force as a member of the ground crew, which was enough to make him occasionally take on a military attitude. This only brought taunts and ridicule from the band, who deliberately contradicted any rule he tried to impose. He'd drive our equipment van and even sleep in it on occasion, but the thought of going on tour to America brought a rare smile from him. He would run his fingers through one side of his moustache as he considered the rich pickings involved in an American trip. It seemed that the only life Ken had revolved around being on tour. He cherished his air-mile upgrades and the perks that came from being associated with a potentially high-profile band. He revelled in getting us cut-price deals on Pan Am. It was a joy to see him get frustrated at check-in if he couldn't get us into the first-class lounge. His deceptively quiet voice belied the fact that Jonesy was a persuasive and intrepid negotiator with airline ground staff. When all else failed, he would simply whinge so much that the airlines would give him what he wanted just to get rid of him.

WE WENT BACK TO AMERICA at the time of the space race, with the *Apollo 11* spacecraft landing Americans on the moon in July of 1969. This made the place even more exhilarating to be involved with. For a while, the Vietnam War and all the racial tension and political unrest in America were eclipsed by the intense excitement surrounding these trips to the moon. It did feel to me, however, like there were two worlds in America. One world was focused on pushing America forward into exploring outer space, accompanied by old-school, conservative candy-floss pop for a world that seemed to be in denial about everything going on around it; as opposed to the other politicised world, with radical antiwar music and the subculture of alternative rock and roll. Bands such as Frank Zappa's Mothers of Invention had come along; their deceptively complex musical structures combined lyrics that actually criticised the establishment with a combination of Lenny Bruce–style comedy and what was an until-then uniquely British comic device, satire. Now, finally, America seemed to have the ability to laugh at itself. Perhaps the British Invaders had inspired antiestablishment radicalism in young America after all. When I first heard the Mothers of Invention singing "It Can't Happen Here" I was convinced "it" could. There was still an outside chance that the Kinks could make it in America.

The Fillmore East was the first Kinks gig on our return to New York City in October of 1969. When we got to town, there was a mass of interviews to do—a press conference was organised with mainly college newspapers, including *Rolling Stone* and *Creem* magazines, all of them wanting to know what it was like for us to be returning to America, where we had been banned. The "ban" had actually made us seem "cool," since many students were critical of American politics at that time.

I was amazed at how organised rock music had become. The American musical scene had certainly changed, and we were taken aback by our own almost naive attempts to conform to the new rock industry that had evolved since our previous American tour. Bill Graham, the promoter of the Fillmore, was one of the pioneers in launching the American music revolution. Since we'd been away we missed this renaissance, which included Woodstock, Monterey Pop, and other big festivals.

The Fillmore itself was situated in New York's East Village, where the hippie culture had fully emerged. People wore caftans and beads, and were smoking pot openly on the street and back stage at the venue. We were ushered back stage by huge security guards—unlike the out-of-shape "bouncers" we were accustomed to in the UK—and they insisted that we show our backstage passes no matter who we were. Our needs were taken care of by the Fillmore staff and, without going into too much detail, I mean *all* our needs were taken care of—ironing shirts, getting refreshments, running errands—which was unheard of at concerts in the UK. There was catering—not sweaty, dried-up cheese-and-Spam rolls like those we would have been given in England, but an enticing array of Asian cuisine and exotic nibbles. Rock and roll had turned into a mini industry in our time away from the United States, but the whole thing had become slightly decadent; as Grenville said, "It's like an empire in decline."

There seemed to be a parallel between the imperialistic qualities of the British Empire and the American "empire" that was under assault in Asia. Moral standards hadn't exactly dropped, they were just there for everybody to see and ignore. Excess ruled, and I was grateful that our dressing-room door had a lock on it. Backstage personnel assisted Ken Jones with equipment; in the UK, he sometimes had to load up the van single-handedly. Onstage we were confronted with freaky light shows and stage monitors so that we could actually hear what we were playing. This was the first time we had ever encountered this new technological phenomenon. On all our other tours, including our recent trips into Europe, we had just used PA and front-of-house systems. There were no such extravagances as stage monitors. It was a completely new learning curve for us as musicians, and it made our performance during sound check seem more amateurish and tentative than usual.

It was the "prodigals'" return, the second coming, but our performance was below par. Unused to the sophisticated stage equipment, we must have sounded like a bunch of skiffle players in the back room of a pub. Our management in all their wisdom had done an endorsement deal with an amplifier company that had an unpronounceable name. We had made our name and reputation using small VOX amplifiers—which had worked successfully all over the world—but in America, for some reason, everything had to be bigger. It was also a time when amplifiers were stacked behind the musicians, but we didn't have the luxury of doing production rehearsals before a tour. We'd literally come straight off the stage of a small provincial theatre in England, only to be thrown into the deep end with a technology that we were totally unfamiliar and unconfident with.

We were promoting our new album *Arthur (Or the Decline and Fall of the British Empire)*, and the Fillmore was to be a tastemaker event that would set the tone for the rest of the U.S. dates. But anyone who witnessed the

Kinks' concerts at that time was astounded by the contradictions in our performance. Foppish, almost effeminate behaviour in some songs and brutal,
brute force in some of the harder rock songs.

We shared the bill with two other acts that typified the extremes in
our own stage performances: Spirit, a jazz-rock fusion band who punctuated their set by playing long guitar solos that went down a storm with
the mainly stoned audience at the Fillmore, and the extravagantly named
Bonzo Dog Doo-Dah Band. The Kinks were familiar with the Bonzos, led by
Vivian Stanshall, who had pop hits in the UK with songs like "I'm the Urban
Spaceman," and they'd attained some cult following in America, which is
why I think they were on the bill with us at the Fillmore on our return show.
The Bonzos were popular because of their eccentric English wit and the
outrageous stage antics carried out by the band members, which included
Vivian, "Legs" Larry Smith, and Neil Innes.

There were two shows a night, and after the first show I was disturbed
to see a punch-up going on near the Bonzo's dressing room between two of
the Bonzos. In what seemed like a girlish spat, they stood in the corridor
throwing punches and swearing at one another, dressed in their full stage
attire. One was wearing a silver suit, and the other was wearing his own silly
outfit. The insults were flying as well as the fists, but very few punches were
landing. Apparently they were breaking up as a band, and this was probably
one of their last tours. This scene was in total contrast to the sombre, laid-
back vibe of Spirit, who appeared to do everything in a completely medita-
tive state. I don't know what sort of food they were eating or what vitamins
they were on, if any, but they must have had superefficient concentration
because when we passed in the corridor back stage, my friendly greeting of
"Hi" was met with glazed stares and unblinking eyes as they walked past.
Maybe intense focus was a new ingredient in rock and roll.

The Bonzos played brilliantly and got laughs and applause in admi-
ration of their musical prowess. However, they were far from being a joke
band; they were all very accomplished musicians. Spirit seemed like the
soundtrack to a nation in turmoil; relentlessly unflinching, complete tunnel
vision. From back stage it sounded like the audience gave an exhausted
but collective "Yeah, man" at the end of each song. Fists punched the air in

acknowledgment, and stagehands nodded in approval, while groupies and friends of the band hovered piously at the side of the stage. Spirit was the epitome of power and psychedelic progressive rock, and they were very influential in their own way. The band made extensive use of amplified gizmos, and while it may have seemed a total mismatch to have Spirit on with the Kinks at the time, the combination of "You Really Got Me" and Spirit's instrumental sound effects may have been an influence on Jimmy Page and Led Zeppelin, who had opened for Spirit a year earlier.

After a short intermission it was time for the Kinks to make their American return. Bill Graham walked onstage and made a speech about how we'd been "away too long" and the time had come for us to return. He paused and then said, "Please welcome to the stage the Kinks." As we walked onstage I tried to thank Bill for the introduction, but the charismatic promoter walked straight past me, his eyes wide open and staring. He must have either been focused on something important like the next event in his busy calendar or what the box-office gross would be or recovering from something he'd eaten back stage. He stood at the side of the stage while we played our first few songs, and then he turned and disappeared with a bunch of minders. It struck me that in the new upper echelons of "Rock-and-Roll" America, even promoters had bodyguards.

The Kinks' set was tentative at first, but then it evolved into something more confident and substantial as we took the audience through a journey of what we had been doing for the past four years. Hard-core fans got it immediately, whereas newcomers to our music looked on warily. Eventually they were won over by the hits we played from the British Invasion days; we then played a few songs from our new album, *Arthur*. The songs that had a more cutting rock edge to them and more complex structures were received with nods of approval, as if they were progressive enough to warrant an airing at the Fillmore. At the end of the show it was clear that we had made our mark—that we had taken our music somewhere since we first arrived in America years earlier, and, more than anything else, we had evolved.

During the show I noticed a row of about eight or ten seats near the front that were left empty. Grenville pointed out that some dedicated fans bought tickets and didn't show up as a sign of protest. They felt we had sold out to the new American corporate rock system by not playing at an intimate venue like a small club or bar. The message got through to me that these devotees would be gathered in one of their apartments to listen to our *Village Green Preservation Society* album rather than attend the concert at the Fillmore, where, in their opinion, the Kinks were prostituting themselves. It was the tail end of the God Save the Kinks campaign that Reprise Records had organised around *Village Green Preservation Society*, which was released a year earlier. It had been taken up by anti–Vietnam War protestors as an alternative to the drug-culture music that was prevalent in the U.S. at that time. The album was more "pastoral," and its wistful appreciation for better times and tranquillity must have seemed an antidote to the drug-induced, quick-fix counterculture America was immersed in.

Our performance at the Fillmore East must have been quite a success because I was told that the "high priestess" of groupies was anxious to give me an audience. In the corridor I was introduced to this tall, lean African-American woman who had a huge Afro and piercing eyes. The whole confrontation was more like an interview than a conversation, except that I was the one being questioned. (I even considered whether I should provide references.) She gave me a few notes on our performance and declared that we should meet later in a bar, where I should buy her a drink. The possibilities were too scary to think about; it was as though she was ready to file a report to groupie central after our "encounter." I politely declined and agreed to meet another time, and later we did have a drink. I soon discovered that there is no confidentiality among groupies; everyone wanted to know everything about everyone in the most graphic and intimate detail.

One of the joys of playing the Fillmore East was that we could visit Ratner's delicatessen to have a meal between shows. Ratner's was renowned for the rudeness of its waiters, who would shout out what they thought you should order if you seemed at all hesitant. Bill Graham claimed that he had once been a waiter there when he first came to the city. Anyone who met Bill Graham would soon know that he did not suffer fools gladly and could outshout any waiter at Ratner's. It was a better, less dangerous option for me to let him promote my concerts than to order a grilled cheese sandwich from him when he'd been a waiter there.

One night when we had come back from Ratner's to the Fillmore between shows, we walked into our dressing room to find a roadie getting "serviced" by a groupie. While the band and I tried to quietly manoeuvre our way around the "event," Ken Jones was disgusted, appalled, and felt professionally compromised by what was taking place. His normally soft-spoken Northern Irish voice was raised almost to a shout. "Streuth, it's blow-job central 'round here; you think they would have had the decency to use the toilet like anybody else! Where do they think they are, Scandinavia?"

Jonesy had a point, but we were already resigned to the fact that this was the "new way" to behave; it was accepted as the new backstage protocol, particularly in the hippie era of free love. Anyway, as Mick Avory astutely observed, "Why hide such an event in a closet when you can perform it in public for the world to see?" The manners of society were breaking down, morals were being destroyed daily by these new liberal freedoms, and there was nothing anyone could do about it. Standards had slipped, the decay had started, and old values were falling into decadence. People could perpetrate any deviance they wanted, anytime, anywhere, day or night; the most outrageous acts were allowed to take place, but not—according to Jonesy—in the Kinks' dressing room.

WHEN THE FILLMORE EAST DATES WERE OVER, the band breathed a joint sigh of relief as we headed off to play a college gymnasium in Potsdam, New York, followed by a club in Long Beach, New York. Then we were off to Boston to play at the Boston Tea Party, a major rock hall that was promoted by Don Law, who, like Bill Graham, had emerged in the late 1960s to turn what was a small pop business into a rock-and-roll industry.

Boston proved to be an unexpected highlight after the tense, insecure performances at the Fillmore East. The audience was responsive to our onstage asides and quips, which almost made it feel as though we were playing to a home crowd. Boston later proved to be a substantial building block to our following in the Northeast, particularly as it was possible to buy decent English beer there—which was at that time a rarity in the U.S.

The tour was a predictable routing, with a few days off during each week while we waited to travel to the next date. This schedule was already beginning to have an effect on the band's morale, mainly due to the fact that we were preaching to the not-quite-yet-converted; also, if we had been on tour in Europe, we would have had less time on our hands because we could have driven or flown home on a night off. Instead, we would have two, sometimes three, nights off in a city before playing.

After Boston, we made our way to Chicago, where I was interviewed by the legendary Studs Terkel. The next day we played a date with the Who, but the night was spoiled when Dave had an accident in the hotel after the show and was unable to play for several days afterward due to a cut hand. He had been partying with Who drummer Keith Moon—an activity that would inevitable lead to disaster. My brother had tried to help Keith throw a television out the window of the penthouse at the Holiday Inn in Chicago, only to be thwarted because the window was too small. (This was the time of the rock-and-roll excesses of bands such as Led Zeppelin and the Who, who were indulging in antics of varying degrees of extravagance, such as driving a motor bike down the hall at the Hyatt on the Sunset Strip in Hollywood and throwing furniture and TVs out of hotel windows.) Dave flew back to Europe for a few days to nurse his wounds while the rest of us stayed in Chicago. Calls back home were becoming more infrequent in the pre–mobile phone and Internet days, when an international call cost around three pounds a minute. Travelling so far west was making me miss home, and Dave was having his own problems. Despite my homesickness and Dave's recovering from his accident in Chicago, we had to get through the tour and were determined to stick with it.

On Dave's return, we travelled to Detroit, where we were to play along with Joe Cocker, Grand Funk Railroad, and the James Gang. I don't know what state of mind Joe Cocker was in, but he appeared to walk through a partition on his way to the stage. I was already feeling slightly alienated by the machismo displayed by the other bands on the bill, so during our own set I slipped into vaudeville mode by telling a few bad jokes by the legendary British comedian Max Miller; I was greeted with stunned silence by the hard-core Detroit rock audience. As we moved on through the Midwest, it was clear that the Kinks had been appreciated but slightly misunderstood at some of the venues. We played Cincinnati, supported by

Humble Pie, and we talked back stage with band members Steve Marriott and Peter Frampton about Steve's time with the Small Faces and Peter's with a band called the Herd.

On the day off before the show, Grenville and I walked around downtown and ended up in a bar listening to a piano player who was performing outstanding renditions of Noël Coward songs. We looked around and discovered that we were in a gay bar. After we had tipped the singer by putting some dollar bills into a glass on his baby grand piano, we politely made our exit, but I was so impressed by that singer's rendition of "Someday I'll Find You" that I still listen out for his voice whenever I play Cincinnati.

No risks were being taken by promoters, and the safe, easy ticket was in smaller venues, which came as a slight shock—particularly as in the mid-1960s we'd played large auditoriums of fifteen thousand seats or more; now we were certainly starting from scratch. A few college venues were thrown in; at one of these we opened for Neil Diamond. The college circuit was becoming more and more important at that time, and playing some college venues—often during the week—helped support the band until the bigger paydays came on the weekends.

It had been an erratic and bumpy ride so far, and it was a relief when we reached Hollywood, where we would be headlining our own show at the Whisky a Go Go. Because the tour was strictly low-budget, even relatively cheap hotels were too expensive, but necessity indeed proved to be the mother of invention when Ken Jones's astute frugality landed us in the then-named Hollywood Hawaiian Hotel at Grace and Yucca Streets, just off Hollywood Boulevard. There we indulged ourselves in mini suites and swam in the outdoor pool, which enjoyed varying degrees of cleanliness depending on whether the hotel staff bothered to clean it. It was worth enduring the erratic AC system in each room, because the price was right at the special rate of fifteen bucks a night.

The hotel lobby was manned by a couple of guys who must have been extras in the golden age of Hollywood. Outlandish dye jobs and obvious plastic surgery made them look like they could once have been stand-ins for Gregory Peck or Errol Flynn back in their day. Their manner was polite and slightly feminine at times, but when it was necessary they would put on scary airs and engage in manly behaviour, to the point that we thought they had split personalities—which Grenville attributed to bad acting classes. Thursday afternoons must have been their days off because then they were replaced by a large, frightening Hispanic gentleman who had scars on his neck and a frail little old lady who wore so much makeup she resembled Bette Davis in *What Ever Happened to Baby Jane?*. Because the hotel was at the corner of Grace and Yucca, it was conveniently close to the head shops and cheap cafés on Hollywood Boulevard, and the lads could always get a cab to Sunset and hang out at Filthy McNasty's and other bars.

The Whisky a Go Go shows were a success, and after a few more fill-in shows in the California cities of Irvine and Antioch, we arrived in San Francisco. While Los Angeles was always a big party town for bands, including the Kinks, San Francisco reminded me of England because of the Anglophile sensibility of its inhabitants. The last time we had been to the city was during the ill-fated '65 tour, when we had been prevented from going on at the Cow Palace. We prayed that this time there would be a much different result.

This time around we were greeted at the San Francisco airport by Reprise Records promotion man Pete Moreno, who had arrived in a massive Rolls-Royce. He was accompanied by Mike and Trish Daly. Mike was a *Rolling Stone* journalist who'd written up a favourable review for our album *Arthur*, and he, Pete, and Trish wanted to make us feel at home. After polite welcomes, Pete took me alone in the large Rolls and left Mike, Trish, and the band to travel into San Francisco by van. Later, Moreno used his powers of persuasion to make us play a few songs from the back of a truck in the parking lot of Tower Records. Trish and Mike befriended me and Grenville, became great supporters of the band and my work, and remain friends to this day.

The billing at Bill Graham's Fillmore West in San Francisco was always slightly unpredictable. During the last weekend of November 1969, we found ourselves playing there with the inspirational Taj Mahal, who had Jesse Davis on guitar, and the burlesque-like Sha Na Na, who with their doo-wop antics seemed like an American parallel to the Bonzos. During one of the shows I was feeling distinctly like a "Brit out of water," and during a lull in our performance the audience was either too distracted or too stoned to understand what I was saying. I shouted to my brother, Dave, to play the English national anthem, "God Save the Queen," and demanded that all the hippies who could get up stand at attention while we completed the song. We might have lost a few passive fans, but we gained many hard-core supporters.

Dave was playing erratically at this time, and before our second San Francisco show I found out that a drug dealer had visited him on our first night. On discovering this, I made sure I was around when the dealer turned up the following day to peddle some more drugs. Dave and I both had shoulder-length hair and looked quite similar at the time, and the dealer came over and asked me if I would like to score. I smiled at first; then my anger boiled over and I clipped him over the forehead with my guitar. It was more like a warning rather than a blow, but it was enough to send the dope dealer scurrying down the stairs and out through the stage door. Extreme behaviour on my part, perhaps, but I would let nobody interfere with the quality of my band's performance. When I think about it, I wouldn't have minded so much if Dave had been able to go off into outstanding guitar solos, but the brutal reality was that on this occasion, the drugs made him play like a prat. Whether I overreacted I am not sure, but from what I understand, the dealer never came back. Our manager, Grenville Collins, was somewhat concerned by my extreme reaction, but at the same time he understood the necessity of the disciplinary actions I took. I felt out of place, dressed up in my '70s flares, polka-dot shirt, and bow tie, but it must have been nothing to how out of place Grenville felt, dressed in his pin-striped Savile Row stockbroker's suit and tie.

WE WERE ACCOMPANIED on many of our subsequent West Coast trips by a local Reprise Records promotion man, Russ Shaw. He always seemed to wear a light brown suede shirt and trousers to complement his cowboy boots, and he topped off the ensemble with a floppy leather cowboy hat. To see Russ and Grenville talking about promotion ideas and the advancement of the Kinks' career was unnerving, to say the least. Russ and Grenville both spoke English, but that is where communication and understanding ended. It was left to Jonesy to act as interpreter between Grenville's King's English and Russ's American version. Russ became the butt of many of our jokes and would often have to duck a can of beer that was thrown at him as we took turns trying to knock his hat off during backstage banter. Still, Russ remained a firm believer in the band, even though his dry cleaning bill must have been difficult to justify to his bosses at the record company.

We flew back east to play the Spectrum in Philadelphia, where we were on the bill with the Chambers Brothers and Spirit. I was nearly electrocuted when my wet lip touched a microphone and triggered a spark from faulty wiring. It was a sold-out show, so at least I would have gone out on a high. After our set I watched to see how the Chambers Brothers reacted to the faulty wiring, but they charged ahead in their own relentless way and didn't appear to feel a thing.

The tour continued in the Northwest, and by the time we played Portland, Oregon, in the beginning of December 1969, the realities of the Vietnam War suddenly hit us again. There was an underlying nervousness among Americans of our age and those who were in their late teens. It was draft lottery time, when all young men of eligible age were conscripted into the armed forces. A lottery was organised and broadcast live on radio, and the names of those chosen were read out—it seemed as if the names were more or less picked out of a hat and read out by a glorified bingo caller. There was a lot of discontent; a number of guys who qualified for military service were leaving the country rather than going to fight in Vietnam. The term "draft dodger" was on everybody's lips. In Britain we had abolished the National Service system in the early '60s. My generation was the last to actually be eligible; the system was rescinded around the time of the Bay of Pigs, much to our relief. It is no coincidence that the National Service stopped around the same time as the new beat-music boom was emerging in Britain. Probably many of the people in rock bands would have been doing their National Service if this had not been the case. In America, however, because of the large numbers of soldiers needed for the Vietnam War, the draft lottery seemed to be the only way the U.S. government could deal with the situation.

THE 1969 TOUR FINISHED with a small club date in New York City at Ungano's on the Upper West Side. It was only a small club, but the show did more to enhance our reputation in America than any of the other dates on the tour. The band was tight and played with real dedication after such a strenuous and eventful trip. More than anything else, we proved that we could get through a tour without being banned.

We had finally finished our six-week tour, but the *Arthur* album had barely made an impact on the charts. Mo Ostin at Reprise told us that while *Arthur* did well enough, he wanted us to do the whole tour again, but this time with a worldwide hit, like the ones we had in the old days. He emphasised the point that despite our efforts and the wide critical acclaim the album had received, it was clear that we had to "do time" in America and not just "show up," as we did on our first tour.

IS THIS THE WAY THAT THE WEST WAS WON?
WINTER 1969—EARLY 1970S

We had to find our audience; so we toured and we toured, and then "Lola" arrived in the summer of 1970. Maybe "Lola" came along as a response to the way the Kinks had been received in America. Tough and aggressive with a sing-along chorus in one sense, and in another respect, touching on subject matter that would not be accepted in most hard-rock circles. I found some of the bands that we'd played with in America to be ludicrously overly macho. Many of our new audiences in the States liked us for our vulnerability and for the edgy content in some of our songs; we were not afraid to show that we had emotions.

I had been cast to play a role in an episode of the BBC *Play for Today* drama series about a piano player who wanted to break the world record for marathon piano playing. I relieved myself of some of my Kinks songwriting and performing duties as I engrossed myself in the part. My second daughter, Victoria, was one year old at the time, and I wanted to write something she could sing along to, so I wrote the chorus of Lola for her. Many of my songs were quite wordy, and I wanted something simple that people could latch onto quickly—and if my daughter could sing it, so could our audience. All I needed now was the content of the lyric; I wanted it to be edgy, a topic that would resonate with the times, and I remembered an incident at a club in Paris years earlier. My manager Robert Wace had been dancing with this exotic beauty all night, but was shocked to discover that his dancing partner was actually a man. I had been through a similar experience, so I wrote the song in the first person. We recorded the song just before Easter in 1970. Everyone at the record company was pleased with the outcome, but something bothered me—it needed a stronger intro. I didn't want to wait till the first chorus—I wanted the song to be a hit in the first few seconds—so I went back into the studio and put on the intro that's now famous: the powerful guitars at the front that would be instantly recognizable and give it that rock-and-roll edge. In May, we embarked on a late spring tour of America. We had just done a date in Minneapolis when I received a call from my management in London. Some of the content in the lyrics had apparently caused raised eyebrows at the BBC. I immediately thought that they must have objected to the song because it was about a transvestite when in actual fact the BBC radio stations were questioning whether they should play the record because it had the words "Coca-Cola" in it. At the time the BBC had a strict rule against advertising of any sort and it might be construed to be that I was advertising Coca-Cola if the record had been played on air. This had to be changed or there would be no airplay, which meant that in the days of the BBC's virtual monopoly of radio that the record wouldn't be heard. So I took the next flight back to London from Chicago to replace the word "coca" with "cherry." This pleased the BBC producers at the radio stations, who started playing the record. I was confused by the contradictions of the BBC's apparent concern about the lyrics of "Lola" and concluded that whilst an innocent reference to a brand of a soft drink was in bad taste, dancing with a transvestite was deemed to be acceptable behaviour. I flew back the next day to Chicago, where we had a concert that night.

BY EARLY SUMMER 1970, the four-piece Kinks had added keyboard player John Gosling to the touring lineup. Gosling was tall and bearded and seemed so biblical in appearance that we renamed him the Baptist, after John the Baptist. When we'd auditioned him he told us about his classical training,

which we assumed was at London's Royal Academy of Music, and we therefore deemed him a responsible, serious-minded individual. It was not until
we embarked on our next North American tour that we realised that Baptist
was prone to inspire John Dalton and Mick Avory to excessive, prankish
behaviour. Ken Jones was by now relieved of his duties as equipment boy
and had been elevated to the position of tour manager. He was replaced by
an assistant whom we only ever referred to as Ashtray. This was because of
his habit of absconding with souvenir ashtrays from every establishment we
visited. Ashtray's other obsession was his girlfriend, and whilst he undoubtedly loved the woman, his description of the sexual experiences he would put
her through upon his return from tour made us all shudder.

Most tours ended up with shows in—or side trips to—L.A., where
somehow there was always more downtime, which gave us an opportunity
to indulge ourselves. In late November of 1970, we were back at our beloved
Hollywood Hawaiian Hotel, where the party could go on all night. With
"Lola" being such a hit, Grenville and I had to entertain Mo Ostin and other
dignitaries from Warner and Reprise while we talked about a new contract.
After a sumptuous meal in Beverly Hills, we all ended up at the Whisky a Go
Go for a nightcap.

Grenville and I were discussing a bigger recording budget and trying to
be on our best behaviour to impress the record company. Grenville spared
no expense—he bought a bottle of fine Champagne and booked us in a
booth. Little did we know that the rest of the band in the club were all in
fancy dress, causing mayhem on the dance floor, led by a riotous Mick Avory.
Grenville and I had just negotiated a crucial deal point when paramedics
arrived to assist someone who had collapsed on the dance floor. A small
group of dancers were in cheap costumes purchased from a novelty shop
on the Boulevard: to my horror I recognised them as members of the Kinks.
There were a few clowns; the Baptist was dressed as a Viking; John Dalton
wore a Donald Duck outfit. There was a sense of concern from all around
as a man dressed as Coco the Clown was carried past us on a stretcher. It
was only when the semiconscious body went by that I discerned it was Mick
Avory. Fortunately, no one else from the recording company recognised
Mick, who was in full makeup, complete with red nose and orange wig. Mick

AMERICANA

saw me and tried to reach out as the stretcher went by, but the situation was too embarrassing, and I chose to ignore him. "Poor fellow," I said. "He must have taken a nasty tumble." It transpired that Mick had fallen trying to do a somersault and had a pinched nerve in his back.

The next day Grenville called a meeting to instil some discipline into the band, but a hungover John Gosling arrived at the meeting still dressed in his Viking outfit, blowing his Viking horn, and carrying a bottle of Jack Daniel's. Grenville just put his head in his hands and left the room, exclaiming, "This is futile. I give up!" It was around this time that Grenville took up meditation to calm his nerves, while around him the clowns partied on whenever they could.

AS TOURING BECAME MORE INTENSIVE, Ken Jones did more and more to undermine the management team of Collins and Wace at Boscobel Productions. By this time he could virtually run a tour single-handedly, without their help. The rest of the band didn't really disagree with this. A parting of ways between Collins and Wace—the two stockbroker types—and the Kinks was long overdue. To their credit, Boscobel was part of the English "team" that had overcome the music establishment by challenging traditional British show-business rules. Collins and Wace, with their public-school accents and upper-class affectations, and the Kinks, with our working-class directness, appeared to be a perfect combination. But during the '60s euphoria, Collins and Wace had, in my opinion, assisted us in making some well-intentioned but naive business decisions that haunt me and the band to this day.

Mo Ostin had been given his worldwide hit with "Lola" and its album, *Lola versus Powerman and the Moneygoround, Part One*. However, the album did not do as well as we'd hoped, despite having a great follow-up single in "Apeman." It also had many other key tracks, such as "This Time Tomorrow" and "Strangers." It was generally thought by the Kinks that it was time, particularly with our new American campaign looming, to leave Pye Records in the UK along with Reprise Records in America. It seemed an appropriate time to bring about a parting of the ways all around. We found it increasingly easier to deal with our U.S. agent, Herb Spar, while Ken did the tour management and I had more direct contact with the record companies.

No one who'd witnessed that disastrous '60s tour envisioned that the Kinks would still be able to tour and make records into the 1970s, but I was determined to get back the success that was taken away from us because of the American ban.

However, it was not certain that we would receive our full entitlement from the business itself. Songs like "Got to Be Free," "Powerman," "The Moneygoround," and "This Time Tomorrow" were indications of our actual plight, and certainly said a lot about my emotional state as a writer. I wanted desperately to be free from the power man and wondered where on earth I would be this time tomorrow. My work was not only defining me as a person, it was becoming my whole life and dictating my future as a human being—which was not entirely helpful to my own well-being. I spent more and more time away from my family, either in the studio or on tour. It was the quest for artistic freedom that spurred us on. Writing songs in order to survive was my only way to take revenge.

6

THE BIG WEIRD

"Another balmy night in old Tremé,
Creole ladies dance and sway,
Look at that girl she looks so young, flirting like she's having fun. She
    says,
'Hey Casanova, look what I have got, there's a ding dong down the block,
Big strong men in party frocks'
Party time in the Big Weird
Whores, punks, pimps, and dancing queers, can't you dig the weirdness,
    come and join the weirdness, don't you love the weirdness of it all?
Fell for this girl she was so young,
Am gonna hate myself when mornin' comes,
But I lost her somewhere in the crowd
With the music playing much too loud,
I can't stand the weirdness, I can't stand the weirdness, I can't take the
    weirdness of it all . . .
I don't know how I ended up down here, it's gonna end in tears
Drifted into this desolate space,
I feel so out of place
I can see it now in a couple more years I'll be stuck in the Big Weird
But she'll be outta here,
Look at me now full of self-destruction, that part of the big seduction
Yeah livin' in the Big Weird,
Another rainy day in old Tremé, even the funeral parlour closed today
But there's a party on just across the way, and there's a brass band
    playin' on a dead man's grave,
No I can't take the weirdness, I can't stand the weirdness, I can't cope
    with the weirdness of it all,
But it's Mardi Gras in New Orleans
All those big brass bands and dancin' queens . . ."

Whether it's Mardi Gras, Jazz Fest, Voodoo Fest, or even a funeral in the French Quarter, there is always a party going on somewhere in New Orleans. It's a city that needs tourists and conventions to exist. During my visits there I had become friends with a local couple, Bob Tannen and Jeanne Nathan, who aside from being creative spirits in their own right were advocates for saving the wetlands of America and campaigning to have land reclaimed from the sea. But despite being below sea level, the ocean's encroachment, and the constant struggle with poverty, crime, and lack of opportunity for underprivileged people of New Orleans, the upbeat atmosphere seems to go on almost relentlessly. Perhaps it only serves as a mild antidote for the more disadvantaged people who live there, but whenever there is a convention or festival it is "party time," and the bars seem full of music and celebration of one kind or another.

I'm not generally a "clubby" person. I like to go to clubs in my own time, unannounced. But my initial stay in New Orleans was not like that. It was impossible to go privately at this time. J.J. took me, Rory, and friends to all the hot spots, and we got in for free, but like the proverbial "lunch" there is no such thing as a free pass. For a habitually private person like me, every handshake seemed like a massive intrusion. In NOLA, or the Big Weird, as I started to call New Orleans, there seemed to be a tom-tom system that told everybody where everybody else would be.

One night we went to a club called El Matador owned by actor Rio Hackford, son of the film producer/director Taylor Hackford. There was a new band in town playing there, a duo called the White Stripes, and I wanted to see them. They were looking for a record deal at the time and their music was incredibly tight—they slotted into each other's playing in a way that made them sound full, so it didn't matter that they didn't have a bass player.

During the intermission after their first set, someone came over to me and asked if I'd like to meet Alex Chilton. I said no—it was my night off and I did not want to meet anybody, I just wanted to enjoy the music. That was a lie. I was just being a misfit and enjoying my own company.

I knew Alex had been in the Box Tops and had recorded one of my favourite songs in the '60s, "The Letter." I also knew that he was possibly grumpier than I was, so I left it at that.

Some of my songs are sometimes better company than real people. Many musical characters inhabit my world: they are good, bad, kind, mean, and sometimes mischievous. I usually write a theme song in my head for nearly every person I encounter in the real world. They exist as part of my musical memory so that afterward I cast them in my own musical version of life, which is often more truthful than reality. Long-term friends are usually accompanied by a good tune. On the other hand, people that don't bring a good theme song with them rarely stay in my life. It's a form of "musical schizophrenia" that evolved in my childhood; these imaginary musical allies are sometimes more credible than the real people I encounter. As a child I was very quiet, very secluded, and it was music that helped me relate to and confront the real world—without music I would probably never have interacted with people.

Alex Chilton brought his own song with him and I respected that. We'd catch up in our own time without the assistance of other people.

Meanwhile, I hid away in the corner of the club and sat behind the bar. Then I heard a voice that sounded familiar. "What you doing in town?" I turned around, and it was Travis Davis.

WHENEVER I SEE SOMEONE FROM MY OWN MUSICAL UNIVERSE, their unique musical theme slips into my head, a theme that represents my perception of their true character. After a while the real person I know blends into the imaginary person I have invented. As sometimes happens in life, often the real person you know disappears—you lose touch, they move on, you move on. But if I need someone, all I have to do is remember their theme song—and some strange musical voodoo brings them to life. Travis Davis was such a person. As a young aspiring guitar player starting out in London I'd once connected with Travis. He was a decade older than I and had played serious modern jazz trumpet when we first met, but he had given up playing full-time when younger rock musicians like me came along. He had been my inspirational guide through my own world of "cool," and I wanted to connect with him again. I wanted to go back to the source of all the music that inspired me when I started out, and after numerous trips across America visiting inner cities that for the most part were desolate and lacking in heart,

I made the assessment that New Orleans was the starting point of all my musical aspirations: country music, Cajun music, Dixieland, boogie-woogie and soul, trad jazz, skiffle, bebop, rock and roll. It all came from somewhere, and it had to be in New Orleans. That's why I went there; that's why people like Travis probably gravitated there.

Travis Davis had become my spiritual mentor and muse; whenever I felt the need to write great riffs, he always seemed to be in my head. His symbolic nod of approval was all the encouragement I needed, and whenever I lost the plot I imagined he was always over my shoulder to put me back on track.

Although he was in his mid to late sixties, Travis exuded a youthful quality. He was not a very tall person, but he had a large presence. His deceptively thin frame looked fit under his dark suit. He was not an expensive dresser, but it was obvious that he had taste and probably knew where the best thrift stores were. There was an air of frailty behind his squinted eyes, as though he'd known hard times. What I admired about him was that, unlike me, he seemed to have confronted all his demons but was not about to let the world know if there were any left. He drank but not to excess. Never saw him tipsy or dishevelled. He told me that he often had a quiet nightcap at the Circle Bar or at Cosimo's Bar in order to get away from his own joint. He'd sit and chew the fat with some of the regulars as a form of respite from the responsibilities of running his own place. He had a good bar manager, but it was T.D. who was the real draw. Not to say that Travis was a people person. Far from it. The locals loved him because they knew that Travis had the knack of picking the right music and used his special touch with people to make everyone feel welcome. He appeared to be in control.

He was Fred C. Dobbs, Lee Marvin, Hoagy Carmichael, and a touch of Stan Laurel all rolled into one. Sometimes I would walk past a shop window, and on seeing my reflection I would turn my face and smile in that crooked way Travis had. He was a striking-looking fellow when he decided to turn on the charm; not outrageously handsome in the classic sense, but Travis looked like nobody else. He never gave the impression he was a ladies' man; even though he had women admirers, somehow he seemed too aloof to participate in sexual banter. Perhaps it was shyness. He confided in me that there had been a special woman once, but it never worked out. I think he was embarrassed to admit that he'd followed her from state to state trying to patch up a relationship that was broken, which ended up making him feel like a complete sucker. Somehow no other woman would ever get close to him again. It's like he knew my story because he'd lived it himself. Despite the differences in our ages, Travis was almost a mirror image of the way I imagined I'd be in ten years' time.

He'd been a bit of a legend when he played clubs, back when I was starting out; that's why I was shocked when he told me that he'd stopped playing. He could have been one of the great players, could have been another Chet Baker, but he'd fallen through the cracks when my beat generation had come along. While Lol Coxhill and Ronnie Scott had cut their losses and gone on their own musical journeys, Travis retreated into the jazz wilderness, changed his identity, and even changed his name. He'd lived in Denmark, Sweden, and Hamburg, Germany, for a while, looking for gigs, but became disillusioned. When I'd played in the Dave Hunt Band in Soho in the early '60s, it was Travis who came to my rescue when the bandleader had reprimanded me for playing too loud. He said, "The solo was slow and full of soul. Even though it was a little too loud it wasn't a solo so much as a great riff." I was sixteen, and hearing that from Travis helped my confidence no end. I'd seen him play on one of those American air force bases that were dotted around the east of England since the Second World War, and he was a hell of a player. Afterward, he'd tried to open his own club in London, but saxophonist Ronnie Scott had it sewn up. He'd moved back to his native Midwest and finally opened his own bar.

It was nice to catch up and reminisce with Travis for a while at the El Matador. Suddenly he stood up to leave just as I was getting engrossed in one of his stories. "I've got to be somewhere soon. Enjoy the White Stripes. See you around town. Oh, and be careful in this neighbourhood. People get shot." He downed the rest of his drink, then disappeared into the crowd and was gone.

AFTER THAT VISIT TO NOLA I went back and forth from the "Big Weird" to England, and for the most part Rory stayed in New Orleans, working as a waitress-manager at a bar near the racetrack. Whenever I came back to town, I stayed in a small two-room apartment down the street from the rambling home of my friends Bob and Jeanne, whom I visited with often. The couple appeared to be in with all the movers and shakers; Bob was a semi-retired architect who was involved in the local arts scene, and Jeanne was a former TV journalist who worked as a community campaigner and broadcaster.

The apartment was very basic, but it had a celebrated list of former "tenants," including Alex Chilton. The front entrance exuded elegance, while the street at the back seemed like it was in the third world. That's the charm and attraction of New Orleans: every door you walk through can lead you to somewhere unexpected. Every morning I would be awakened by the distant sound of the marching band rehearsing at John McDonogh High School, which was on the next block. The sounds—naive beginners, crumbled notes, and musical promise—fascinated me so much that I asked Bob to arrange for me to meet the head of music at the school. I'd seen the marching band at Mardi Gras and thought I had found the connection I was searching for—the connection that had made my journey worthwhile.

THE MARCHING BAND

During my visits back and forth from London to New Orleans, I had entered into discussions with the head of music at White Hart Lane, a secondary school in a working-class area of North London that somehow reminded me of John McDonogh High School. The head of music at White Hart Lane was enthusiastic about my idea to start a music program at the London school and work out some sort of exchange program between them and John McDonogh.

Somewhat audaciously, I decided that it might be easier to bring New Orleans to North London—to entertain, educate, and in many ways liberate London schoolchildren from the constraints of the politically correct bias that was beginning to engulf every aspect of British life. I had no idea where the money would come from to make this musical exchange happen but I started to move forward with blind faith hoping that somehow this would be funded from somewhere.

As far apart as the two schools may have seemed geographically, there were many similarities and a few major differences. At White Hart Lane I was told that more than fifty languages were spoken by children from many different countries and cultures. Also, after I went to the school open house, it was obvious to me that although the music played there reflected the multi-ethnic diversity of the school, there was no sight or sound of anything that represented traditional British culture. More importantly, there was nothing that brought the different cultures together. The nearest it came was when the Irish headmistress got up on stage at the end of the afternoon to sing a stirring version of the folk song "The Irish Rover." However, it felt like the London kids still had interracial divisions between them and that culturally there was no common ground, apart from what they saw on TV.

John McDonogh, on the other hand, seemed to have the marching band as a unifying force. It was a way of giving many deprived kids in New Orleans an opportunity to engage with the local culture. Local kids could join the marching band when school started in August, and by early in the following year could conceivably be performing in the Mardi Gras parade. There was also a healthy competition between the various school marching bands, whereas healthy rivalry was probably frowned upon by the overly politically correct powers of the London education system at that time.

In my own naive way I saw music as a means to break down barriers put up by racial stereotypes and cultural separation. I wanted to see diversity as well as a healthy fusion between children from Jamaica and those from Eastern Europe, and music could help do this. Perhaps then a new British music might emerge. The golden age of Britpop had been long gone by this time, and popular music was in a wilderness. When I inquired what local kids were writing and playing, I was told that for the most part it was rap—nothing that vaguely resembled English or even British traditional culture. Not that I wanted children from Serbia or Poland to dance around the maypole and sing English folk songs, but it worried me that a generation was emerging that had no awareness of the musical history of the country they chose to live in.

Kids in New Orleans, on the other hand, if they were lucky, had extensive access to the city's jazz and blues heritage. Rap and jazz seemed to go hand in hand. There was also no danger that I wouldn't know the right buzzwords. The kids knew instinctively what a "groove" was; I wouldn't have to learn a new urban street talk or have to come up against the argot of the London inner-city hip. There was no danger of being overly nationalistic or jingoistic in New Orleans because of its desire to promote its own musical heritage with such energised abandon. As poor as the city was, the New Orleans school system seemed to have a way of plugging into the musical culture so that the kids could connect with the local jazz heritage. I watched the marching band rehearse at the school and was inspired by the energy and dedication of the teachers and the efforts and commitments of the pupils themselves.

There was another difference: I was told that in America, many of the schoolchildren still recite the Pledge of Allegiance every day, which I think in a strange way helps form a bond among all new Americans. I still got the sense that there was a possibility that the American dream might still exist. In other words, a person will always feel like a misfit when there is nothing to fit into.

7

THANKSGIVING DAY

"Are you going on Thanksgiving Day to those family celebrations?
Passing on knowledge down through the years at the gathering of
*   generations,*
Every year it's the same routine, all over the American Dream.
Papa looks over at the small gathering remembering days gone by
Smiles at the children as he watches them play, and wishes his wife was
*   still by his side*
She would always cook dinner on Thanksgiving Day
It's all over the American Way."

When the Kinks first went to America in the '60s and early '70s, we always thought Thanksgiving Day was just a day off, like a bank holiday. The first time I was actually asked to somebody's house for Thanksgiving dinner was when the Kinks played the Felt Forum, underneath Madison Square Garden, on November 27–28 in 1974. The venue held about three or four thousand people. Ronnie Delsener promoted the show but he must have felt sorry for the Kinks—despite the fact that we had sold out two nights—because he invited us to his house for Thanksgiving dinner. The real significance of Thanksgiving didn't strike me even then. It wasn't until I spent more time in the States in the late '90s and early in 2000 that I realised the holiday's significance to families: Thanksgiving was, in a way, more important than Christmas.

I had been to a family Thanksgiving dinner in New Jersey and as I'd come from a large family myself, I appreciated the ceremonial gathering.

On a visit to New Orleans in 2002, I spent Thanksgiving in New Orleans at J.J.'s place, where she had invited a bunch of people over. The thing that struck me about this particular dinner was that no one was related; there were no family members. Everyone was too far away from home, unwilling to travel, or, more likely, just plain lost. This was J.J.'s finest moment because she acted as a surrogate parent to all who were present, even me. While some of the assorted characters were hungover or out of it for one reason or another, she managed to bring them together as a family. It made me painfully aware of how much I missed my own family at this time. J.J. must have recognised this in me and provided some measure of humanitarian warmth towards me that I had not recognised in her before. I almost christened her "Saint J.J., patron of the lost souls." There was no dining table as such; as a result, everyone sat on chairs with food on their laps or sat cross-legged on the floor.

I don't usually eat meat (although I occasionally eat turkey), yet I was taken aback that J.J. had purchased a hybrid dish called turducken—a mixture of turkey, duck, and chicken that had been pressed together in order to form some sort of mutant bird. The dish was apparently quite popular in the South but was inedible to a finicky North London eater like me. I politely "passed" on the turducken and headed for the roast vegetables. As the meal came to an end people started to leave and just as I was about to get up from my seat next to J.J. she took my hand and squeezed it tightly before kissing me gently on the cheek.

"Happy Thanksgiving, hon." Her voice was soft and a little croaky. "That's one for your family who can't be here."

"And for your family also," I replied.

I was unsure how to react but I have no doubt that her intentions were honest and sincere. Underneath the tough veneer there was a once gentle soul that was now almost afraid to come out. She must have worked in some pretty tough environments to get that edge to her personality. When she got up to show some people out, she straightened her tight skirt, which had slipped up her legs while she was sitting down next to me, and for the first time I noticed what great legs she had. She turned and smiled, showing those incredible white teeth, which were framed by her rich deep red lips. Her mascara had smudged slightly, probably because she had become slightly emotional when she was talking to me about her family. I'd never thought about her age before, but she couldn't have been more than forty. I could hardly believe it but there I was being seduced over a stuffed turducken dinner from Winn-Dixie.

After the dinner J.J. and I escorted all the stragglers and strolled over to a nearby bar lounge owned by the late legendary blues singer Ernie-K-Doe with his wife and co-proprietor Miss Antoinette. We'd been there a few years earlier when Ernie was still alive. Now we thought we'd stop by and pay our respects and reminisce about Ernie. The lounge was still the same; the bar was upfront, but the back room, which had only held about twenty or thirty people, was where the music happened. On most nights Ernie would have been the star attraction. The night that we'd seen Ernie play, Miss Antoinette must have taken a shine to me because she led me to the front row centre so that Ernie could sing straight at me. Ernie was small in stature; he resembled a miniature James Brown with shoulder-length black hair that must have been a wig. He wore a velvet cabaret-style jacket, a frilly shirt on top of the obligatory flares, and boots with Cuban heels. His fingers were covered with rings, and his nails were perfectly manicured; he made expressive movements with his elegant hands as he moved in a slightly effeminate way and sang into a large retro microphone.

Ernie sang his hit from the dawn of rock and roll, "Mother-in-Law," followed by a new song that preached racial harmony, "White Boy/Black Boy." It wasn't until the second chorus when Ernie had reached out and shook my hand as he sang the words "white boy" that I realised I was the only white boy in the back room. It was a sincere gesture on Ernie's part, and it touched me deeply, because I never thought for a moment he knew who I was, I had the feeling Ernie didn't know any musicians who appeared after 1962. When Ernie died in July 2001 he would have the full New Orleans funeral marching bands and a parade that marched all through the streets of the French Quarter, totally appropriate and befitting a great New Orleans musician. The only thing that bothered me slightly was that after Ernie's death, Miss Antoinette commissioned a life-size statue of him that she placed at the entrance to the bar, so it would seem to greet punters as they walked in. The statue was dressed in Ernie's stage gear and was so lifelike that some cruel patrons said she had Ernie's body stuffed and mummified.

Now Ernie was gone. We stayed and had a few drinks with Miss Antoinette, who was working behind the bar by herself that day. She complained it was hard to get bar staff to work on Thanksgiving so she relied on friends to help out. As we left I looked at the statue of Ernie smiling and dressed in the same outfit and wig he'd worn when I'd seen him perform a few years earlier, but it freaked me out when I thought about the stuffed turducken dinner I'd just been to.

Then we took a trip to visit Alex Chilton in his little house on Prieur Street. By this time Alex had become a notorious shut-in. He had been invited to J.J.'s gathering but had failed to turn up, which led everyone to fear that he may have died lying on his couch, reading Thackeray, of whom he was very fond. A few of us knocked on his door, but there was no response from within. We were thinking about calling 911 when a meek-sounding "Who is it?" came from behind the door. We stepped back as the door to the shotgun-style house slowly creaked open, revealing Alex looking somewhat disoriented. He ushered us in to reveal that he was indeed reading Thackeray. The television, which must have dated back to the 1970s, was on the local news channel, but the sound was turned down.

"I like this newscaster because he's got a great mullet" was Alex's explanation. I looked over at the small couch and noted that there was an imprint of Alex's body where he must have sat—and probably slept—day after day. When we asked why he didn't come to Thanksgiving dinner, Alex made his way to the microwave to produce a single chicken potpie. "Why travel across town when you can eat in the comfort of your own home?" We stayed for a while, then left him to finish his chicken potpie in the peace and quiet of his own home.

MEANWHILE, I HAD MORE than chicken potpie on my mind. I had to get back to London to put a band together and take care of many business issues. My deal with Guardian Records was over, and their owners, EMI, had not yet committed to releasing my next record, so I was considering talking to other labels. I was even being courted by the Sanctuary Records Group, who wanted to manage me as well as acquire all my publishing. They had already purchased the Kinks back catalogue from the previous owners, but I was determined to retain my independence.

Back in the old days, the band would complain about the business chaos around us, have a few beers, and then move on. In those days I could confide in my band, then we would regroup and after considering the latest errors and disasters, I'd write another song and we'd do some gigs.

Things were always put in perspective because I had the Kinks. We were comrades. Now I was struggling, using session players whom I was trying to mould into a unit that resembled a band. The songs were, for the most part, finished, but a few more still had to be written. I already had enough songs for nearly three albums, but they didn't seem to connect. Another thing about being a solo artist is that I had to work around other people's schedules and availabilities. This required me to stay in the UK for longer than I'd intended, which increased my travel load. Flying back and forth from the UK to New Orleans was becoming a drain. Meanwhile, I was looking for someone to produce my record with me.

In fall 2001, I had flown down to Nashville to see Jim Pitt, who had organised a tribute album of my songs called *This Is Where I Belong*. Jim knew lots of studios and producers in Nashville, and he would show me around. On this trip, I met Ray Kennedy at his studio in Nashville. Ray had produced Lucinda Williams's Grammy-winning album *Car Wheels on a Gravel Road*, and he had always expressed an interest in producing a record with someone from the British Invasion. Ray was going to be in Europe at Christmas because his wife came from Liverpool, and we thought it would be a good chance to do a tryout track, so we arranged for him to come to Konk Studios in London during the holidays. The track we recorded was called "After the Fall"—one of the first songs I had written for my solo record. We used some of the session musicians I had either auditioned or worked with during my demo period. Ray liked Konk and thought about working there. We stayed in touch, but nothing really developed because of our various schedules.

By the spring of 2002, I had a bunch of musicians I thought I could tour with, and I wanted to record with them. I met with British co-producer and engineer Laurie Latham, and we started laying down some tracks. He didn't want to use my musicians for various reasons, so we used session musicians of his choice. I felt I needed a co-producer: before now, with the Kinks, I'd always produced our albums myself, but being a solo performer I needed the objectivity and another pair of ears. After I put down our first track I realised how nervous I was. This was a complete change for me; I was a solo artist and these were great session players, but was it a group yet? These questions were still unanswered. Also, the song choices I agreed on with Laurie were very British songs. We didn't record anything that was written in New Orleans because Laurie thought that American songs would not be relevant to what he felt should be a classic British album.

The recording was sporadic during the summer due to various scheduling conflicts and prior commitments. In the fall I toured the UK with my touring band, which also cost us some momentum in the studio.

It wasn't until December that Laurie and I agreed to try some tracks with my touring band, and we put down the rhythm tracks to "The Getaway," "The Tourist," "Next-Door Neighbour," and "Run Away from Time."

I also took time out of my own recording to participate in a collaboration album that Laurie was producing. I did a song called "Yours Truly, Confused N10," which I'd sung on Jools Holland's New Year's show the previous year.

Principal recording on my album stopped at Easter of 2003, when Laurie and I parted company. I continued working with other engineers in between tour dates in the UK, which concluded at London's Royal Festival Hall.

During the late summer I took some recording equipment to my house in Surrey to do some demos with my brother, Dave. This would be the last time we would work together. They were inconclusive songs but powerfully played, and they exist to this day on a computer hard drive. When Dave left my house, I continued to make demos on my own. I wrote a song about trusting relationships called "Honest," which I would later demo with Dick Nolan and Toby Baron, who were becoming regulars with my tour band. The song had a prophetic and telling last lyric:

"And when love dies, lay flowers upon it
I really tried. . . . Honest."

The song was probably a last-gasp attempt to show in musical terms how impossible it was to stay in a relationship while I was struggling with my career. Rory was a straightforward, sensible person with no pretentions, while my life was too chaotic at this time. Just the same, she was good to have around whenever I got back to New Orleans. She was easy on the eye with that flowing blonde hair combined with her confident midwestern swagger that made heads turn. I had no worries in that area because I trusted her enough to know that she was loyal to the person she was with, but the problem was that because of my travel schedule I was not able to be there all the time.

I was also progressing my musical, *Come Dancing*, at this time, as well as taking meetings with record companies about my album distribution. This was punctuated with trips to Ireland to visit my daughter and to New York to meet with music publishers, potential managers. On a few occasions Rory would come to New York from New Orleans to offer some support but as loyal as she was, I could sense that she was becoming impatient about where I was going to settle.

Thanksgiving Day 2003 was coming up, and I was planning to mix my record in the UK. One of the new songs I had recorded in London was "Thanksgiving Day," which at the time had a happy ending as all loved ones finally resolve their personal differences in time for Thanksgiving.

"In a dark apartment on the wrong side of the town
A lonely spinster prays for a handsome lover and a passionate embrace
And kisses all over all over all over her American face.

Today she seems so far away
From the friends in her hometown
So she runs for the Greyhound
She'll spend hours on the bus but she reached town
For Thanksgiving Day.
Come on over, come on over, it's Thanksgiving Day."

DESPITE THE OPTIMISTIC SENTIMENT IN THE SONG, I was beginning to accept that another personal relationship was doomed, and I needed a few days alone, so I drove to a secluded house at a seaside resort town a few hours away from London. I'd just pulled into the drive when a call came on my mobile. It was my office; they said I was needed in New York for some important meetings at Universal. I explained that I was too tired and emotional to travel. My work commitments were building up, and I said that right now it would be impossible to fly to the States from the UK. But they were insistent.

I was still standing in the doorway of the house, in the tranquillity of rural England. It was like another world from America. Many of my projects were coming to a head, and the last thing I needed was to go on another international flight. Part of a typical week in October of 2003 went as follows:

Day One:
10:30 a.m.: A meeting with Bill Taylor from Andrew Lloyd Webber's production company and Sonia Friedman to discuss a workshop for the musical *Come Dancing.*, 3:00 p.m.: A meeting with a new engineer-producer to continue the recording of my solo album., 6:00 p.m.: An event sponsored by Granada television about Arsenal Football Club. At that time Granada was interested in doing a Kinks video retrospective.

Day Two:
9:30 a.m.: In my studio with the new engineer and my studio band., 1:00 p.m.: A meeting with an architect to discuss the proposed renovation of Konk Studios., 4:00 p.m.: A meeting in an editing room with producers of a documentary about me to edit down scenes from my *Storyteller* tour.

Day Three:
10:00 a.m.: A meeting at Konk to play some of my new material for potential publishers., 1:30 p.m.: Back in the editing room for the day to cut down the footage for the documentary makers.

On October 28 I had a casting meeting at the Old Vic in London to look at possible actors for the *Come Dancing* workshop, then I went straight to the editing room to continue cutting footage for the television documentary.

I rearranged everything as best I could, and on November 12 I flew to the States. After arriving in New York I decided to book a flight to New Orleans after my business was concluded to see Rory one more time. I had dinner with an old friend in New York who advised me to forget New Orleans and go home and finish my work. But I felt I had to resolve the relationship in one way or another. On Friday the fourteenth I got a flight down to New Orleans, but not before I had a meeting at Universal Records, where they informed me that they had just passed on my album. This was not great news to receive, but I just put it to one side. I knew there would be an outlet for my record at some point; meanwhile, I had to take care of unresolved business.

When I got to New Orleans I checked myself into a hotel on Canal Street. On the way, I drove past the house where Rory had moved to but there was no one at home so I went out for a drink. My spirits were lifted by the sight of a large fellow wearing a Masonic fez. He was a mixture of British vaude-ville comedian Tommy Cooper and Raymond Burr in the Hitchcock movie *Rear Window*. He was a doctor at a local hospital but was also a part-time promoter of rock events. He was dancing and jumping around the dance floor like a huge loveable elephant. He lightened up my night and I hoped that if ever had to meet him in his professional capacity he would still make me laugh. Later, I finally got a hold of Rory and we agreed to meet the next day at my hotel to discuss our situation, but when it was time for the meeting she was a no-show.

She said she would meet me in a couple days' time, when she felt a bit more centred. So I had to hang around this hotel on Canal Street. This enforced downtime gave me the opportunity to mull over my predica-ment, and my prognosis was not great. I felt I had really screwed up. Some Thanksgiving this would be. I sat and wondered how I got into this situation. Even the problem with the record companies and my own career seemed insignificant but nevertheless all these issues whirled around in my mind while I sat in my hotel room. My life was in a complete mess. I headed to the French Quarter hoping to find Travis Davis, but as always when you need people the most they are never there. I went to the Riff Club but found out that he was out of town for the weekend. Smart move; I wish that I had done the same.

I wandered around the Quarter in a fugue state. I didn't know where I was. I thought about when I had first met Rory and how we danced and laughed to the song "Big River" by Johnny Cash. The song was about this woman he'd met in St. Paul and how she'd make him eventually cry so many tears that they flooded the Big River. The world started to spin round. It was as though I was everywhere at once, but was actually in meltdown. First, in my hometown at Muswell Hill . . . then the Hollywood Bowl in L.A. . . . nearly crashing my car in a dark road in Surrey . . . then confronting some buskers singing in my face outside the House of Voodoo in the French Quarter. I hadn't been drinking, but I found it hard to stand up straight; it was a mixture of jet lag, concern, and exhaustion.

I walked past the New Orleans Athletic Club and considered going in for a workout and possibly drowning in the pool there. "Big River" went through my head, then segued into my song "The Tourist." As dissonant chords went out of key in my head, my brother Dave stood in a doorway when he was a child playing a banjo, while my youngest daughter skipped around the pavement singing *"Oh, let's go to the Mardi Gras . . . ,"* but I was too tired to go anywhere. The French Quarter seemed full of noise but no music. I thought I saw Travis on a street corner but just as I managed to cross the busy street, he must have ducked into a shadowy doorway.

It was not so much as whether Travis was real or not, but more about whether I existed at all without a good tune to accompany me. My inner musical world that had comforted me for so long was suddenly imploding. I wanted two notes that had soul rather than a perfectly worked out song that had no emotion. Without my shadow man to guide me I was a lost, clumsy imitation of a person.

Like Travis, I'd rather have disappeared on that street there and then than leave the city with no creative resolution or even a glimmer of inspiration. I would not write great songs but like Travis, I could still dream them. Perhaps my life was becoming like a good demo record—full of sketches and promise but destined to be unresolved. Instead of a series of flawed, cheap-sounding melodies, I had wanted to leave New Orleans with a great opus but my songs, like my life, had become only an impression of something worthy. My ideas were full of ambitions and aspirations that were the size of a continent bigger than America but I simply hadn't the ability to deliver the musical goods. Not for any publisher or record company, but to myself. Schooled, classical players are blessed in that they can blithely follow the notes placed before them and surrender to the score, knowing and trusting that the song journey has been written out for them by the composer's desire. My song world, in contrast, had become totally improvised, with no theme or direction. I was inventing my musical formula as I went along.

It didn't matter to me whether Travis was really there or not. He'd pop back into my life when he was good and ready in between the cracks of my reality. Some real people can talk the talk, bleed when they cut themselves, have feelings and emotions that pronounce them normal, but the payback is that they can only dream symphonies that simulate the normal world, while Travis brings a new riff every time he arrives, offering possibilities I could have never envisaged without him.

THE STREETS WERE CROWDED so I walked down Rampart Street and came upon a church. I went in and talked to the priest, explaining to him how confused I was. We sat in the peace and tranquillity of his church and spoke for about an hour, which seemed to give me strength and clarity. A few days later I met Rory at the apartment she was staying in, where she explained that she would like to give us a try but she was tormented by things in her own life. We decided to take more time to figure things out.

I would have stayed longer, but I had to be back in London on November 20 for meetings about my musical *Come Dancing*, and for another recording session with the band. I also had to get back to London to take care of many personal and professional issues that had built up—but most of all, to spend Christmas with my daughter. Rory and I agreed to meet up in New York between Christmas and New Year's.

"Now papa looks out of the window
The sight brings a smile to his face.
He sees all his children coming back home
Together on this special day.
Come on over, come on over, it's Thanksgiving Day."

I'VE HEARD THAT BEAT BEFORE, DECEMBER 2003

A few weeks later I found myself on a whistle-stop tour of Ireland to visit my daughter for Christmas, before going on to London, then back to New Orleans via New York, where I would meet Rory after she came back from spending Christmas in Minneapolis. Now it seemed as if I were flying every day, but at least the drive and ferry trip over to Ireland offered some respite from the bad conversations I had been having with Rory over the phone. It was dark as I approached a small Irish village near my daughter's house, where I was staying in a small cottage. The mobile phone reception there was, to say the least, erratic, and it often cut out just when an argument was reaching fever pitch. If it had been a landline phone, I could have slammed the receiver down, and that would have been it, but unfortunately mobile phones do not allow you that luxury. On a cell phone, it's unsatisfying to say, "I hate your guts," and then politely press the END button; the little click seems inconclusive.

There was better mobile reception at high elevations, which would at least give more clarity to the next argument, so I drove to the top of a nearby cliff, where it was pitch black. I reversed into what I thought was a cul-de-sac when suddenly my car keeled over backwards. I looked over the backseat and discovered to my horror that I was balanced precariously over the edge of a cliff. The back wheels were hanging over the edge, dangling in thin air, while just the front wheels were connected to the little gravel road at the top of the cliff. It was Christmas Day, and no one was about; no one could help me. I suddenly remembered the advert for the film *Alien* when it first came out: *In space no one can hear you scream.* No one could hear me scream at the top of the hill in Ireland.

After five minutes I started to panic. I turned off the engine and put on the hand brake, but the car still appeared to want to keel over backwards as I tried to get out. On a normal day, people would be passing by in their cars on the way to the village, but on this cold Christmas night there was no one about. Even the mobile signal had disappeared. I was completely trapped and isolated, stuck in my car. A car did come past, but the driver just waved his fist at me and shouted abuse, thinking I was badly parked. If only he'd known how desperate I was. My situation seemed perilous, but a rhythm came into my head. A sort of tip-tappy vaudevillian soft-shoe shuffle beat to help take my mind off the seemingly near-death predicament I was in. I thought, if I'm going to fall off this cliff it's going to be while I'm tapping a happy beat. Then, a miracle—a police car turned a corner. The police officers got out and approached the car. First they asked for my documents and wanted to Breathalyze me, thinking I was a local party reveller who'd gotten lost. I tried to explain my geographical situation: perched precariously at the top of a hill. The officer who addressed me was very nonchalant. "Yes, it looks like we have a problem here, so, but we can't help you. We can't pull you out; our car is not strong enough. We'll go into town and see if there is a garage open. Just hold it there, stay where you are, stay in the car, and we'll send help. No problem." No problem? I could feel the vehicle gradually slipping backwards.

I sat for what seemed like hours. Then I saw headlights appear at the top of the hill. A large figure got out of a van, silhouetted against the night sky. I was beginning to panic at this point.

"Who are you? Can you help me? I'm going to fall off the cliff if I get out of the car!"

Then a friendly face appeared in my headlights. It was Danny, a large, burly Irishman wearing a flat cap who specialised in breakdowns and accident recovery. The police had chosen the right man. Danny secured a large chain around the front of my car and hooked it onto the back of his recovery truck. After several desperate attempts he finally dragged me off the top of the slope. I was saved. I was leaving town over the Christmas holiday and offered to pay there and then. He quoted me a price for cash payment in euros. I fumbled around in my pockets but could only come up with half the amount in euros; I had some U.S. dollars and sterling to make up the rest. Danny may have looked like a working man, but when it came to money he assessed the exchange rate of the various currencies like a city trader.

"Now," he said sharply, "that's the amount down to the penny." Then he went on his way.

The next day I was really in no condition to drive, but I got the ferry and somehow made the return trip back to London just in time to get ready for the flight to New York. At the airport I had to have a stiff drink before boarding. On the flight I was given a newspaper that announced the death of actor Alan Bates, who was the star of some of the finest New Wave films of the 1960s. I put the newspaper in my travel bag so I could read the great actor's obit at my leisure when I reached New York. I actually got a couple of hours' sleep on the flight, but that "tip-tappy" beat from the clifftop in Ireland kept going through my head.

On arrival I was met by a concerned-looking Rory, who hardly spoke a word. I even took her to a swanky Midtown restaurant that served Scandinavian cuisine, where she sat stone-faced throughout the meal. Then she announced she'd been offered a high-paying job as a translator in Asia and was deciding whether to take it or not. We sat in silence for awhile. That beat from the cliff started going through my head. I started tapping out the beat on the table, only to receive a reprimand. We flew down to New Orleans on New Year's Eve and went straight to the apartment in the Tremé. Bob and Jeanne had invited me to a New Year's Eve party, but I decided that it was too late to go, so we stayed at home and quarrelled, finally calming down as the church bells from across the road announced that the New Year had begun and that 2004 had arrived. We turned off the lights to go to sleep, but a light shone through the floorboards, as though someone was living silently in the basement, spying on us. Someone paced around quietly in the apartment above. Outside on the street, a bottle smashed against a wall as a couple of drunks fought. It was going to be a long night, but it was just a prelude to what was to come. A melody shuffled around in my head along with the jet lag. A dope dealer's four-wheel-drive vehicle hovered on the corner outside. The *boom, boom* from the rap music playing in the car thumped, but thankfully Rory slept through it. Then that beat from the cliff top in Ireland started going through my head. I'd heard that beat before now, and it wouldn't go away until it became a song.

> *"The neighborhood's really going down since that couple upstairs*
> *arrived in town,*
> *Ain't never seen what they both look like*
> *But I sure can hear them when they start to fight*

They go at it.
He shouts at her and she shouts back, he slams the door and she starts
*   to pack,*
You know I can't help thinking starts me thinking you know I can't help
*   thinking*
I've heard that beat before.
And when he goes out to get drunk with friends, there's a record she
*   plays over and over again*
It reverberates and the bass end booms, and the window starts shaking
*   in my bathroom.*
It reminds me of a life I had, before the good times turned bad
And my heart starts aching, when the floor starts shaking,
And there ain't no mistakin' the beat I've heard before
I've heard it all before."

I quietly searched the darkened bedroom for some paper to write the lyrics on. I found the newspaper with Alan Bates's obituary in it, but it would be disrespectful to write on that. Eventually I found a long letter a fan had given me, so I started to scribble on the back of it.

"If you were still around you'd understand what I'm feelin'
Hearing that old familiar sound
The good and bad of all the love that we once had,

You know I can't help thinking,
I've heard that beat before."

The person in the apartment above must have been an insomniac, too, because he was still shuffling around—but amazingly, he was shuffling in time to that "beat" in my head. I scrambled around in my suitcase and found my Dictaphone. Now I was thankful for the light shining through the floorboards from the basement so I could find my way through to the bathroom. Once inside I could sit on the loo and whisper out the lyrics as they came into my head.

"What can I say what can I do, like me and you it's déjà vu
Those memories keep reappearing, another day, another night another
   row another fight,
Just can't stand what I'm hearing,
And I've heard that old beat before."

The following morning I went out for a ride on Rory's pedal bike. The great thing about the city is that it is almost totally flat, which makes it easy to cycle around. My mobile rang with Rory on the other end; she'd been unpacking my suitcase and she found a harmless letter from a fan whom she immediately accused me of having an affair with. I'd only met the woman once, when I was signing autographs after a show, but the letter did say that the woman loved me—meaning she loved my work. That was enough to send Rory on a tirade. I told her to rip up the letter, but then I realised it had my lyrics written on the back. Then she said she had discovered a woman's bra and panties tucked away in my suitcase. To lighten up the situation I tried to tell her I was a drag queen, but she wouldn't buy it. Then she remembered that in the rush to pack in the hotel in New York she had thrown a pile of some of her own clothes, which must have included her underwear, into my suitcase rather than repack her own. She realised her error but refused to see the irony. Things were going from bad to worse. I was considering getting hold of a flight back to London just until this all cooled down.

The next night I went for a long work out at the New Orleans Athletic Club. I stayed on for a swim and a steam bath. Rory had gone missing completely; I looked in the closet and her suitcase was gone. She'd done a runner. I went across the street to Cosimo's to kill some time and to my relief I saw Travis Davis. I told him about the situation I was in and my concerns about Rory. Travis stared at me as he spoke. "Your girl, she's got a Scandinavian background right? Well, they say that to most people love is a matter of life or death, only Scandinavian girls think it's more important than that."

I didn't get the joke. I tried to explain the difficulties Rory and I were having because of my lifestyle.

Travis stroked the day-old stubble on his chin. "That's what you get when you fall for a musician. A musician can go away and play the blues; sing

'Your Cheatin' Heart' or 'Frankie and Johnny' and somehow get away with it. Musicians are expected to be flawed. That's why women fall for them. A horn player can play 'The Saints' in F, but an angel never played the blues."

It would have sounded like a clichéd load of gibberish if it had been spoken by anyone else, but Travis had a way of delivering a story. Then he spoke as if he was setting up a coda for the final bars of a song; his verbal beats resounded powerfully as if to hand over to me to play the final chord, but I couldn't work out which key his song would end in.

"Maybe you and your girl are finished." He just sat there and read me the riot act.

This time his implied melody was full of questions that I could not respond to, full of unresolved phrases that defied musical genre; it was not the blues, ballad rock, or any other form. The song came in without a key signature or chord structure, yet it quoted a theme that had been in my head since childhood—only now I understood its journey and where the theme was taking me. It was a sad phrase that was coloured with occasional notes of optimism, indicating that there would be a resolution at the ending. Travis brought more than a simple song, it was a jigsaw puzzle. It was a complete symphony that was challenging me to fill in the musical gaps to his improvised score. I had set myself an emotional challenge that was impossible to finish. I had neither the technique nor the compositional skills. I had a vision full of resounding ideas but not the ability to transfer it to a song.

Then he got serious. He waved his hand like a conductor bringing an orchestra to its end.

"You need to find the right woman and settle down with her. Maybe this town is not for either of you. If you can't take it, then get out of New Orleans. It's a tough town, even if the music is good." Then he smiled and said, "Love is never a simple song, but when it goes wrong it's an all-too-familiar beat." I was tapping nervously on the table, which made Travis stop talking. Then he continued.

"Oh, by the way . . . I've heard that beat before. See you, kid."

We shook hands, and he left the club. There was a woman playing poker on the slot machine. Travis smiled at her, shook his head as if to say "sucker," then walked out. It's finito.

I HEADED BACK TO THE APARTMENT. I was still in a daze from jet lag and the sleeping pills I had taken, which rendered me even more sleepless and disoriented. Not a good way to feel, particularly in New Orleans. I thought about Rory, and how when we'd first met she'd talk to me in what little she knew of the Swedish language. Then, how her face would break into an enormous grin as she snapped back into her midwestern accent and joked about taking me down that "Big River." How I'd been inspired by her sense of discovery and adventure and how she had instilled it in me. But now I wondered if it had been real. Sometimes when people are together, they become the person the other one imagines them to be and vice versa, until eventually, the real person disappears and only the memories are left. I thought about that big river. Well I was on it now, but in a boat without a paddle and the current was getting stronger and stronger.

Like many other exiles in New Orleans, I was running away from something. Maybe I felt safe in knowing that America is so large that it is possible for a person to get completely lost and take on a new identity there. Gamblers come from Cleveland, Ohio; Portland, Oregon; Coney Island, New York; and even Anchorage, Alaska, to start new lives in what they refer to as the Big Easy. Then, as reality hits, truth comes knocking like an unwanted ghost.

I took my digital video camera, went out onto the street, and filmed around the Tremé area. The setting was on night vision, so everything showed up negative. White became black and vice versa. A celluloid fantasy. The church bells chimed and the streets seemed haunted as I filmed the houses near where we were staying and committed them to my cinematic fantasy world.

JANUARY 3

I had already set up a meeting with Walter Goodwin and the music department at John McDonogh High School for January 3, the Saturday morning before the term started. Mr. Goodwin was accompanied by his assistant and by the head of the music department, Mr. Jefferson. We went through my goals and aims; they all listened intently to what I had to say, and I was greeted with polite support from all concerned. I explained my credentials: fifteen years of running music courses for songwriters in England and a career as a musician, which, thankfully, Mr. Goodwin seemed to know something about.

Bob Tannen accompanied me on the trip to the school and was enthused by what I was trying to do. He occasionally interjected his own interpretation of what I had said, just in case Mr. Goodwin might have missed the point. Bob was a great boost for my PR.

"Ray, my friend, you're not like other people that come to this town. Most people want to just take things from New Orleans, but you are trying to give something back. That's rare."

I went to great lengths to explain that I was there to celebrate the local music and hopefully inspire the kids to make new music of their own. Then I explained that I did not want to pass myself off as being an authentic jazz player. I just appreciated the influence and inspiration the place had on me. I also made the point that "you can take the musician out of London, but you can't take the Londoner out of the musician." Everybody liked that thought.

Mr. Goodwin and Mr. Jefferson smiled. Even if they only half understood what I was on about, in a tentative way I think I had passed the audition. I had their approval to be in attendance on the first day of rehearsals the following Monday, when the semester started. There I was—an outsider coming in without any corporate backing but offering all sorts of creative support. At the very least I offered a plan that would raise enough funds so that the band uniforms could be repaired along with the band instruments, which were always in need of maintenance. Bob was convinced that together we would find a way to organise some sort of local event to raise these funds.

Mr. Goodwin expertly wrapped up the proceedings in a professional and diplomatic manner, as though he were bringing an end to an important debate on a PBS arts show. I knew he had a schedule to keep.

"Hey, it's all music no matter where it's from, ain't that the truth, Ray?"

Amen, I thought. We had connected.

As Bob and I left the building, we saw a couple of kids hanging around outside. They were not loitering by any means. Bob spoke in his loud, friendly way, as though he knew them.

"How you doing?"

"Doing good, mister."

"You know, school doesn't start till Monday."

"We know that, mister. Just getting used to it."

Bob told me that school was the only home some kids had, and when you said something simple to them, like "How are ya?" it translated as "You exist as a human being." This was the validation and acknowledgment they sometimes didn't get at home. If I needed opening lines to the first song I'd write for the school kids at John McDonogh, it would be just that.

Bob and I left the school and walked the short distance back to his house.

The fact remained that while the project was possibly starting up, my personal life was in a chaotic state. It was clear that my relationship with Rory was over, but I took comfort in knowing that the school music project could still happen and that was probably the real reason I was meant to be in New Orleans.

On the drive back to the apartment, Bob took me on a tour of the sights of the New Orleans and as I looked at the place it made me more determined to continue my mission in the Crescent City.

I thought about the school marching band at John McDonagh and the great possibilities in store for me in New Orleans. Then I thought of the band I left behind years earlier, the Kinks. I longed to recapture that feeling of inspiration I'd had during the actual beginning of my relationship with Americana. I thought of how against all the odds the Kinks had been rediscovered by this vast, complex continent.

8

CELLULOID HEROES

"Everybody's a dreamer and everybody's a star,
And everybody's in movies, it doesn't matter who you are . . .
There are stars in every city, in every house
    and on every street
And if you walk down Hollywood Boulevard
Their names are written in concrete."

CELLULOID HEROES, AMERICANA, LONDON, 1971–72

Whenever I was in Los Angeles I noticed that most of the people who lived and worked there were in one way or another connected to the movie industry, or had been at some point; and if they hadn't, they dreamed of being in the movies. As a result, I imagined that nearly everybody I saw resembled a star. I devised a game called "'tis 'im," in which I would spot some anonymous person sitting in a bar or café, and if, for example, that man had a large nose I would say to whoever I was with, "Jimmy Durante, 'tis 'im," even though the person didn't resemble Jimmy Durante in any way other than having a large nose. The theory was that if you took the time to study that person eventually he or she would resemble a celebrity even more. I knew that one day I would write about the whole star system, given the opportunity.

The Kinks had given Reprise Records their worldwide hit with "Lola" in 1970, but deep down we realised that we were coming to the end of our recording contract with them. At the end of 1970, we were approached by Ken Glancy of RCA Records, who wanted to sign us to the label. There was no bidding war; there were no heavy negotiations. We asked for a fee per album and a six-album solid guarantee, and RCA was willing to pay a fair advance, not too large, not too small. It was the beginning of a new era for the Kinks; we now only played in Europe very sparingly—it was America that we were focusing on, and as a result America was starting to be more interested in us.

I was beginning to feel more at home in the States. A new Kinks image had been reinvented for our new musical adventure. The signature album to accompany this change of image was *Muswell Hillbillies*, released in 1971. Ironically, *Muswell Hillbillies* was inspired by London more than any other album we had recorded to date and much to our surprise the album received relatively good reviews in Britain particularly after the BBC had broadcast a television special based on the album. My family had come from the North London area of Holloway and Islington, where decades before cattle drovers herded livestock down to the markets to be sold and the railroad transported goods to and from the inner city. The album was also about urban renewal; in the late 1960s and into the 1970s, inner-city neighbourhoods were being torn down, particularly in Holloway and Islington. People were being sent to new towns in the countryside, where they must have felt out of place in the more modern post-war communities. The *Muswell Hillbillies* title itself was obviously a play on the American TV show *The Beverly Hillbillies*, about a hick family from the South that discovers oil and moves to a life of luxury in Beverly Hills. The naming of our album was no accident. The analogy was deliberate, but totally out of keeping with the rest of the English musical establishment at that time; while the mainstream British bands were breaking away from their roots, the Kinks were celebrating theirs. One friend described me as an existentialist. We were desperately trying to shake off the original Kinks image, which we managed to do to a degree but the cost of reinvention would be high. Commitment to longer tours and separation from family were bound to take their toll on the personal lives of the band.

On our first extensive tour to support *Muswell Hillbillies* I bought a 16mm Arriflex movie camera and took it with us on the road, along with a cameraman. The success of "Lola" had drawn many borderline fans out of the closet to come to concerts, and I wanted to capture this new era of the Kinks on film. We arrived in New York to kick off our American tour on the morning of November 18, 1971; that evening, RCA threw a large party in our honour at a chic Midtown restaurant hosted by Lisa Robinson. Everybody who was anybody was invited—including Andy Warhol and many of his starlets. Later that night we went to the infamous nightclub Max's Kansas City, where the famous back room was full of underground celebrities—from the drag queens Jackie Curtis and Candy Darling to then-aspiring singer Patti Smith, who at the time introduced herself to us as a poet.

At our Carnegie Hall show on the twenty-first, I wore a newly made cowboy shirt with incredibly detailed embroidered patchwork, which we jokingly dubbed the "colossal shirt." The front row of the concert hall was populated with more underground New York stars, including the transvestite performer Wayne, also known as Jayne County, and rock royalty such as Lou Reed.

We made our way to California the following March, whereon there was another party thrown for us at the Hyatt House on the Sunset Strip in L.A. Again RCA mustered as many celebrities together as they could, including '50s heartthrob Tab Hunter and legendary country-and-western costume designer Nudie Cohn, who all willingly gave interviews for the documentary I was making. The Turtles also came to the party with their entourage; two years earlier I had produced an album for them called *Turtle Soup*. The Cockettes, a drag queen group, arrived from San Francisco with their whole troupe of performers.

The party, which was a huge success, was only marred by an unfortunate error on my part. I was so exhausted from the journey and went to my room to go to bed early only to find a few people in there talking and drinking. I called hotel security and had them escorted from my room. One of the women, who had very curly hair, looked like then-superstar Julie Christie, in her curly-haired *McCabe & Mrs. Miller* role. In Los Angeles there are so many look-alikes. Who knows?

Our concert at the Hollywood Palladium the next day was an unqualified success. We had been joined by the Mike Cotton Sound to provide Dixieland style feel to some of our songs. The old Kinks of the British Invasion were now consigned to history as the Muswell Hillbillies arrived with a vengeance. On our travels we had acquired the services of violinist David Sewall, who could perform an entire opera, singing all the parts, while accompanying himself on the violin. After the Palladium show we took our camera crew

down to Hollywood Boulevard and shot David playing violin in various locations. Hollywood Boulevard inspired me because it was full of decadence but
strangely innocent at the same time; sad as well as inspiring. What added
to the bizarreness of the shoot was the fact that David was dressed in full
evening dress—white tie and tails, finished off by a pair of flip-flops on his
bare feet. This, combined with his Harpo Marx hairdo, made him look even
more incongruous among the deadbeats and desperate souls who were scattered around the Boulevard at two in the morning. We had the following day
off, so I went back to the Boulevard with my cameraman and shot in various
locations, just concentrating on people in the street. There were wannabe
Bette Davises, Joan Crawfords, and Errol Flynns on every street corner.
During the remainder of the tour I started making notes about Hollywood
Boulevard—people still aspiring for fame after a lifetime of being nobodies.
The song—which I thought I might call "Celluloid Heroes"—had several
verses, but I didn't have the chorus yet.

A few weeks later when I was back in London I started to edit the film
in a cutting room in Covent Garden. During a break I held up a piece of film
and asked my film editor what it was actually made of. "Celluloid," he replied.

The song had already been named, but this was a confirmation of the
title. I knew I had a song, but would it make a record? We wouldn't know
until we went into the studio. We had recorded most of the tracks for our
next still-to-be-titled album at Morgan Studios in North West London, and
it was getting close to the delivery date. I knew I wanted the backing track
of "Celluloid Heroes" to be a continuous piece of music with no stops and
starts for edits.

I asked Dave Rowberry, Mick Avory's flatmate and ex-member of the
Animals to play organ, which would allow John Gosling to play the harmo-
nium live on the track. I wanted there to be interaction between the two
keyboards that can only be naturally achieved by playing live. Mick Avory
played drums, John Dalton played bass, and my brother, Dave, put down an
acoustic guitar that complemented mine. I didn't sing the lyrics to the song
because I wanted the music to express what the song was about without me
having to just spell it out in lyric form. I coaxed the guys over the headphones
to "play louder," "play softer," "louder here," "bigger," "smaller" . . . and they

responded brilliantly. "Celluloid Heroes" was done in two passes, and the second one was the best. I had too many lyrics and hadn't edited them all down yet, so I went home with the backing track.

My three-year-old daughter, Victoria, was playing on the floor of my living room, where I had my tape recorder. This was the same daughter I had tried the chorus of "Lola" out on a few years earlier. She played with her toys while the backing track played, and when it came to the chorus of "Celluloid Heroes," she turned around to me and smiled. There were no lyrics on the track yet, so there was nothing to tell her what it was about, but her smile told me everything. The song shape had a resolution and it felt right—all the passion, all the poetry, was contained in the backing track. Now the words would provide the icing on the cake.

Delivery time for the album was rapidly approaching. "Celluloid Heroes" was the last backing track we put down, but we still had to do all the other overdubs and lead vocals. There were several other tracks to finish, including horn overdubs on tracks such as "Maximum Consumption," "Unreal Reality," and "Look a Little on the Sunny Side." Also, keyboard, guitar parts, and backing vocals were needed. On top of all this work, the album had to be mastered and delivered to New York the following Monday, so we booked the studio time at Morgan from Friday night through Sunday night and worked nonstop.

Some of the band went home at night, but as I lived nearby, I would sleep for a few hours in the early morning and then go back and continue to work. The engineers took shifts around me. At one point I had a nap on the sofa in the studio office, and after a few hours of sleep I felt ready to do the lead vocal on "Celluloid Heroes." It was Sunday, the day before the delivery day for the album; I asked Dave and the others to come in to do their backing vocals. I thought that there was still something missing on the track, so I asked Alan Holmes, our baritone sax player, to come in and play a foghorn-type sound at the end to give the track a climactic ending. The studio was booked by another client on Sunday night, so we had to move to a smaller studio across the road. There I started mixing the rest of the tracks with my engineer, Mike Bobak. It was five o'clock on Monday morning when we started mixing down the last track, "Celluloid Heroes." Mike was exhausted from working almost continuously for three days and nights, and he kept nodding off over the console. We knew there was another band due to come in at ten the following morning and that I had to get a flight out to get the tapes to Masterdisk, the mastering studio in New York, the same day. Then at seven a.m., I spotted a vocal line that needed redoing in the last verse. I suddenly remembered a line that would work better, one I had written in Hollywood: "Everybody's in showbiz, it doesn't matter who you are." This last-minute change to the vocal had provided the album with its title.

I asked Mike to set up a microphone, which he reluctantly did. I sang the appropriate lines, and we started mixing again. The fade-out on the final note was done by me, because by this point Mike had fallen asleep. By now the cleaners were banging on the door; they needed to get in and set up for the ten o'clock session so I quickly wrapped up the quarter-inch stereo master tapes in tinfoil to protect them against airport scanner X-rays, put them in a box, put the box in a bag, and left the building. I walked into a bright sunny morning but I didn't notice that one of the lenses in the sunglasses I was wearing had fallen out; I must have looked a bit dishevelled and eccentric, but that was the pressure I was under.

I went home for a shower, then got a car to the airport, where I caught the next Concorde flight to New York with the tapes snugly tucked in a bag next to me all the way. The supersonic Concorde at this time was the elite way to travel and the song it inspired, "Supersonic Rocket Ship," was also on the album. When the stewardesses came by and asked me if I wanted Champagne I took a glass, but when the caviar, prawns, and all the accoutrements of luxury dining were offered I politely declined.

"What do you want to eat, sir?" the pretty stewardess asked.

"Please just give me two aspirin."

I took the aspirin and fell asleep on the flight. It wasn't until we deplaned at Kennedy Airport that it was pointed out to me that I had been sitting next to the actor Warren Beatty the entire trip and hadn't even said hello. There I was carrying a song about Hollywood Boulevard, sitting on the Concorde next to a real-life movie star, and I didn't know it. I got to the mastering room in time, and the engineer cut the album. RCA signed off on the delivery. Job done.

"I wish my life was a nonstop Hollywood movie show,
A fantasy world of celluloid villains and heroes
Because celluloid heroes never feel any pain
And celluloid heroes never really die."

THE CONTENDER, NEW YORK, 1971

While I was writing about and singing the praises of Hollywood's golden age, America had been changing into a more political, radical place. The Black Panther movement had come to prominence, and there were civil rights demonstrations across the country. Angela Davis had emerged as an educated, politically driven, female black activist with the coolest Afro; she was named a "dangerous terrorist" by Richard Nixon. There were anti-war demonstrations in Washington, Gay Pride protests and marches in New York City, the Kent State University riots, and a small burglary at the Watergate hotel that would in time bring down a president. Change was everywhere as the 1970s seemed to explode in the face of conservatism.

On March 8, 1971, Joe Frazier beat Muhammad Ali at Madison Square Garden in what promoters called the "Fight of the Century."

Three years later, Ali beat Frazier in a nontitle fight in New York City. Then they fought each other in the "Thrilla in Manila" a year after that; a grueling match that Ali won. At the time there was a common denominator between a great fighter and what seemed to personify the Kinks: a will to battle against all odds to win, to stand up there and give it your all. This was the spirit I embarked upon with the Kinks at this point.

Several weeks after the Fight of the Century, the Kinks played Lincoln Center's Philharmonic Hall (now Avery Fisher Hall). I took what I thought was a sip of lemonade just before I walked onstage. The drink must have been spiked, as it turned out. Perhaps it was karmic revenge from the drug dealer whom I'd knocked over in San Francisco, but less than four songs into the show, I started reeling. I couldn't speak, I couldn't see; I fell into the amplifiers. I am told that I collapsed halfway through the song "Apeman," but I can't be sure. Some of the fans feared that the large stack of amplifiers behind me would fall forward and crush me as I lay flat on my back, but miraculously the amps did not tumble over. Apparently, I still had the microphone in my hand, attempting valiantly to get through the song even though the band had stopped playing. This was supposed to be a prestigious return to a classy New York venue, but instead it turned into a free-for-all, with confused roadies running around and fans clambering onto the stage. A couple of well-meaning concertgoers jumped down from the upper tier to drag me off the stage by my feet, risking their own lives in the process. I do remember someone fumbling through my skintight flares, which added extra confusion. The band tried to resume without me while the audience sang along. The theatre was in chaos, and I flashed back to the time when there had been a ban on the Kinks all those years earlier. I was convinced another ban would ensue because of this incident.

The promoter was major New York rock impresario Ron Delsener, and it was one of the first times he had promoted the Kinks in the city. It was destined not to be the last, even though even he was now running around back stage in a panic. Ronnie was pleased because the show was sold out, and hopefully there would be no union repercussions this time. Somehow I managed to stumble back onto the stage and finish the set, which by now had descended into a pantomime, although some people who were there remembered it as being one of the best shows they had ever seen.

Afterward, my manager, Grenville Collins, took me to Elaine's, the well-known restaurant on the Upper East Side, and we had dinner. I sat next to famous people but I didn't care; I was so distressed that after dinner I walked the streets all night. Maybe it was the effect of the drugs in the drink, but I couldn't sleep. I ended up at the Howard Johnson's coffee shop on Eighth Avenue at about eight o'clock the next morning; it was a bright, sunny day. I sat down at the bar and tried to order some breakfast. I was still reeling a little from the effects of the spiked drink. The man with a gravel-deep voice to my right said, "I'm next to order. Who do you think you are? You jumped in ahead of me." I said that I was sorry and that I was just trying to order breakfast.

I turned to look at him. He seemed as wide as he was tall, and he was dressed in a smart three-piece suit, which looked a little bit formal for an

8:00 a.m. breakfast. There was no confusion as to who he was. His face was one of the most recognizable in the world at that time. Still, I had to ask the question.

I said, "And who do you think you are?" in my politest of voices.

"My name is Joe Frazier and I am the heavyweight champion of the world." I wasn't going to argue. He looked kindly at me. He seemed to recognise my pain and embarrassment. I was sure that if I needed more actual pain he would gladly inflict it upon me, but it was no coincidence that I sat next to him that day. I had met Muhammad Ali at check-in at the Ramada Inn, also on Eighth Avenue, a few years earlier, and had wondered why such a great man was staying at a relatively low-rent hotel frequented by rock bands on a modest budget. I guess he was on one also. At that time he was going through his problems with the U.S. government for refusing to fight in Vietnam.

It was almost prophetic that I met those two great fighters. The boxing ring was symbolic of what it was like to tour at that time. Each show night was a big fight. You couldn't win on points. Victory only counted when it was a knockout performance—whether or not the records sold, and whether or not the concerts were well attended, the Kinks had to win by a knockout punch. That was the quest—victory or nothing. I saw the Ali-Frazer fights as similar to our own battles to win over audiences and achieve some redemption for our shattered past. The Ali-Frazer fights were inspiring, violent, at times beautiful, and yet brutal at the same time. Just like a Kinks concert. A group of talented musicians can get together and create fantastic music, but they might not have the fighting spirit. Bands with strong-willed musicians—as opposed to session players—can cover up each other's inadequacies and create a performance, a process that ultimately defies all musicality. It is a pure united spirit and will to achieve a goal. That's what a band like the Kinks is. It's what built and sustained our fan base through the ups and downs. It was not just the music; it was the cause behind it. It's like a big fight. Eventually, though, the punches take their toll.

105

PRESERVATION, 1974–75

As casualties go, mine was the first marriage to fall apart. Between the wrapping up of *Everybody's in Show-Biz* in 1972 and the recording of our third album with RCA, *Preservation Act 1*, my marriage to my first wife had come to an untidy end. I was only in my late twenties but felt like retiring. I almost quit the band, but the road was always beckoning. I sat down with my brother, Dave, and said that the only reason I would keep going is if I could get off the rock-and-roll treadmill to do the rock-and-theatre concept shows that I always wanted to perform. I saw the theatrical aspect of what I was writing to be important to the band's evolution. I had nearly completed the album when Dave and I decided to turn *Preservation Act 1* into a total rock opera, released in 1973. *Preservation Act 2 was* released in 1974, and the two albums combined were transformed into a touring multimedia musical. With all our fringe-theatre, low-budget-production guns blasting, we toured America, starting at Colgate University in November of 1974.

The audience of primarily college students sat comfortably, expecting to see the Kinks perform as the Muswell Hillbillies. After playing some of our well-known material for forty-five minutes, we launched into our new opus, *Preservation.* Jaws dropped in the audience as the young, hip college students seemed totally overwhelmed by the political satire they were witnessing. The show had a Wagnerian opening, with a chorus singing "Morning Song," and then images of my alter ego, the villainous Mr. Flash, appeared. Mr. Twitch was played by Dave; Big Ron, the Minister of Punishment, was played by Mick Avory; the Minister of War was played by John Dalton; and the Drunken Bishop was played by John "the Baptist" Gosling. The band donned various outfits befitting their roles, and the show itself—which depicted the struggle of the proletariat against the cruel capitalist dictators—was Brechtian and minimalist. Mr. Flash was eventually overthrown by the mysterious Mr. Black (also played by me), who seductively promised a new society—only to lead the city of Preservation into becoming a dark totalitarian state.

As the drama unfolded in the performance, which lasted more than two hours, we saw the audience start to engross themselves in the story line, which seemed to resonate with them. They obviously saw parallels between Mr. Flash and Richard Nixon (the Colgate show took place only three months after Nixon had resigned). However, *Preservation* was not a protest against the Nixon administration specifically; it was a protest against abuse of power everywhere. When the show reached its climax there was a hushed hall and then rapturous applause. We had created something new, and despite our madcap antics on stage, it was totally original. As word about the show spread, other acts, including Pink Floyd and Alice Cooper, began using similar theatrical devices in their own shows.

Even though the *Preservation* shows were an amazing success, and our cult following grew, the album failed to connect. The same fate befell our subsequent album, *Soap Opera* (1975), an even more outrageously conceived parody of a television soap opera. I was originally commissioned to write a television show based on a song I'd written called "Starmaker," and the show was first broadcast by Granada television as an "experimental" musical play. The original outline was written in the Chicago Hyatt hotel while I was recovering from a bout of flu brought on by extreme exhaustion, hence the somewhat psychotic nature of the story: a man with a split personality who wanted to be a rock star instead of an accountant. I played both roles, of course: Norman, the schizophrenic accountant, and his alter ego, the Starmaker, who exploded into the unsuspecting accountant's world, taking over his identity, and sleeping with his subject's wife. The TV show was reworked, and with some extra songs added it was renamed *Soap Opera*. We added a horn section to the lineup as well as three backup singers—Shirley Roden, Pamela Travis, and Debbie Doss—who also played character roles.

In May of 1975, promoter Ron Delsener brought us back for two nights at the Beacon Theatre in New York on the Upper West Side, and we also took the show to the Spectrum in Philadelphia as well as to other cities. The show itself was a mixed-media event that utilised rear-projection screens and special effects, including two large cardboard ducks that were supposed to fly off the wall to terrify Norman the accountant while he was going through a nervous breakdown. The highlight, however, was that the band got to dress up in spandex suits as well as coloured Afro wigs. My biggest delight was to see my brother, Dave, play great blues solos while dressed in this outfit. We were touring more extensively at this time, and we took the show to Florida, where we all got sunburned after a day out on the beach. Needless to say, at the next show, in Tampa, we displayed red faces—sunburned, painful, peeling skin— and everyone on the stage was covered in calamine lotion during the show, much to the confusion of our opening act, rocker Bob Seger.

At the end of *Soap Opera*, Norman abandons his dream of becoming a star to return to being an anonymous face in the crowd, a story line that mirrored my own internal confusion at the time. Norman's metamorphosis into the Starmaker was symbolic of my situation: when I started in the Kinks I was a reluctant lead singer, shy and unconfident, very much like Norman. As time moved on I became more outgoing, like the Starmaker. There was more to these concept shows than just fantasy. I know now that they had profound psychological significance for me. Without realising it at the time, I used these characters to express deep-rooted inner conflicts. Innocence overwhelmed by corrupt power, money, greed, loss of identity; followed, finally, by acceptance—but then after all this artifice I was just an ordinary bloke. Was I really trying to take the band all the way to the top in America and as a result pushing myself over the edge or were these roles just camouflaging my fear of returning to my own nonidentity? I don't think the band even understood what I was on about, but the core cult Kinks fans totally got it. They knew that success in a way frightened me, despite my attempts at frivolity. The audience knew and understood my frailty through the character of Norman, and that's why our cult following grew. They saw us as having flaws just like other people instead of posing as rock gods like other bands. We filmed our London performance of *Soap Opera* as a lasting document of this insanely ambitious piece.

Later in 1975 came the follow-up to *Preservation*, *Schoolboys in Disgrace*, which was set in a secondary school that had a sadistic headmaster who wielded the firm rod of authority over the audience as he sang the pre-punk "The Hard Way." This show required the band to dress up as schoolboys, complete with short trousers and caps. The female backup singers were dressed in skimpy gymslips and cavorted around the stage with whips and bamboo canes to beat the naughty schoolboys if they misbehaved. The climactic moment came when the headmaster humiliated a prostrate schoolboy in front of the entire audience. Needless to say, both the headmaster and the schoolboy were both played by me.

The scene that involved this difficult act of self-flagellation was cunningly conceived: Debbie Doss (who was as tall as I am when she wore high heels) played my double; she wore the same headmaster's mask and robe. As I delivered a mock Shakespearean speech, a tape took over halfway through. A slick lighting effect enabled me to be replaced by Debbie, who mimed the rest of my taped speech. This gave me enough time to change into my schoolboy's outfit back stage before running back on in time to be flogged by the headmaster, played impeccably by Madame Doss. There was one problem in that Debbie herself had to make a quick change from her dancer's outfit, and observant members of the audience could see that Debbie's headmaster was wearing women's stiletto heels. This detail was lost on most members of the audience, who were so engrossed in the show that they did not notice this error in the costume change . . . but it was greeted with howls of delight by bondage fans, who loved this moment of S and M. The headmaster's mask became my constant disguise at after-show parties, and I would even wear it when I checked into hotels—which bewildered the hotel staff.

Theatrical insiders who came to the show said that had *Schoolboys in Disgrace* run on Broadway it would have been nominated for—and undoubtedly would have won—a Tony Award. The problem with these shows was that while they contained some of my favourite Kinks songs of the period, including "No More Looking Back" and "(A) Face in the Crowd," the songs were completely overshadowed by the insanity of the shows themselves. Even though the albums contained key radio tracks and gave us Top 40 status, they didn't contain the old-style stand-alone "pop" hit singles that we'd had with Reprise. The music industry still wanted us to give them three-minute singles while I wanted to give them three-hour rock operas. It was also significant that the band was playing more tightly than ever during this period, as opposed to the sloppy drunken antics we displayed during the *Muswell Hillbillies* era, when many shows degenerated into glorified boozefests. Our audience grew with us as our cult status grew, and our live shows became so strong that when we were put on to support other bands we gained a reputation as being impossible to follow.

WE WERE NEARING THE END of the RCA days and it was time for a change. Enter Clive Davis, who had departed from Columbia Records in a blaze of publicity to start a new company called Arista in 1974.

It seemed like the perfect fit: Clive, the enigmatic, maverick music businessman who had steered Columbia Records through the '60s and '70s with phenomenal success, paired with the Kinks, who had amazing chart success initially but who at that point were also maverick outsiders. I cherished our days at RCA. I made a good friend in Ken Glancy, the head of the company. Rocco Laginestra, who took over from him, was a good supporter. Mike Everett, Olav Wyper—all of them good record men, all workers in a large company that seemed disorganised. RCA was at its best when someone like Tony Defries, who managed David Bowie, could go in and muster up a marketing campaign for his artist and get the label to implement the plan. The Kinks had none of this machinery. We tried desperately, but found no coordination between the record company and the promoters. There was no synergy.

It didn't take a rocket scientist to work out that the RCA years were an artistic triumph, but in the conventional music world they were considered to be a commercial failure. After the product commitment was fulfilled, RCA executives submitted an album for release called *The Kinks' Celluloid Heroes—The Greatest Hits*. I politely pointed out that none of these songs had been massive hits, and we would be in breach of the Trade Descriptions Act in the United Kingdom if we released it. The title of the album was subsequently changed to *The Kinks' Greatest: Celluloid Heroes*, and released in 1976. It gives a really accurate representation of some of the fine songs we produced for RCA during this period. The Kinks' live shows were always well attended, but the production costs outweighed the profits.

I had been introduced to Clive Davis by Allen Klein in the '60s, when Clive was running Columbia Records. At that time, Allen had his offices in a suite at the Warwick, a hotel on Sixth Avenue. He actually walked me the few blocks to the former Columbia headquarters at the CBS Building, known as Black Rock, so I could meet Clive. This was a measure of the importance and esteem that Allen must have held Clive at that time. There I was, almost a decade later, staying at the Warwick, and this time it was Clive who knocked at the door of my hotel room. Gone was the corporate air and pomp; leaving Columbia seemed to have made him stronger and down to earth. We talked briefly about our goals and realised we had similar views. Even though I joked that I would like to make *Preservation Three*, the fact that Clive got the joke meant that we had connected.

A few weeks later Clive and I were having dinner in a Chinese restaurant in Greenwich Village when he asked me what it would take to finally commit to Arista. I knew that he knew that I was keen to sign but nevertheless I mischievously played along. "I'll sign the deal if you sing me a Barry Manilow song," I said. Clive thought for a moment then in front of the crowded restaurant he came out with a stunning cabaret version of "I Write the Songs," complete with Bill Murray-as-the-"Lounge Singer"–style vibrato at the end of the line. I knew that at that moment I would refuse to record for no other company but Arista. We decided that we wanted to work together.

The Kinks were without management, so I needed to find someone to put a deal together with Arista. I had met L.A. attorney Mickey Shapiro via Tony Dimitriades in the mid-'70s, when he'd helped broker the deal for a small indie label we ran from our studio in London. Near the end of the RCA contract I contacted Mickey again to see if he could bring in the Arista contract for me with Elliot Goldman, head of business affairs at Arista. All the preliminary paperwork was done by the time I and the rest of the band sat down to have a meeting with my accountant in his London office in the summer of 1976, when I knew he was going to declare that the Kinks were about to go broke. I trumped him by suddenly producing the Arista contract at the very moment he was going to give us the bad news. Mick Avory was at the meeting and was taken aback. Dave, however, sat in his chair and took the news with a grain of salt. Dave was no longer the "Dave the Rave" character he was in the 1960s. He had become a family man with kids. He somehow knew that I, the big brother, would always come up with something to sustain the band, so he accepted this latest development with equanimity, as was his optimistic nature. At least I had some insight into the big picture; all the prancing around on tours as Mr. Flash, Norman, and the Starmaker had not killed my sense of survival. During the negotiations with RCA I had, out of necessity, picked up some do-it-yourself idea's about the contractual process. In my years with the Kinks I had taken a tip from my character Mr. Flash and had also developed the art of self-preservation.

We had to keep moving ahead; otherwise the Kinks would never have survived. The Arista contract meant that the Kinks were to do battle yet again, but the body of music I produced throughout the RCA years made it evident that it was uncertain where we belonged—did we make mainstream pop, progressive rock, or eccentric art house music? The Kinks were a mixture of all three. Between us, Clive Davis and I would hopefully devise a plan to give us more focus. The question still went through my head. Where did we belong? Where did I belong? Maybe I was just on a continued journey to somewhere. This willingness to recapture the Kinks' former glories overtook the fact that I was lost as a person. Maybe my search, my quest for success in capturing the American market, was really a subjective, subliminal attempt to try to find a real-life character for myself.

9

LIFE ON THE ROAD: DIARY OF 1977

After many months in the studio recording the *Sleepwalker* album we finally got ready to tour America. Things were not well within the band itself, particularly as we had to replace John Dalton at the last minute. An acquaintance of John "the Baptist" Gosling, Andy Pyle, had been recruited. He didn't sing but he played a proficient finger-style bass, unlike Dalton's plectrum-heavy bass sound, which added more punch to the bass and kick drum. *Sleepwalker* had quite layered backing vocals and so I kept two girl backing singers in the tour entourage to make up for the absence of Dalton's backing vocals and Baptist's unwilling meandering attempts to sing along.

Touring was not only necessary to promote the album but essential in order to pay for the band retainers. Clive Davis was not only good at spotting a song but an astute businessman who had signed the Kinks at a more-than-reasonable rate. It seemed to me that the recording fund for each record barely paid for studio time, and if we hadn't had Konk Studios we might not have been able to make records at all. Nevertheless, the gauntlet was thrown down; the challenge was there; the band took a collective deep breath and battle would commence.

JANUARY

Monday 24th/ Long rehearsal at Konk Studios to remix the end of "Brother" as Clive requested; it sounded much better. Phoned the U.S. but found out that they have held up the album and we have committed to a tour. I get drunk in the evening.

Tuesday 25th/ I started to panic about getting ready for the tour. Went over to Dave's house and he was still angry about Mick and Baptist. He's not happy with either of them.

Wednesday 26th/ Strange atmosphere at the airport, everybody is uncertain and unsure. We have a great album but there is so much insecurity in the band. Had very little sleep the night before and have too much to drink on the jet. I have a long talk with Mick, Baptist, and Andy Pile (who stood in for John Dalton for the tour). It's like a sparring session—everyone being intimidating, on the verge of arguing.

Thursday 27th/ When we arrive in Philadelphia I stay up the whole night, the room spins round, and I begin to hallucinate with exhaustion. I feel remarkably fresh when I wake up though. I go out with some of the crew to see a movie called *Network* in the afternoon, and then we rehearse with the band in the theatre in Philadelphia; it's a very cold place, hope we can warm it up.

Friday 28th/ Everyone a little bit tense today, obviously, the first day of the tour since we recorded the album. Felt very exhausted near the end of the show, especially in "Lola." Some things never change—Mick's still playing untidily, Dave was glaring at him—still it's been a long time since we played. I really hope the record company can deliver and achieve a success for this record after all the effort we have put into it.

Saturday 29th/ Meeting with Chip Rachlin regarding representation of future tours. 1:30 p.m. radio show with Ed Sciaky of WMMR in Philly. Fairly good show that night, though not as together as the night before. If nothing else we work for each other.

Monday 31st/ We play a college in Connecticut near Hartford. There's an excellent band on before us, Jean Luc Ponty; they're very fast and technical but the music seems to have no soul to it. Somehow though they're very compatible with the Kinks, who are untidy and ragged. Try to raise the band during the show and we play "Brother" for the first time. Dave and Mick had another ruck on the stage; the band is still a little disjointed. I think Dave has lost all confidence.

FEBRUARY

Tuesday 1st/ The Palladium in New York. Dave's tuning really off. After the show we have to go to a reception with Clive and the Arista people and lots of reporters. Feel a bit embarrassed because the show was not up to standard.

Wednesday 2nd/ Better show.

Thursday 3rd/ Day off. It's Dave's birthday. I spent the day mostly in bed and went out to buy Dave a birthday present. Dinner with Clive, Bob Feiden, and others, and then drinks with Chip Rachlin at Maxwell's Plum. There I met Randy Newman's manager Elliot Abbott, who is interested in managing the Kinks. Then I bumped into John Reid, Elton John's manager, near the hotel.

Friday 4th/ Capitol Theater, Passaic, New Jersey. The tuning was bad. Andy the bass player said afterward "Sorry Ray, I blew it." Completely out of time, time, time. He's concerned about his future. "I need to know where I stand, Ray." I said, "I'll tell you where you stand, next to the bloody drummer, now get on with it."

Saturday 5th/ Fly up to Boston with Mike Kleffner to do radio stations and then two concerts that are sold out. The second set is great, a standing ovation. I love Boston. It's like playing the home counties in England.

Sunday 6th/ Rhode Island theatre holds 2,600 but we squeeze in 3,000. Five hundred people are locked out. Not a bad show considering.

Monday 7th/ Drive down from Rhode Island to the Warwick Hotel in New York, and then to *The Mike Douglas Show* in Philadelphia. We play "Sleepwalker." Chat with Mike Douglas and Arnold Schwarzenegger and the great Tony Bennett. Feel very good about the show. Dave might have more confidence now, he looks good on TV.

Tuesday 8th/ Day off. Go with Feiden to see *The Night of the Iguana* starring Richard Chamberlain and Sylvia Miles at the Circle in the Square. The play is long in places but really good when it starts to kick off. Afterward Feiden took my tour assistant Barbara Bothwell and me to the Backstage Diner to have dinner. Very theatrical people there.

Wednesday 9th/ New Jersey, William Paterson College, small theatre, close to the audience. Band is really untogether; I tell Andy Pile off for not doing his homework and learning the songs.

Thursday 10th/ Day off. Travel to Cleveland. It's a very depressing town to me; whenever a restaurant closes at 10 p.m. there is nothing else to do.

Friday 11th/ Cleveland. Maybe the best show so far. You know what? It's great to play depressing towns because they know how to rock. It's all they have sometimes. Strange how the band seems to play well when it doesn't matter.

Saturday 12th/ Chicago. My guitar let me down. I have got to get a better guitar. Another big row after the show with Dave and Mick.

Sunday 13th/ Fly to L.A.

Monday 14th/ Sunbathe for an hour, get burned. I do three interviews. Went with Brian Wilcox to see a film called *Rocky.* I fell asleep during the big fight sequence but I enjoyed what I saw.

Wednesday 16th/ A lazy day around the pool at the hotel. Everyone becoming more relaxed. Went to the Palm restaurant with two Arista people, and then to see the Ramones play at the Whiskey. Who says I don't go out to see other bands?

Thursday 17th/ Santa Monica Civic Auditorium. Good tidy show. No major cock-ups or disasters. Did a song called "Life on the Road" from the *Sleepwalker* album as an encore. This is very rare for new untried songs. This record must have potential.

Friday 18th/ Santa Monica Civic first show recorded for *King Biscuit Flower Hour.* First show was a disaster, the second show almost catastrophic. Dave and Baptist were arguing over the volume of the organ, which was, I have to admit, very loud. At the end of the show I threatened to hit Baptist when he refused to go on for an encore.

"Will you go on?"

"No, do I have to?"

"Yes, please come on sir," I said politely, "or I'll thump you."

Then I coaxed Dave on, who was also reluctant to play an encore. The audience was going mad. And Mick was at fault for missing beats. We did the show and somehow got off, and finished the evening without a fight. What a relief!

Saturday 19th/ San Francisco. A live broadcast for KSAN. A very tense atmosphere, but the show itself was possibly the best we have done on this tour. Maybe it's good to be stressed out; it's good to be tense. That's when the good shows happen.

Monday 21st/ George Washington's Birthday and I'm very depressed. Have to sleep all afternoon. I went to eat with Mike Kleffner at the Palm. I actually passed on lobster for a steak, which is very rare for me . . . ha ha. At one of the other tables I saw George Raft eating. Man! If only Travis Davis would have known. I went to Beach Boy Carl Wilson's house, got home about 4:30 a.m.

Tuesday 22nd/ Day off in L.A. I spent the morning getting brown, the afternoon doing interviews. One guy didn't know I wrote the songs, so there is still a reason to do press.

Wednesday 23rd/ Fly to New York. Out to Ashley's Club for a drink and a bite. Meet some people from *Saturday Night Live* show.

Thursday 24th/ A *Saturday Night Live* rehearsal at S.I.R. studios. Afterward I go out with some of the crew to see *King Kong*. Can't sleep. Scared of heights, must be the gorilla.

Friday 25th/ Full rehearsal at NBC for *Saturday Night Live*. Fingers crossed. Something inside me still draws back from showbiz for some reason. I do not want to become a rock-and-roll relic.

Saturday 26th/ NBC, *Saturday Night Live*. Dress rehearsal was disastrous. Dave and I had an argument seconds before we went on. But the show itself was ok. I thought I did a lot of good. Had words with the AFTRA union man about the old days; we had to join and I signed this time. Afterward we went for drinks with Clive and Feiden where I met a famous actress.

MARCH

Tuesday 1st/ Fly to Atlanta for radio interviews. Picked up by the local Arista man, who was really together and organized, He carried a small gun in his glove compartment. He kept asking strange questions to see if I liked girls. I said I didn't mind girls. After Atlanta we flew back to the UK for more press interviews to promote the new album.

APRIL

Tuesday 5th/ First date in Houston. Good show, more together than the last tour. Michael Kleffner called me at the hotel to say he is leaving Arista.

Wednesday 6th/ Dallas-Fort Worth, the Will Rogers auditorium. A great show even though I am very tired.

Thursday 7th/ Oklahoma City. Good energetic gig even though the theatre was only about half full. Everybody keeps saying it will be full next time. I hope so!

Friday 8th/ Oklahoma to Kansas to Minneapolis. A long gruelling journey. We arrive at the hotel after being met by a local promotion man. They take us out to eat with Barbara Bothwell and Ken Jones at a very upmarket Italian restaurant with rude waitresses. Apparently a burglar walked into one of our roadie's rooms in the night and stole 300 dollars while the roadie slept. An ominous sign perhaps?

Saturday 9th/ Minneapolis sold out. Great crowd. Good show.

Sunday 10th/ Fly to Kansas City. Seemingly a nowhere town, a nothing gig, but a great audience.

Monday 11th/ Iowa. We take the bus all the way. A good gig and a really great university. Beautiful concert hall. Iowa City is a wide-open town, grass fields everywhere. American paradise.

Tuesday 12th/ Road to Milwaukee, gig very good indeed. Everyone getting a little tired though. Dave and I had a shout out after the show. He accuses me of being a manipulator. Drive to Chicago by coach.

Wednesday 13th/ The album is no. 21 with a bullet in *Billboard* magazine. Record company excited.

Friday 15th/ Fly to Portland, Oregon. The gig is a disappointment for me for some reason. First time since San Francisco in '69 that I lost my temper with an audience. I swear that the show will be better next time; somehow we get through the show.

Saturday, 16th/ Seattle. Fly down to do a great show in front of a sell-out crowd. The promoters take us out for a meal to a superb restaurant, had the best white wine I have ever had, which I find out is locally made.

Sunday 17th/ Vancouver. Strange show. Meet my uncle Albert Crocker afterward with Keith, his son.

Tuesday 19th/ San Jose, a beautiful green theatre—at least the seats were green. But the monitor man let us down big time with an over-ambitious mixing. The sold-out show was a great success, went for a quick meal before going to bed. Early start tomorrow.

Thursday 21/ Did an interview panel for *The New York Times*. Bill Graham, Linda Ronstadt, John Rockwell, a nice chap I think, and Tina Turner. We talk about music, we talk about our various lives, and Bill comes out with an amazing quote. "Ray Davies tours because he's got a family to support," people don't understand that the road musicians actually have families and have obligations. It's a remarkable and insightful comment from him. Fly to San Diego. Excellent gig. The best so far. Good Arista people there.

Friday 22nd/ Santa Barbara; even better show than the night before. Play in a little Mexican-type church that has balconies. Stay up late drinking with a reporter from the *Daily Mirror* from London then go to a noisy room where the band are drinking the rest of the liquor from the gig.

Sunday 24/ Fly to Denver. Unbearable backache. Can't get rid of it, take painkillers. Very good show. Fly back at 3:15 a.m.

Tuesday 26th/ Midnight Special TV show in Burbank. We play "Sleep-walker," "Jukebox Music," and "Life Goes On." The first two are okay, the last one is bad.

Thursday 28th/ Detroit at Cobo Arena with Heart, topping 10,000 people. Many see the Kinks for the first time. It's heavy going but keeping my cool. Crowd response great. Show served purpose, which was to play in front of a lot of people. And steal the show from Heart—which I think we did. Not sure if we have the same fans though.

Later on that night I do a personal appearance at Peaches record store, and in return I get the *Ring Cycle* by Wagner box set. What a heavy box that was.

Friday 29th/ Toronto, Canada. Very good audience, good show, nearly 5,000 people. Twice as many as we played to last time.

Sunday 31st/ Fly to New York and have dinner with Clive, Janet, and Feiden at Tavern on the Green. Have a long walk and talk with Clive. I made the mistake of asking why Michael Kleffner left and Clive talked about it for what seemed like hours. He's obviously hurt because Mike left. See Grateful Dead concert in the evening. Too many drugs, too many people onstage. I am a little concerned they will stop working on my record at Arista now that Michael has left.

MAY

Tuesday 3rd/ Washington, D.C. A good feeling at the gig until the last number. Some of the president's aides have come to the concert to take us on to the White House afterward, but Mick and Dave have a row onstage. Baptist joins in, and then falls asleep and bangs his head on the piano. Needless to say we didn't get to the White House.

Thursday 5th/ Fly to Atlanta to do TV interviews on channel 36. Go out to a few bars afterward and at one, listen to a bluegrass band with a great steel player.

Friday 6th/ Atlanta Fox Theatre, fine show.

Saturday 7th/ Miami. I am only in second gear until halfway through then I charge up for the last part of the show and go over the top to what seems a largely blasé audience wearing too much suntan lotion.

Sunday 8th/ Tampa, Florida/ Fly back to London the following day.

JUNE

Friday 17th/ It all starts again: Fly to L.A. via New York.

Sunday 19th/ Play Anaheim Stadium with Alice Cooper, surprisingly good show. Although something went wrong; my headmaster's mask I wear for "The Hard Way" was stolen. Play from day till night. The first band to use lights. My favourite time.

Tuesday 21st/ Day off L.A. Not much to do or see. Try to work but nothing comes of it. Have lunch with Tom Ross and Rob from our agent's office at Le Restaurant. Go to bed and I forget I just missed my birthday.

Friday 24th/ Day off in Troy, Michigan. Bit of sunbathing, bit of work, then go see film Dave recommends called *Star Wars*. Found the music to be pretentious. To me sounded like fake Wagner and Walton.

Saturday 25th/ Fly to Chicago for a show at the Aragon Ballroom. The best show for a long time. High energy.

Sunday 26th/ Fly to Philadelphia. Full circle.

Tuesday 28th. Reading, Pennsylvania. Seemed to me like a pit of a theatre, tacky dressing rooms with rat poison on the floor, the champagne is too sweet. Great show.

Wednesday 29th/ Merryweather Post, Columbia, Maryland. Drive to N.Y. after the gig.

JULY

Friday 1st/ Mid-Hudson Civic Center, Poughkeepsie, New York. Feeling depressed.

Saturday 2nd/ Cape Cod Coliseum, the finest reception of the year. Holiday crowd and the fireworks, straight into a limousine afterward. Back to the pub in time for the last drink—can't do no better than that.

Sunday 3rd/ Asbury Park, New Jersey. Playing at the Convention Hall was like playing at Southend-on-Sea at an English seaside resort. Great audience; say no more.

Wednesday, 6th/ Last day in New York. Met with director Peter Medak, whom I have known since the '60s. Fly back to London.

Thursday 7th/ The seventh second, the seventh minute of the seventh hour of the seventh day of the seventh month, in the year seven-seven, I was just flying over Iceland.

AUGUST

Monday 8th/ Went to the Upper West Side to see an apartment that Clive wanted me to sublet; an apartment nearby that Arista held for visiting artists. Walked around Columbus Avenue. A little worried about the district, not sure if I like it up here. Go to Bert Padell's office to talk it over.

Saturday 13th/ Moved into the apartment on a very rainy day. Went to see Phoebe Snow in Central Park.

Monday 15th/ Writing new songs.

Tuesday 16th/ Elvis Presley died at 4:30 p.m.

Friday 19th/ Groucho Marx died.

Tuesday 30th/ Meeting with Bert Padell says we should have manager. Go to see *Side by Side by Sondheim* in evening.

Wednesday 31st/ Go to East Hampton to play Clive some new songs, new ideas. But will he like them?

NOVEMBER

Monday 31st/ The final assault of the year. Catch Air India flight to New York. Will promote new Xmas single "Father Christmas."

Tuesday 22nd/ First date in Trenton, New Jersey. Fabulous opening show; the band is really up. Best first show on tour for ages. "Magic," as our saxophone player Nick Newell put it. I like New Jersey.

Wednesday 23rd/ Brooklyn College. Great crowd, good show, but not as spontaneous as night before.

Thursday Nov 24th/ Had a good day. Woken up by people at the parade singing the Mickey Mouse theme. Had a turkey dinner and the best hot chocolate in the world at Rumplemeyer's. Went to see *Close Encounters of the Third Kind*. Then straight on with Bob Feiden to see *Looking for Mr. Goodbar*. Some heavy day.

Friday 25th/ Fly to Cleveland to support Hall and Oates in an arena. Hard time with tuning up, hard time with everything, hard time with stage crew. Wear Father Christmas outfit for encore.

Saturday 26/ Indianapolis. Drive there on coach through the snow. Do reasonably well. Hall and Oates roadie brings up the lights before we leave stage. Bad aggravation backstage with Hall and Oates crew. I rush on as Santa Claus to do Father Christmas, but am held back by roadies. Barbara Bothwell tries to step in but gets stopped by a member of the stage crew. Bad vibes all round.

DECEMBER

Friday 2nd/ Rhode Island. Great show, everything seems right. The song "Full Moon" is really perfect.

Saturday 3rd/ Second Rhode Island gig nearly as good as the night before. Theatre really packed. 1,000 people "walk up" at the last minute and hundreds locked out.

Sunday 4th/ Drive to gig at Massachusetts college. Great gig, big party afterwards.

Monday 5th/ Day off in Providence. Get drunk at hotel while the others have a party.

Tuesday 6th/ Drive down to Westchester Premier Theatre in Tarrytown, New York. Cold and snowing, a dire atmosphere backstage, but we get up for the show.

Thursday 8th/ Fly to Rochester to play a great college crowd of 3,000 in a small indoor running track.

Saturday 10th/ Landover, Maryland, near Washington. Hall and Oates bus fiasco, the crew pulls our plugs and makes our life miserable. How childish can you get?

Sunday 11th/ Stockton State College in Pomona, New Jersey. Good end; everyone happy to go home.

10

SLEEPWALKER

"Everybody got problems, buddy, I've got mine
When midnight comes around I start to lose my mind
When the sun turns out the light
I join the creatures of the night
Oh yeah.
I'm a sleepwalker
I'm a night stalker."

ARISTA, 1976–79

Arista Records, with Clive at the helm, seemed a perfect destination for the Kinks. RCA had acted like gentlemen throughout our whole time with them, allowing us to make the music we wanted to make regardless of whether it was successful or not. They knew and understood that I was trying to push the boundaries artistically with my overachieving stage shows and concept albums. We may have deviated slightly from the plot as a conventional recording unit but the amount of artistic freedom we had been given allowed us time and space to reinvent ourselves. The Kinks came out of the RCA period a tighter musical unit and I was allowed to experiment with subject matter that would have been impossible at our previous labels. RCA gave us free rein, and I will always be grateful for that. But there would be no such indulgences from Clive, who was his own A&R man, always at the ready with an opinion for better or worse. In fact, even the day that we signed with Arista, at a meeting at the Dorchester hotel in London, Clive brought over a songwriter to play me some songs he'd written for the Kinks. We were in a penthouse suite to close the deal. Clive was with Elliot Goldman and my attorney in the dining room finalizing the last few points of the contract. I was left talking to him.

"What do you think of this?" he said as he put on the tape of a musical backing track, as though he was a magician about to pull a rabbit out of a hat. The sound of drums thumping filled the plush suite. Chandeliers rattled as a loud, cranking guitar, similar to my brother's onstage sound, thudded around the room. Then I turned around and found myself face-to-face with him; in order to perform the song, he had transformed himself into a gyrating rock singer as he started singing over the track. His gesticulations and animated actions shocked me somewhat, given the genteel surroundings we were in. I stood and listened while he performed a fine rock ballad, but while it was excellently structured, it all seemed to be an impressionistic version of a Kinks song that was being pitched to me. I nodded politely and tried to turn down the volume of the system, but he immediately stepped in to turn it back up again; by now I'd heard enough and promised to play it to the band but he was in full flow. I pleaded for him to quit, but he kept going regardless, so I picked up an apple from a bowl of fruit and laughingly threatened to throw it at him. But he was still not deterred; on the contrary, it only made his performance more animated and robust. Something came over me, and this time I threw the apple at him, which, miraculously, landed in his mouth while he was in full vocal flow. He fell backward onto the sofa, took out the apple, and continued to sing the song. By then I was riled. I ran over to him and picked up a large cushion, as I thought I might smother him. The faux Kinks song was still playing, and his stifled vocals could still be heard through the cushion. I shouted half jokingly to Clive and the others. "Bring in the contract: I'll sign anything. Just stop this and I'll sign the first piece of paper you give me." The paperwork arrived in a heartbeat. The deal was closed.

CLIVE WANTED THE KINKS to make the more middle-of-the-road, commercial music he thought we had left behind since our early hits. The only problem I could foresee was that whatever we were, the Kinks were never middle of the road, so we settled for the term "accessible." This might become a bone of contention between me and Clive, but I put that thought to one side for the time being. The great attribute Clive had was that he would listen and take council whenever it was offered, even though often he would eventually revert to his original decision. He had put together a great marketing team of Michael Kleffner and, later, Richard Palmese in promotion and Abbey Konowitch and Dennis Fine (supposedly of the Fine & Schapiro delicatessen dynasty on West 72nd Street in NYC) doing publicity; it felt like a team that would lead us to success. *Sleepwalker*, the first album, released in 1977, was Clive's pet project.

One of the joys of working with someone like Clive is that he responded to the music in a very articulate way, unusual for an executive with a record company. *Sleepwalker* had a great selection of songs—"Life Goes On," "Life on the Road," "Stormy Sky," and "Sleepwalker" itself—but there was one song that Clive was passionate about called "Brother." It was one of those stream-of-consciousness songs that I write from time to time, but Clive made a connection with the title "Brother"; I had intended it to be a generalisation implying "humanity," that all men are brothers, as opposed to Clive's interpretation—that it was about Dave and me. Clive must have concluded that it would make a great publicity angle as well as a great record. I would have mixes and updates of the tracks couriered over to him, and we would speak for what seemed like hours on the transatlantic phone. Clive was passionate—no expense was spared—but I hate to think what his telephone bills were. He wanted an epic ending, but I hadn't yet achieved it on the track, so I brought the band back in to try to fulfil his wishes, overdubbing the outro and layering the track with sounds to build a massive ending.

Clive had a reputation at Columbia for inspiring A&R moments on tracks, as he had on occasion with acts such as Simon and Garfunkel, and he wanted the same amount of input on the Kinks album, particularly a song called "Brother." Yet suddenly, after almost a month of negotiations, countless guitar overdubs, and endless transatlantic telephone calls, his attention shifted to another track, and "Brother" was forgotten. We even dubbed an orchestra onto the end, but Clive was by then focused on "Sleepwalker," a more conventional rock track. I had to admit I agreed with him.

Sleepwalker was double the sales of our last few RCA albums, partly due to Michael Kleffner, who was a real powerhouse of a promotion man. He had to be; he weighed nearly fifteen stone and was a former bouncer for

Bill Graham at the Fillmore. One day I was enjoying a rare morning off in my hotel room when the phone rang. It was Kleffner. Without introducing himself he blurted out in his New York accent: "Do you want to lie in bed and sell two hundred and fifty thousand units for the rest of your life or do you want to come to Boston with me in half an hour and do some record promotion?"

For a second I thought about telling him to get lost, but then I thought about the great promotional opportunities I had at my disposal. I was waiting in the lobby within forty-five minutes to get the air shuttle to Boston.

IN CONTRAST TO THE TOUGH, MACHO, Kleffner, Bob Feiden was a slightly built, well-spoken, articulate, fast-talking New Yorker who knew all the connections and contacts vital to assist Clive. Feiden was also a complete insomniac. He would often call me in the middle of the night to see if I had any "dolls," meaning sleeping pills, to help him through the night. This had backfired the first time he required a doll, when I misunderstood the meaning of the word and asked my tour manager if he knew of any groupies he could send over to Feiden.

Bob, whom Kleffner referred to as "the count," was an old friend of Barbara Bothwell, my tour assistant during the RCA days. Barbara was a southern belle, a true femme fatal in the tradition of Blanche DeBois from *A Streetcar Named Desire*. When her hair was newly shampooed and well groomed it hung down onto her shoulders in ringlets and waves. When it was unkempt and matted she turned rodentlike and was a caution. She said that she hailed from Atlanta, Georgia, which she pronounced as "Hatlanna" in a breathy Southern accent. She had married the pop singer Johnny Tillotson when she was only around sixteen and described herself as a child bride but even so, I couldn't help thinking she was probably lying about her age. Whilst I wouldn't have known Johnny Tillotson from Adam, I had heard his hit song "Only Sixteen" on the radio when I was a kid. I didn't ask how long the marriage lasted and she didn't offer up any more information so I didn't enquire further.

Barbara was a typical American beauty with a pert, upturned nose, even though her slim face showed faint scars on her cheeks from what must have been bad acne marks left from when she was a kid.

She knew how to enter a room and even when she'd had a few drinks, she managed to give off a superior air as if waiting for a servant to open the door for her. Like so many people I met along the way, she arrived in my life a fully formed character; whatever her journey had been it would remain a secret to me. She had made her way to New York City, where she had ended up working in A&R at RCA Records, which is where we first met. She had become friendly with my tour manager Ken Jones, and came out on many of our New York–based dates; even then she had an eye for musicians (particularly British pop invaders like myself) even so, she would often be seen drinking with the dregs hanging around at the end of a party. She inspired many sordid rumours in the tour entourage, and despite all the distasteful gossip relating to blow jobs and sex—which she helped circulate—I suspect that she invariably ended up alone.

She would often come to concerts with Bob Feiden. It became obvious that they were not a couple as Bob was overtly gay, but they loved one another's company because they understood each other. They had christened themselves "Mama and Papa." When they were together, Mama and Papa gave the impression they were a very well-spoken and articulate couple, who in another life would've been ideal partners.

As time went on it became clear that Mama, or as Ken Jones referred to her as "Aunty," was becoming obsessed with being around the Kinks, and myself in particular. Once when I had foolishly run off with an American girl, Mama went to great lengths to convince me that such American women were dangerous predators and any such liaison would inevitably end with me being destroyed. "If you want an unhappy but passionate liaison with an American girl who will destroy, then I'm available and at half the price," she told me. Nevertheless she become a devoted ally and would often come on trips with us when we played the East Coast. I don't know whether it was a result of corporate restructure or their life-style, but both Bob and Barbara left RCA. From that moment on Mama's life started a downward spiral, and she saw the Kinks as a lifeline. She eventually started touring with us as our tour coordinator and assisted Ken Jones. She was also very helpful when it came to liaising with the record company due to her experience with corporate America. When we released *Low Budget*, Mama had insisted that she had posed for the photograph on the front cover, and whilst on tour she would wear exactly the same shoes as in the photograph so that people would think she was the model on the album cover.

In the heady days of the Konk Club, our former nightclub at Konk Studios, Mama came to stay in London and frequented the bar at the back of the club, where she would talk until the early hours with musicians and the bartender, Frank Smyth. One night she had to be forcibly ejected after a romantic interlude with a roadie on the snooker table. Smyth was concerned that any such shenanigans would possibly damage the snooker table, which was due to be used for a club tournament.

Mama was not a spring chicken, but nevertheless she insisted on adopting a rock-and-roll lifestyle and had become good friends with the late Hilly Kristal, the founder and owner of CBGB in the East Village in New York. She straddled pre-punk with rock-and-roll aplomb and had befriended many of the new young bands; needless to say, she had crushes on all of them and never turned down a good party. Once, at the airport in the baggage claim area we'd heard a buzzing sound go off in her case conveyer belt, and although Mama insisted that it was just her alarm clock, others in the band swore it was a dildo.

Mama was a real confidante, and even during the low-life days of debauchery in the 1970s she was level-headed when it came to business matters and always had my best intentions at heart. Nevertheless she was becoming a true rock-and-roll victim, and while with successful albums like *Misfits* and *Low Budget* the Kinks cachet went up in terms of touring and record sales, Mama's emotional state was deteriorating.

At the beginning of one tour we arrived in New York and were alarmed to discover that she had been living with nuns in a convent. This was a genuine cause for concern but she said she was happy there and it helped prevent sins of the flesh. She remained steadfastly loyal to us, even when she had to accompany Mick Avory and members of our horn section to porn movies. She still hadn't lost her corporate ethos, when she came up with commentaries like "that stud's got no staying power." Once when we arrived in Chicago she had seized the initiative and brought the whole band to see a porn spoof version of the movie *Shampoo*, entitled *Blow Dry*, starring "Warren Piece"—she thought the band would be entertained by that. Avory and one of the horn players went along for the treat while the rest of us slept off our jet lag at the hotel. Perhaps she wanted to be considered as "one of the boys." I couldn't help but observe that in this regard, Mama was turning into a fallen woman. In time it got to the point where Ken Jones felt that Mama was unreliable with her advance work and so made the suggestion that we shouldn't employ her anymore. I insisted that we keep Mama around because she had a good heart and when she was capable of being sober she was very sensible about business matters.

Events eventually took a turn for the worse when she didn't turn up at all at the beginning of a tour. I caught up with her several years later and discovered that she had gone down to Florida to be a teacher and then had helped start a food channel on cable TV and had successfully reconnected with the corporate world.

The turning point in her life finally came when her beloved Bob Feiden died tragically of cancer. Bob and Mama were always inseparable, and somehow helped one another get through their excesses. The situation was not improved when I remarried and had what was a seemingly happy home life. We stayed in touch on and off; she would write beautifully structured letters and gave continual advice on what I should do with my business and personal life. Last time I saw Barbara she was living up near Colombia University, and I took her for a Mexican meal at a nearby place appropriately called Mama Mexico. That was the last communication we had. A few months later I got the news via one of my old road crew that Barbara had "fallen" from a window on the eleventh floor where she lived. I thought back to the good times we all had and all of the laughter, which was often at her expense. It was not easy for a woman to be around and function in what was at that time a male-dominated industry. Like Blanche DuBois, no one ever found out the true source of her sadness. Whenever I said goodbye to her and bade her a fond farewell, it never seemed enough. There must be a darkness inside some of us that never knows the sunlight and a sorrow that can never seem to be comforted. Or maybe I was more unfeeling and insensitive than I ever thought I could be.

SUNDAY AFTERNOONS IN THE SUMMER OF 1977 were spent with Feiden and Mama at Clive Davis's beach cabana on Atlantic Beach, in Long Island. Feiden, Mama, and I would stop off at Barney Greengrass on the Upper West Side to buy gefilte fish and bagels, which happened to be Clive's favourite. We would then drive out to Long Island, where we would find Clive already sunbathing outside his cabana—referred to by Bob as "the beach property." With a mix from the latest Barry Manilow recording playing loudly in the background, Clive's young son, Fred, would build sand castles at our feet. When Clive's elderly neighbours, with their glistening faces covered in Hawaiian Tropic, would complain about the noise level from Clive's boom box, Clive would simply gesture to Feiden, who would explain to the sun-worshipping neighbours not to interrupt while Clive's decision-making was in progress. It transpired that the neighbours, who Feiden referred to as "the leather faces," were Barry Manilow fans, so there were no further problems. I think they may have even been responsible for choosing "Copacabana" as a single. Whether this was true or not, Clive would watch out of the corner of his eye to see if Feiden's "leather faces" next door would tap their feet whenever a new Manilow album track played, as if to make a mental note for his next marketing meeting at Arista. Clive knew his artists' audiences.

Journeys out to Long Island and the beach property seemed to be as far as Feiden wanted to venture out of New York. He was a Manhattan animal through and through, and he stated in no uncertain terms that he always needed to feel concrete beneath his feet. Feiden was a good old-fashioned big-city socialite. On occasion, he would invite me to parties to mingle with New York "society" and to the theatre, where he'd introduce me to film stars and socialites such as Jackie Bisset, Candice Bergen, and Sabrina Guinness. Richard Gere became quite a fan of the Kinks at the time. These were heady days. Baked Alaska at Tavern on the Green, brunch at the Plaza Hotel, drinks at the New York Athletic Club, dinner at Elaine's. A far cry from a Sunday pint with my dad in the Clissold Arms in Muswell Hill. These were the days of Studio 54 and other chic clubs. We would often meet fellow West Siders

Michael Kleffner and his wife, Carol, for a night out. There was a club at the corner of 72nd Street and Columbus Avenue called Trax, where I would eventually meet Chrissie Hynde. When he discovered that Hynde and I were seeing one another, Feiden took us both out to dinner at a swanky Midtown restaurant. Chrissie must have been eating bad road food at the time, because she not only scoffed down her meal but seemed to enjoy it so much that she innocently mopped up the remains of her food with a piece of bread. Quite acceptable behaviour in my opinion, particularly after being subjected to road food for months on end, but as we walked home, Bob took me to one side and whispered firmly in my ear. "She's a great singer, an emerging talent, and quite possibly a Grammy winner, but with table manners like that she is definitely not for you." Bob's words were prophetic, but it wouldn't hit home until many dinners later.

It seemed that every few blocks there was a good club to go to. Back then, there was minimal enforcement of the old cabaret law that banned groups of more than three musicians from playing in clubs unless they had a specific license. There were so many great bands playing about in bars and back rooms, including Weather Report and other jazz fusion and progressive rock bands of the period.

New York can be spellbinding, not just because of its spectacular skyline but also because there are so many different types of people, cultures, languages, styles, and a seemingly endless array of cuisines. To me, the city resembles a giant overpopulated pizza with ingredients thrown in from all over the world.

ON FEBRUARY 26, 1977, THE KINKS had just done *Saturday Night Live* to promote the new *Sleepwalker* album for Arista. *Saturday Night Live* was by then an American TV institution, and it was considered to be a real coup for us to be on. It was hosted by Steve Martin, with the classic cast of Dan Aykroyd, John Belushi, Jane Curtin, Gilda Radner, and Bill Murray, with special guest Lily Tomlin. The Kinks were having problems with the sound, and this took all my attention, so subsequently I declined to be included in the Coneheads sketch that came on immediately before the Kinks slot. It was a strange contrast—me grumpily storming off the soundstage complaining about the lack of professionalism on the show as I walked past two men wearing cones on their heads and talking in strange, high-pitched, alien accents. The rehearsals were barely over when it was time to go live. We performed a couple of songs; an old hit and the title track of our new album, *Sleepwalker*. Clive Davis and Bob Feiden attended the show with us, and afterward they walked us through to the after-party. The Kinks were a coveted signing for Clive's label, and we were shown off proudly by him as newly acquired members of his roster. Clive was particularly pumped up after our performance, and when the elevator man asked if we were going up or down, Clive remarked, "We are in the music business, and with the Kinks, the only way is up." At the *SNL* party, Clive and Bob were accompanied by a well-known Andy Warhol actress known for her sexy, racy roles, whom I will call Ramona. On the surface, Ramona's persona seemed not dissimilar to the stereotypical gravel-voiced, hard-edged, New York "babe." I suspect these elements of hardness were designed to counteract any vulnerability that might result from having a classic tits-and-arse figure, big lips, and the rest of the whammeroo. Deep down she was obviously a serious actress who probably had become typecast as a sex bomb.

As we left the studio, Clive asked her what she thought of the Kinks' performance. She rolled her eyes and pouted her lips in her own inimitable way, then she compared it to a recent chart-topping record. "It was hardly *Frampton Comes Alive!*, but it was passable." I took this to be a direct comment on my performance, which probably was nervous and, in her eyes, lame. This was said in that jarring theatrical twang that is so typical of New Yorkers who speak to be heard above the crowd in restaurants, to be quoted in *The New Yorker*, to be noticed as part of the New York party that never stops in the swirling milieu of Manhattan society. Ramona would shoot from the hip and was never one to pull any punches when her turn came to critique. I detected that she had some interest in me and I flirted with the situation but rather than repel my ridiculous innuendo, this only served to whet her appetite.

We were also accompanied by my devoted assistant, Barbara Bothwell, who was very mindful that I should not drink too much or get into any bad situations. Ramona seemed to be in a particularly predatory mood that night, and it appears that I was on the menu. Barbara did her best to intervene and step in whenever Ramona came too close to me, and I tried to explain that I was already spoken for. But Ramona was on a mission, and her voice became more breathily seductive. The harder Barbara worked to dissuade her, the more Ramona blanked her out. Eventually the party was over and we all three decided to go back to Ramona's apartment in Midtown Manhattan to have a nightcap.

It was a cold winter's night in New York, and I had made it clear that I wasn't going to stay long, so I kept on my blue Crombie overcoat with my scarf firmly wrapped around me. I heard some talking in the kitchen. Barbara was being quizzed by Ramona. I don't know what was said, but shortly afterward, Barbara left me alone in the apartment with the charismatic actress.

On the one hand I was flattered; on the other hand I was terrified. I'd once been in the Plaza Hotel with Clive, having brunch seated next to the writer Truman Capote and listening as he gossiped about other members of the literati and spread rumours about his latest would-be romantic conquests.

New York was that kind of place—everybody knew everything about everybody else, and everyone was fair game when it came to scandal. It was the beginning of celebrity culture, and if I had stayed in Ramona's apartment too long I could possibly have ended up as one of her conquests. Other people—probably very normal people, ambitious people, people with futures, people wanting to get in the public eye—would have jumped at the opportunity to spend the night with the voluptuous Ramona. Her engine was still revved up, and her tank was far from empty, but all I could think of was a way out. I looked for the nearest exit—or, if things got to a desperate state, I thought I might try to climb down the fire escape forty floors down to the street.

I buttoned up my Crombie coat, wrapped my scarf around my neck even tighter, and headed for the door, ready to go out into the cold night. I turned around, and at the far end of the room I saw a sight to behold: Ramona draped seductively across her chaise lounge. An exquisite-looking mature woman indeed, a nice bit of old, but I couldn't stay. I felt like a real wimp saying I had to get up in the morning to go to Boston, but Ramona was unrelenting. She got up and smooched from across the room, her unblinking eyes firmly fixed on mine. For a moment I was taken in, completely transfixed by her hypnotic look. "Are you gonna stay or are you gonna run away like a scared rabbit?" As she spoke, a whole series of images went through my head—a scared rabbit; did I really look like one? Well, I certainly felt like one. I explained that I was about to come down with a cold and had to leave immediately. She sidled up to me again at the door, breathed in my face, batted her eyelids, and took a deep intake of air as she drew her pouting mouth upward and closer to mine. Our eyes were less than an inch apart, and she spoke in that breathy, gravelly voice. "Before you go, tell me one thing. What turned you off?" I mumbled a series of pathetic schoolboy remarks. "You're a great actress; I'm not worthy; and you're so, so . . . New York." She inquired what "so New York" meant. I thought about it for a minute, then an image came into my head. I tried to make this as polite and complimentary as possible, but I blurted out in a somewhat clumsy way, "You look like a pizza, because that's what New York reminds me of, and Miss Ramona, you're so New York."

Ramona's jaw dropped, and her face froze in a shocked expression. As the Sleepwalker walked into the cold night, the actress might have looked in the mirror for a hint of pepperoni. It was a narrow escape for all concerned. After that very brief encounter, we would often bump into one another at various events, and we even became good, if only occasional, friends. Sometimes I'd see her walking around near my apartment, and we would stop in the street to chat. She often used to show me clippings in a scrapbook that for some reason she always seemed to have with her. She was and still is a proud and dedicated actress, but more than anything else, and in the sincerest possible way, she is a great and lovable "dame."

ROCK-AND-ROLL FANTASY, AUGUST 1977

The first album for Arista, *Sleepwalker*, had set us up very well. Clive and his team were satisfied and eagerly awaited the follow-up album. I was staying on in New York to write new songs, and as a result this created an uneasiness in the band at this time as certain players were complaining about the long tours we were doing. It was clear to everyone that Clive and I were going to see this six-album commitment through to its completion, and this in turn would require the minimum of one U.S. tour with each album. On top of this my brother Dave and I were falling out about various issues concerning songs and production.

One night I started to write a song about Dave and I when we first started out; how we enjoyed playing so much as kids but how the fun was tainted slightly because the band was working within a business structure.

"Hello you, hello me, hello people we used to be
Isn't it strange, we never changed,
We've been through it all yet we're still the same
And I know, it's a miracle we still go
For all we know, we might still have a way to go.

Hello me, hello you. You say you want out, want to start anew
Throw in your hand, break up the band, start a new life, be a new man
But for all we know we might still have a way to go
Before you go, there's something you ought to know . . . "

By the time I'd written the first couple of verses and started a pre-chorus it was about 2:30 a.m., still quite early for New York nightlife, but it was quiet and dark on my block. I looked out of the window from my apartment, to the building across 72nd Street, which was dark apart from one lit window. I imagined the person inside to be an insomniac like me, up playing music all night and hiding away from the world, so I christened him Dan the Fan. The Kinks were finding a fan base that could see a meaning in our songs far and beyond the music itself, almost as though there was a coded message of hope in the songs. People like Dan the Fan seemed to know us better than we knew ourselves.

"Dan is a fan and he lives for our music,
It's the only thing that gets him by.
He's watched us grow and he's seen all our shows
He's seen us low and he's seen us high
Oh, but you and me keep thinking
That the world's just passing us by.

Don't wanna spend my life living in a rock 'n' roll fantasy
Don't wanna spend my life living on the edge of reality
Don't wanna waste my life hiding away anymore
Don't wanna spend my life living in a rock 'n' roll fantasy."

It was now around 3 a.m., but I was only halfway through the song so I decided to cut my losses and decided to call it a night. The lyric was done and all I had to do was write a final verse and wrap it up with a chorus, but thought I'd mull it over it and finish the song after a good sleep. The next day, August 16, I heard the news that Elvis Presley had died. I tuned in to see all the latest TV and heard the endless stream of radio reports, which started to make me a little emotional, so I got back to writing. I thought about the Scotty Moore guitar solo on Elvis's recording of "I'm Left, You're Right, She's Gone" and how as a teenager I'd tried to copy it note for note. Then I recalled my brother trying to sing "One Night with You" when he was barely a teen-ager himself.

I looked out the window at that same apartment I had been staring at the night before as I reached a moment in the song where the two people, Dave and I, were thinking of breaking up and finishing with the band (which despite our new lease on life with Arista was a real possibility at the time). I began writing an ending that simply catalogued the break-up of our band, but then thought about Elvis Presley and how he symbolised the American Dream. I wrote the final verse and then went into the last chorus of the song, which seemed to write itself after that. It was all written in about twenty-four hours from that first moment I had dreamed up Dan the Fan playing records in the apartment opposite until I'd heard the news of Elvis Presley's death. The King's death had in a strange way instilled in me more belief in what I was doing, and I finished the song partly as a tribute to him:

"Hello me, hello you
You say you want out, want to start anew . . .
The king is dead, rock is done
You might be through but I've just begun."

11

THE BIG GUYS

"Everybody's afraid of the Big Guy called the 'Gorilla' but he was never heavy out of hand—
In fact he was a gentle as a lamb.
Tony, Tony you gave me security, you know, Tony, Tony you gave me security
Minder extraordinaire, I miss you now that you're not there.
No you're never alone as long as the Big Guy's there."

MINDERS, 1977–1983

On the *Sleepwalker* tour, Steve Harley & Cockney Rebel opened for the Kinks. Their minder was Tony Gibbins, a bodyguard from South London, who with his bushy beard and large physical presence resembled Bluto on *Popeye*. Someone in our band blurted out "Who's the gorilla?" at Tony as he walked around backstage after the show. Bands are like kids sometimes: they can seem very cruel, and because their observations can be accurate and telling, like children's, they can come across as blunt and unsympathetic. After that tour we enlisted the "Gorilla"—or Big Tony, as he was lovingly christened—to look after our security. His job was more to look after and pander to our daily needs rather than keep admiring fans away. Tony was a true gentle giant. He looked the part, but I never saw him lift a hand to threaten anybody. His presence was enough to frighten any potential wrongdoers away. That was the beauty of "the big guy." Other bands' security guards sometimes carried guns, but to Tony, "shooters" were off-limits because he considered them totally unnecessary and very "old school." He had an elegant, Zen-like calm—but if things got out of control he would be there to intervene when trouble beckoned. He also had a problem pronouncing his *r*'s and pushed his jaw out when he spoke, which gave the impression that his speech impediment was actually worse than it seemed.

I struck up a great bond with Big Tony. When we went out on a night off, he was under firm instructions from me that if I'd had more than three drinks he was to threaten to break my arm—a threat he had to make on several occasions. He was there to protect me from myself more than from anyone else. His threats were all communicated with a lighthearted banter, but deep down I knew that, if need be, Tony would follow my instructions and implement the punishment.

It was also Tony's duty, on Ken Jones's order, to come into the dressing room before shows and to tell us it was time to go onstage. He would walk up and say in his broad South London accent, "Come on, it's time," in a manner resembling an executioner telling us it was time to be taken to the scaffold.

SOMETIMES ON TOUR YOU JUST FALL INTO SITUATIONS without knowing what you are getting yourself into. You meet up with some people who seem like nice folks after a concert, and they say, "You've got a day off tomorrow, and if you're in town, come over for dinner with me and the wife."

Some unsuspecting members of the crew welcome such hospitality only to find that on occasion they are subjected to unexpected erotic adventures. In the case of one member of our touring entourage, it transpired that the happily married couple who asked him to "come over" turned out to be a pair of swingers, and the husband wanted the unsuspecting fellow to have sex with the missus while he observed from inside the wardrobe—although it was unclear why the wardrobe had to be the vantage point. The next day we had a postmortem on the roadie's unsavoury exploits and realised that the fantasy was more complex than it seemed.

Our "ravers" adjudication committee, chaired by bass player Jim Rodford, reached the conclusion that the husband wanted it to appear that he had secretly discovered what was happening. But under rigorous cross-examination by me, the hapless crew member revealed the true story. Apparently, after the crew member had "done the business" with the woman in question, the husband popped out of the wardrobe and the wife "confessed." The husband then proceeded to put on his wife's clothes and wanted the roadie to make love to him also, only this time the wife would invite a woman neighbour 'round to have sex in the wardrobe with her while they watched events unfold in the bedroom. It was a bizarre tale, but apparently the Jack Daniel's had been flowing, and crew members rarely turn down a free drink. As the story went, the husband then tried to hustle some money from the unfortunate roadie when they discovered that he didn't have any drugs. It all started to get out of hand when the husband took out a revolver, pointed it at his own head, and began to play Russian roulette. The terrified roadie managed to get away and escape by the skin of his teeth. Apparently the husband had just found out about his wife's lesbian affair, and the "gals" wanted to put on the charade just to cheer the poor fellow up. Needless to say, the roadie breathed a sigh of relief and was advised not to go out unaccompanied in the future.

That's why Big Tony was necessary to the Kinks organisation. He wasn't there to keep screaming fans at bay—he was there to protect us from getting into unsavoury scrapes. Big Tony was more a part of the band than anything else. Nobody could work as part of the Kinks entourage if they didn't fit in with Kinks "culture," and that culture was exclusively British. It was a cure for homesickness as well as our way of protecting ourselves against any influence that wasn't uniquely British. When our contemporaries reverted to the use of "man," "buddy," and "brother," the Kinks stuck rigidly to "mush," "cock," and "mate." We made no attempt to be anything other than ourselves. John Dalton even kept his watch on UK time and carried his own supply of HP sauce to put on his eggs and bacon at breakfast so that he still felt that he was at home in the local working man's cafe.

Tony would withstand endless taunts from the band because he was in our employ. If, on the other hand, the derision was directed at him by others, Big Tony would simply escort the person out of the room, often with a word in the person's ear: "Now, don't do that again."

Once at a small venue someone said something that upset Tony, but he didn't blow up and smack anyone; he stayed in one of the dressing rooms, where he sat looking lost, near the point of breaking down. "I just need to be left alone, so go away, please," he said. Later we went into the dressing room to find that he'd completely wrecked some of the chairs, breaking them into tiny pieces. Tony thought that it would be better to demolish the chairs rather than some poor bystander. We left it at that and never got to the bottom of his anger.

As the Kinks played bigger and bigger venues, it became necessary for us to hire a second security person—an "assistant" to Tony. Hence the arrival of Chris Jerome to the fold.

A strong lad from London, he was into martial arts and was a biker. Chris appeared to be as square as he was long, and according to Tony could "march on" a bit. In other words, he could look after himself and anyone else who happened to get in the way. This contrasted with the fact that Chris was a highly intelligent chap who always did the *Daily Telegraph* crosswords whenever he could purchase British newspapers. He had bright red hair, a seafaring mustache, and a beard, which made him look like a fit version of King Henry VIII—except that he was tattooed. On Chris's first trip to New York City, Tony made him walk alone from one end of Central Park to the other in the middle of the night as a test of character, bravery, and stealth. The event was not witnessed by anyone, but according to Big Tony, Jerome passed with flying colours. Whilst Chris didn't need to prove to us that he was a tough guy, Tony insisted that he needed to prove that he was made of the "right stuff."

On one tour, Tony had trouble with his diet and started getting an upset stomach. Everyone assumed that the Big Guy was overdoing it, particularly as the parties in the hotel "noisy rooms" were happening every night. After a show we would assign somebody's hotel room to be the noisy room, and there we would take all the leftover drinks from the dressing rooms. Tony often offered his own room for this purpose, but his physical discomfort was beginning to show. The upset stomachs turned out to be terminal cancer, and once diagnosed, its progress was sharp and sudden. On our August 1981 tour, Tony was unable to make the trip over to the States. We missed him sorely; he'd been with us all the way on the past few years' tours and dates with the likes of Blondie, Tom Petty, Ian Hunter and Mick Ronson, the Cars, John Cougar (Mellencamp), and numerous others.

The last time I saw Tony Gibbins was when we flew back to England from a U.S. tour on Sunday, August 30, 1981, to play the Reading Festival. He was barely recognisable as the strapping South London lad we'd once known. He'd lost weight, he'd had chemotherapy, and was a shadow of the person he used to be. His head was shaved. His beard was gone, and he was not the old scary "Gorilla" anymore. He was obviously no longer able to work with the Kinks on tour, but he did act as backstage security guard at the festival. Tony stood outside our dressing room and tried to be authoritative as he told us to go onstage. The words were the same: "Come on, then, you're on," but they weren't as forceful as before. We used to joke that the only thing missing from Tony was a black executioner's hood. Now the baseball hat he wore seemed too big for his head. He waved his torch around to point the way to the stage, but there was no strength in the way he led us to the concert. Big Tony died a few months later.

An American, Bobby Suszynski, took over as the Big Guy after Tony died. We struggled long and hard to find a name for Bob that would fit the legacy left by Big Tony, and after hours of deliberation we settled on Big Bob. It was a no-brainer. Big Bob had been shot in the leg while serving as a cop in Chicago, and he displayed the wound above his right knee with pride. He rolled up his trouser leg to show me his scar—the dent in his thigh muscle where the bullet had entered—and gave me a precise blow-by-blow breakdown of how the incident occurred.

In the tradition of our Big Guys, Bob had a speech impediment. It made him slur his words, particularly the letter *s*, and even though he was big and menacing this gave him a childlike demeanour. He took the place of Big Tony with pride, and he felt that even though he was an American he blended in with what was a British entourage. The decision to take Bob on was based on the way he adopted our Brit humour.

When the road is all you've got, sometimes it becomes overwhelming, and resentment and self-loathing kicks in. It's a good idea to have people like Bobby around to take the brunt of the abuse and absorb all the negative feelings. We gave Big Bob the same instructions as we had given Tony. "Break an arm if Ray steps out of line on a night off. You got that now, Fatso?"

Bob simmered away his anger and popped a diet soda as he spoke. "I'm too big and stupid to be upset by anything you say, but I'll gladly follow your instructions and break his arm if he really annoys me."

The road is a complete lifestyle. All those one-nighters can come back to haunt you. When you are stuck in a hotel on a night off, there is no one to call except other band members or crew who are in a similar position. Nights off, for some reason, do not typically take place in glamorous penthouses or exotic nightspots. They're usually spent in the back of beyond, at a no-name bar near the hotel. The only females to chat up are the female bar staff, who don't give a "monkey's" about you anyway—and why should they? They're too busy trying to earn tips to respond to the pathetic advances of old roadies who have had too much bourbon. At these types of places, any pretty woman who arrives on the scene is usually accompanied by some beefcake guy. Occasionally an exuberant superfan will find out that members of the band are there and will turn up to buy a round of drinks. Just when you think you can talk to the lone intelligent young lady at the bar, you're confronted with this well-meaning superfan, who wants to know the details of a track you recorded fifteen years ago. There's no escape from that. Best thing is to cut your losses and go back to the hotel to phone up other members of the tour entourage and divvy out the remnants of the dressing-room booze and food from the night before. This would be a mixture of half-finished bottles of cheap wine drunk in somebody's noisy room. Then when the drinks are finished, it's time to raid the minibar. By now desperation sets in, and even one of the monitor guys starts to look attractive from the back because his long flowing hair vaguely resembles that of a woman's. Time to hit the sack and watch *The Tonight Show*.

Then there are the calls home to loved ones who are not at home.

One night when we were on tour in Melbourne, Australia, I was having childish telephone spats with my girlfriend at the time, who was on the other side of the world. I decided to drink away my sorrows, but only on the condition that Big Bob was with me.

I went to the bar with Big Bob to try to get through the night, and found myself being hustled into a game of pool by an ex-pro. By the end of the game it was obvious I couldn't win. I had way too much to drink and was throwing up and acting unruly, to say the least. Bob put me to bed and sat next to me so I wouldn't choke on my own vomit; such is the lot of the devoted security guard.

Another time when I was in Ohio and my girlfriend was in Australia, there was a repetition of the same scenario—only this time I had cracked my kneecap really badly and was forced to walk around in a cast. I was under stress because the venues were sold out and could not be cancelled and I was taking painkillers to get through the shows. I couldn't get my slim black stage pants on over my cast when I performed, so I wore wide-cut 'loons, which were enjoying a fashion renaissance at that time. Our monitor man, Bob Pridden, said that watching me take the stage was both inspiring and sad at the same time.

One night on that tour, one of the crew had a birthday, and the group decided to go to the local strip joint. Rather than stay at the hotel room, as my manager advised, I insisted on hobbling along to the party on crutches, where I had an argument with a man who turned out to be a pimp. I was in a reckless mood and was acting foolishly, so Bob reminded me that not only would he break my arm but that the pimp would probably stab me anyway if I misbehaved. I was a pathetic invalid who had had too much to drink and was hobbling around in a seedy strip joint with a cast on my leg. I was in terrible pain, angry, and obviously very vulnerable. Bobby picked me up and carried me out of the club over his shoulder as I protested. He took me back to the hotel and threatened to throw me off the balcony from the tenth floor if I didn't behave.

"Go to bed, take your painkillers, and get some sleep—and if you don't you'll have a broken arm to match the kneecap and you won't even be able to do the show tomorrow night." Bob stayed on the sofa in my room to ensure I couldn't escape. He not only saved me from myself but probably saved my life in the process. As he was putting the blanket on his makeshift bed, he pondered my recklessness.

"What's scary about guys like you is that as big and strong as I am, you'd still keep coming at me. It's like you got nothin' to lose. You get a thing in your head and you won't stop 'cause your willpower won't let you see sense; like you got a demon inside you that won't lie down. The only thing that'll stop you is yourself."

I pretended I was asleep.

Bob opened a bottle of soda and turned the TV on low volume so that

I wouldn't be too disturbed by it, but later he woke me up because he was snoring and farting so loud.

Big Bob himself later died of cancer before he was thirty.

The Big Guys, Bob and Tony. I hope someone is watching over them right now.

> *"Minders extraordinaire*
> *I miss them now that they're not there."*

12

MISFITS

"You're a Misfit
Afraid of yourself so you run away and hide.
You've been a Misfit all your life
So why don't you join the crowd and come inside
You wander round this town, like you've lost your way
You had your chance in your day
Yet you threw it all away
But you know what they say,
Every dog has its day."

THE MUSIC OR THE WORDS, NYC, SPRING 1978

Legend has it that a journalist once asked the great American song-writer and lyricist Sammy Cahn, "What comes first, the music or the words?" The celebrated writer of the words to "All the Way," "High Hopes," and other classics paused for thought before replying nonchalantly, "The phone calls."

I was asked the same question and answered diplomatically by saying that with the best songs the words and music come together. That answer is factual for the most part, but the reality is simpler. If I were really hard-pressed and forced to scour my inner depths so that I could actually say something remotely truthful, I would have to confess that with me it is what I refer to as the "doo-di-dum-dums."

I usually find that I can't "dum" without a "doo" first, or the idea ends up a fragmented piece of noncerebral dumbness. Sometimes a song comes as a response to a situation I have found myself in or a comment someone has made either to me or about me. I can even be inspired by a character I see walking down the street or an overheard conversation; everybody walks and talks to a beat. When I'm blocked—and I sometimes am—I'll take anything I can get. For now, though, the doo-di-dum-dum will be as good as any. It simply means, "I am attempting to be creative."

It goes back to when I had a small daughter who said, "Dad, I want to do a poo." I would sit at my piano and say, "Okay, but Daddy got to doo-di-dum-dum now, so ask Mum." In other words, "Don't bother me now; I'm working." The "phone call" Sammy Cahn referred to probably related to a deal he was hoping someone would offer him or a request to write a new song—a request that probably would have been based on the assumption that Cahn would only write if commissioned. Unlike that wily old campaigner, I would simply look at a ringing phone in a panic state, too insecure to even answer it. If I were in the middle of working on a song, I would pick up, say that it was not a good time to talk, and hang up. No wonder people stopped calling me.

In the spring of 1978, New York was buzzing, but I was not. The sidewalk was vibrating with scintillating contrapuntal rhythms, bristling with multilingual effervescent melodies everywhere—except in my world. I was in a nonproductive phase. Nothing I wrote worked. The old doo-di–dum-dum was definitely not functioning as it should. On good days the songs can sometimes start in my head and quickly form lyrics and melodies before scrambling through my mouth and out onto the keyboard or guitar, where they turn into eloquent musical phrases. That spring, my ideas didn't even warrant a "scooby-doo" from my lips.

I was living awkwardly and was not in a good place emotionally. Clive Davis was keen for me to write and record, so at his request I had stayed on after a tour in New York in an apartment on the Upper West Side to be "close" to my new record company, Arista, whose offices were on West 57th Street. I also needed to get away from the UK, where the music scene had turned into, on the one hand, a pompous parade of pomp-rock Eurovision and disco and, on the other hand, a morass of designer-clad postpunk. The British Invasion was over, but ironically I found that staying in America did in some way help me stay in touch with my Britishness because I was so detached from it geographically. The Kinks were in the middle of rebuilding their career in the United States while New York City danced to a relentless disco rhythm. I sat in the apartment on the Upper West Side looking at a blank page. I would get up early and try to psych myself into creativity, but usually I'd end up watching the *Today* show for inspiration. I pondered how, if given the opportunity to do so, I might ask the show's cohost, Jane Pauley, for a date. In my fantasy she would blush while I propositioned her live on the air, but then my illusion would be shattered by her guard-dog partner, Tom Brokaw, who would remind the pretty talk-show host that they had a brunch appointment at the 21 Club. In my crushed fantasy she would then bring the interview to an end by announcing a station break, and during it she would politely blow me out. At the apartment I would scribble on a notepad through the news update, before watching Phil Donahue nod his head politely in response to irate guests on his talk show.

In a creatively nonproductive phase, my body almost mirrors my emotional state and I can become uncoordinated and a risk to myself and others as I bump into tables and walk into closing doors. When it gets like this I forget which side of the Atlantic I am on. I invariably trip up on the pavement, drive on the wrong side of the road, and generally become a danger to anyone who happens to be walking near me. I become a cause for concern among all those who care about me.

I might do things out of clumsiness, like accidentally cut myself shaving or pour salt in my coffee instead of sugar—only to realise that I do not take sugar in any event. I spill soup over my shirt in fancy restaurants. This segues into being stood over by an intimidating Manhattan waiter as I break into a sweat while nervously trying to think of something to order. As the deadline imposed by the glaring waiter comes, I crumble up my bread into hundreds of tiny pieces. Then I realise that I don't want what I've ordered, but I can't face the ensuing confrontation. On days where there is no doo-di-dum-dum to sing home about, I can descend from Cary Grant suaveness to Stan Laurel ineptness in a heartbeat. I might doodle on a complicated contract that just arrived via special delivery from the UK—a contract that I was supposed to proofread by the end of that day so that it could be picked up by a courier in the evening. Is it any wonder that over the years I have signed some dodgy contracts? Sometimes the inspiration gene kicks in early in the morning like a randy rooster crowing a new beat. That's the time when it is important to start writing. When the dum-dum explodes it is usually accompanied in my head by the *William Tell* overture, that tells me I have to write—which I do at maniacal speed, stopping only in response to exhaustion or physical pain. A period of nonproductivity, on the other hand, can sometimes necessitate a jug of coffee before I can even put on my dressing gown and get out of bed. That's the creative curse.

In March of 1978, my life in New York—and everywhere, for that matter—had come to a little bit of a standstill. I would literally and emotionally stagger my way through each day. Two steps forward, one step back. By the end of the day I had progressed only to the elevator located outside the apartment. Then it would be time to go to bed and try again another day. I should have taken a holiday somewhere exotic instead of staying indoors trying to write in my exhausted state. Cole Porter would have driven up to Connecticut and thrown a lavish party; Noël Coward would have jetted in to join him, and they would have sung witty lyrics on the veranda of Cole's beach house. But yours truly, Ray Davies, stayed on 72nd Street, where the highlight of his day was an excursion to Columbus Avenue to share a cup of coffee with a Ukrainian newspaper seller who spoke ten words of English.

I was in between albums, and touring was not happening until later that year. I had just been introduced to Mike Stoller of the classic songwriting team Leiber and Stoller. Mike was the musician of that team and had composed classics like "Kansas City," "Jailhouse Rock," and numerous hits for the Coasters, who were one of my favourite American groups when I was a kid. The Coasters' "Poison Ivy" was one of the songs the Kinks covered back in the beginning. Without knowing it, Stoller's writing partner, Jerry Leiber, had written lyrics to some Coasters songs that connected with my North London sense of humour. His Ealing "pie-in-the-face" slapstick comedy on songs like "Charlie Brown" blended with Stoller's sophisticated musical grooves.

Mike Stoller did not look like the sort of person I had imagined had written these songs. He was a dapper and knowledgeable New Yorker who met me on the Upper East Side, where he took me to eat at a smart Italian restaurant. He was educated and spoke like an attorney, and I felt a little bit of a roughneck in comparison. I was stunned when he told me that he considered my own songs to be sophisticated. We went out to a few bars before ending up at a nightclub, where we listened to some jazz. He made me feel relaxed and part of that exclusive "club" of songwriters associated with the famed Brill Building and Carlin Music, the publishing house owned by Freddy Bienstock. I never ever wanted to be in a club, let alone an exclusive one, but that night I went along with it, and I even tipped the waiter. I behaved and handled myself as though I were an exclusive kind of guy—even snapping my fingers to the music on a few occasions.

During the set the groovy jazz musos played a Weather Report–style version of "Kansas City," and Mike grinned as he sipped his drink. "They're playing my tune." I smiled at his one-upmanship and tried to look exclusive as Mike explained how he'd first encountered Jerry Leiber, who had thumped on his door late one night. When Mike, still in his dressing gown, opened the door, he saw Leiber's unnerving stare. One blue eye, one brown eye. "You're Mike Stoller, right? Well, I'm Jerry Leiber, and I've written some killer lyrics, and I hear that you're the guy who can put them to music." That was, according to folklore, their first meeting and the beginning of their relationship. Rough and smooth. Fire and ice. A complementary pair, even though no one would have thought of putting them together—except, as Mike went on to say, "possibly a publisher like Freddy B." I felt a little envious that Mike had found Jerry and that they had written great songs together, unlike the solitary predicament I was in at that time. I did it all by myself. I had no one knocking at my door with an idea.

That night, just for fun, I went back to my apartment and wrote an homage to Leiber and Stoller in the form of a chorus to an unfinished song called "A Gallon of Gas." I wanted it to be in the style of the Coasters. Throwaway, low-slung harmonies that slid into one another without quite hitting the pitch. It was early morning, not quite day, and night was still claiming the city as its own. I slept in the hope that the morning would bring forth new and exciting songs. The next day I woke, but the "rooster" didn't crow, and I knew it was going to be an unproductive day. I wanted to feel hungry for a song again. I needed new songs for an album, but there was no theme yet, and I wanted to write a one-off single. I was in need of a shock of inspiration that would jolt me into action.

I went down to midtown, where Carlin Music was based. I was signed to Carlin Music in the UK but had never visited their U.S. offices. Because no

LEFT A family portrait from c. 1955: me (standing); Dave Davies (sitting on floor); our sister Gwen, seated in center; and our niece Jackie.

BELOW Left to right: me, Mick Avory, Pete Quaife, and Dave arrive at JFK Airport in New York City for the Kinks' first appearance in America on the NBC musical variety show *Hullabaloo*, February 10, 1965.

LEFT, TOP With Ann Chapman and Linda Lawrence in the Granada TV drama *Starmaker*, July 1974.

LEFT, BOTTOM The Kinks perform on *Hullabaloo*, February 12, 1965, taped at NBC television studios.

BELOW The Kinks meet with Clive Davis to sign with Arista Records at the Dorchester Hotel, London, June 23, 1976. From left to right: John Dalton, Mick Avory, Dave, John Gosling, Clive Davis, me.

ABOVE The Kinks perform on *Saturday Night Live*, February 26, 1977.

BELOW Me and tour assistant Barbara Bothwell talk with CBGB founder
Hilly Kristal, in 1978 at CBGB, in New York City's East Village.

LEFT Passport photos c. 1970s of tour manager extraordinaire Ken Jones, "Jonesy."

BELOW Big Guys: Tony Gibbins, c. 1979; and [*bottom*] me with Bobby Suszynski on the road, c. 1982.

ABOVE The Kinks perform at
Madison Square Garden in
New York City on October 3, 1981.

LEFT Me and Keith Richards
take a break during filming of my
Charles Mingus documentary
Weird Nightmare, June 1990;
Keith and Charlie Watts performed
the Mingus song "Oh Lord Don't
Let Them Drop That Atomic Bomb
on Me" for the film.

RIGHT The Kinks perform at
Cleveland Stadium for the inaugural
concert of the new Rock and Roll
Hall of Fame Museum on
September 2, 1995—the band's
last U.S. concert.

ABOVE A solo performance at the Voodoo Experience music and arts festival at City Park on October 30, 2011, in New Orleans, Louisiana.

RIGHT My daughter Eva and I at Buckingham Palace in London on March 17, 2004, after receiving a CBE (Commander of the Order of the British Empire) from Queen Elizabeth.

one knew me there, I pretended to be a rookie songwriter. I played a game of "looking for a deal" as I walked into the office. I went to the reception desk, and a pretty girl asked me what I wanted. I shuffled around in an unconfident way and explained that I wanted to be a songwriter like Leiber and Stoller and had a few ideas of my own that would be good for one of their major artists to cover. I said that I had flown over from England especially. The receptionist stared at me in a suspicious way, and I half expected her to call a security guard. Instead she went along with my charade and asked if I had any material to leave. I explained that I didn't have any material, but I always carried my pen just in case. She pointed to the sofa by the entrance and said she would get someone who could help me. I sat in the lobby for some hours, and my confidence crumbled. Other people came into the building and were ushered straight into meetings while I just sat there like an unwanted dog. I thought that I would rather not be in a "club" that treated people like this. Who were music people, anyway? It's just another business, after all, and I don't have to put myself through all this. I wanted to cry out, "I am a successful songwriter with many songs to my credit. I am an artist. I deserve to be heard." The reality was that I didn't feel like a songwriter because I couldn't produce at that time. Questions kept running through my head. What are you trying to prove, anyhow? You just got lucky a few years ago, so why should the world open up to you just because you wrote a few hits in the distant past? I thought about going home to get trade and a day job. I was ready to quit the music industry altogether, and by putting myself through this experience I had proven to myself that going home to get a proper job would be the right decision.

I was just about to walk out the door when I heard a familiar voice—authoritative, with a mixture of European and Manhattan exaggerated vowels but yet full of warmth. "Raymond Douglas Davies, my most successful and famed songwriter, what are you doing sitting around my reception area?" The receptionist looked up and stared at me as the man spoke to her. It was a major screwup on her part, but her boss was aware that she had no reason to know who I was. "My dear child, please do not allow rock-and-roll royalty like Raymond Douglas to sit around my office without telling me." Freddy Bienstock still had a touch of a Viennese accent, and he pronounced "Raymond" so it sounded like "RaymAND" every time he said my name. He looked at me with the same expression that Orson Welles gave Joseph Cotten when they were reunited in the movie *The Third Man*. The only thing missing was a quick blast of "The Harry Lime Theme." "My dear RaymAND, we pride ourselves at Carlin that we are able to hang on to our writers. I hope you didn't get the wrong idea, my friend. To avoid further confusion and embarrassment I will have my secretary put your picture on the wall immediately." The whole speech was choreographed so that Freddy had time to walk from his desk over to where I was sitting and shake my hand.

Publishers like Freddy Bienstock were a new breed when they came into the business. Rock and roll was just starting, and the phenomenon of the singer-songwriter was just emerging, so it meant that publishers had to relate to artists who were beginning to demand a say in their own musical destinies. Writers also demanded better deals, and Freddy's company was one of the first to acknowledge this, embracing the new world by giving writers a small stake in their own publishing. Fred was never afraid to play on a hunch. When I signed with his company in the mid-'60s, my money was tied up by a massive lawsuit between my previous publisher, Kassner Music/ Denmark Productions, and Boscobel, and my royalties were frozen in escrow at that time. When at that time I asked him how we would resolve the situation he simply said, "Stay hot, kid, because I've got a feeling you'll still be writing great songs when all this litigation shit is over." I like to think his hunch paid off.

Freddy was a mixture of Eastern European count, Mississippi riverboat gambler, society banker, and consummate diplomat—Rhett Butler, Vatican bishop, and Harry Lime wrapped up into one. His accent made it seem as though he had just walked out of a successful central casting audition for the part of a flamboyant Viennese gigolo. He was dapper, and his smart appearance could not disguise the fact that he was always hungry for more success. He claimed he had been poor when he was younger, and once confided in me that he never once wanted to go through that experience again. Freddy claimed he once stacked boxes in the stockroom at Chappell Music, which was one of the reasons he enjoyed buying the company when he became successful. He was as at home in the smart restaurants of Mayfair and

Manhattan as he was in the seedy bars of Memphis and Nashville. He was able to socialise with cardinals and cardsharks, and in the crapshoot that is the music business they are often seated at the same table. He knew how to treat a waiter who was not giving good table service while at the same time reward a pretty waitress with a flirtatious smile. He loved a gamble at the casino and the races. His stories were endless and legendary, particularly yarns about Elvis Presley, Colonel Tom Parker, and the Memphis Mafia. Elegantly dressed and always ready with a bright quip and slick anecdote, he dazzled lesser businessmen with his wit and effortless charm, but at the same time he never let an adversary off the hook without a cutting remark that could stop them dead in their tracks. As far as I was aware he was not a musician, but he could spot a good tune and had the ability to inspire. He could also spot a bore from a mile off. He gave the impression that he obviously loved to make money and did not pretend otherwise. For some reason I admired and respected him as a man of his word, and when I suspected him of owing me money Freddy would say, "It's nothing that cannot be worked out," as if he were doing me a favour.

I asked if there was anyone he could put me together with who could help me write some songs. He took out a cigar and cut it as he spoke. Lights; camera; action. "I sometimes see writers who can write to make money or fulfil a deal or product commitment, or even to pay off an ex-wife. And brother, I've seen plenty of those. There is a magical moment when the great writers are like chefs. They just turn on the heat and cook something up. You, Raymond Douglas, write because you cannot live without it. I watched you as you survived all that legal stuff. . . . Your work stopped you from going mad. You got through it. Now, for some reason, you have to prove this to yourself every day. You know you can do it. Don't fight it. It's nothing to do with money. It's your entire personality that is at stake. You want to be creative like it is an addiction. Like you need to be creative in order to stay alive and prove something to yourself. That and your uncanny desire to cut a deal make you almost impossible to do business with at times. You don't have to become hungry to want to write so much, because you are always hungry." Freddy paused, then puffed at his cigar. "Now, let's eat." He took me to a nice restaurant near his office. He told me all the latest music-biz gossip and spun me some terrific yarns. I listened to him with rapt attention, and even though I had heard them all before I sat engrossed like a child being told a bedtime story.

Then I noticed a small figure approaching from another part of the restaurant. This little guy hovered around us and then sidled up to Freddy. In between mouthfuls of food, Fred introduced the man as his brother, Johnny. We made polite small talk about a deal Johnny had recently done, but Freddy cut it short and said we needed to be alone. Johnny understood. "Okay, okay, Fred, you are a busy man." As he left, Johnny came up to me and whispered in my ear, "You know my brother, Freddy, is the greatest publisher in the world." Who was I to argue? I thought about Freddy, who along with a few other mavericks had helped build the modern music industry. He'd helped "write the book" of music publishing. When I had first signed with him he asked me how much of an advance I wanted. I looked around the plush Savile Row office in London that he occupied at that time and spotted an original painting by Francis Bacon on the wall. I said that I wanted no monetary advance but would like the painting. He smiled and said that he didn't own it, but if it were his he would have handed it over to me because he had a hunch that I would earn back the value of the painting. He said he'd never met a writer quite like me. I said I had never met a publisher quite like him.

Freddy B. was an original, but he could have only existed as a by-product of Americana. Freddy had put me back on track and, without knowing it or even thinking too hard about it, had told me a lot about myself. Later that night I went to the apartment and started banging out a new tune. It wasn't to celebrate the fact that I had been accepted as a member of any club. It didn't even start as doo-di-bloody-dum-dum. It bypassed all that creative bull. It was because I felt that it was good to be me again, and I was not like anybody else. I felt like an original, and I would defy any bastard who thought otherwise. I was a musical prizefighter who spat words out like left hooks and uppercuts. I was psyched up.

There was a crusade to fight and a war to win. Something inside had triggered me, and more than anything else, I loved writing songs. It was fun again.

I sat down at the electric piano in the apartment. I smiled. I wrote.

"Here's wishing you the bluest sky
And hoping something better comes tomorrow.
Hoping all our verses rhyme
And the very best of choruses to follow
All the doubt and sadness I know that better things are on the way.
It's really good to see you rocking out and having fun
Living like you've just begun
Accepting life and what it brings
I hope tomorrow you find better things
I know tomorrow you'll find better things
I know tomorrow you'll find better things."

BEFORE THE SECOND ARISTA ALBUM, *Misfits*, was released in May 1978, I met with Elliot Abbott, who had managed Randy Newman to success with "Short People," and a former agent, Chip Rachlin, who had started working for Elliot. We hit it off really well and decided to give our business relationship a go. Chip took a backseat and allowed Elliot, a cantor's son from Chicago, to do all the talking. Elliot shared my desire to crack America, and Clive embraced this new managerial relationship, which became our all-American team. More than anything else, besides music, Clive knew how to handle America as a market. *Misfits* did well, and we toured with high-profile support acts, such as Blondie and Tom Petty.

When we had returned to touring America with the 1970 Reprise album *Lola versus Powerman and the Moneygoround, Part One*, we had taken on board John Gosling on keyboard to join John Dalton on bass. Dalton had left in the fall of 1976, right before the release of *Sleepwalker*. Gosling and Dalton's replacement, Andy Pyle, both quit to form their own band before *Misfits* was released. In a strange way, "A Rock 'n' Roll Fantasy" had predicted this break up; as sad as it was, we had to keep going; we replaced Gosling with Gordon Edwards (briefly) and then Ian Gibbons on keyboard, and replaced Dalton with Jim Rodford on bass. The addition of Gibbons and Rodford, in my opinion, made us a winning team. Gosling and Dalton had "lost the faith," and as much as I did to try to convince them otherwise, Dalton firmly stated that he wanted to concentrate on his family and future in England and not be away for such long periods of time. I understood him totally and wished my priorities had been the same, but I was already on a mission to conquer America. To their credit, both Gosling and Dalton are still with the same wives they were with at the time and are in great family units, from what I gather; so in many respects they did the right thing by their personal lives, even if it meant they wouldn't be involved in the final comeback of the Kinks in the United States.

As for the rest of us, it was like we were all living two lives. I still lived in suburban England, but my career was firmly focused on America and based out of New York. The next casualty was Dave's marriage. It began in L.A.—where else? I saw this girl walk into the Hyatt House hotel on Sunset Strip. We didn't speak, but I knew where she was headed and what the result would be. It was almost a prophetic moment. The whole American experience would never be the same without the Americana girlfriend. Our personal lives exploded as a result. It wasn't just my struggle; Dave and the others were having their own personal issues, too, but somehow it was all forgotten when it was showtime. Even Ken Jones, our loyal and trusted tour manager, had succumbed to temptation with a couple of girlfriends in different towns, and he would often arrange tours so we could include those towns in our schedule, along with the obligatory day off afterward. Poor Ken: the rest of the band and crew would speculate that on such days Ken would stay in his executive mini-suite, probably sipping from a bottle of Blue Nun with his admiring and devoted conquest. Eventually, though, each of these women wanted a commitment, and Ken couldn't really offer one. Deep down he loved his family, but even for Ken, the road took its toll.

AS OUR STATUS GREW AND THE VENUES GOT BIGGER, we were able to fund our own sound-and-lights production and carry the equipment with us on tour. We used the Showco company, based in Dallas. Tour manager Ken Jones was instrumental in setting up this arrangement, and he often did advance work that required frequent trips to Showco (and perhaps a visit with a girlfriend on the way). Consequently most of our crew came from the Dallas area. They were a great set of characters in their own right: Larry Raul, our guitar tech; Kevin "Roadhog" Brown, who handled the production backline; Ken Byrnes, on lights; and Mike Ponczek, who handled front of house. Our newly elevated status, which came with all the trappings of a high-tech production, enabled us to transport our equipment in articulated lorries while the crew rode buses. It was a far cry from the old days, when Ken Jones and an assistant travelled in the back of a van with the band. We needed a small army of lighting and sound technicians to set up for huge auditoriums; this meant a larger entourage, and new positions were created. Roadies had specific roles—guitar tech, lighting tech, security man; they were part of a whole new ball game. Soon there were limousines to take us from the hotel to the venue; it was expected that the promoter would absorb this expense as part of the production cost. The whole event was getting bigger and bigger, and it was becoming increasingly difficult to keep track of the costs. Fortunately we had a good tour accountant in Lynn Walsh, who worked for Bert Padell, based in New York, who was in turn advised by Elliot Abbott and Ken Jones. The Kinks no longer just turned up, set up, and played without any fuss before a tour; we would do a couple of days' rehearsal in Fort Lauderdale or somewhere near Texas in order to put the production together before starting a tour. It didn't necessarily improve our performance, but it made it more of a spectacle. We had come on a fascinating journey so far. Like a wagon train, we found the way west open to us. I only hoped the journey would be worth it.

13

LOW BUDGET

"Cheap is small and not too steep
But best of all cheap is cheap
Circumstance has forced my hand
To be a cut price person in a low budget land.
Times are hard, but we'll all survive
I just got to learn to economise.

I'm on a low budget
I'm on a low budget

I'm not cheap, you understand,
I'm just a cut price person in a low budget land.
Excuse my shoes they don't quite fit
They're a special offer and they hurt me a bit
Even my trousers are giving me pain
They were reduced in a sale so I shouldn't complain
They squeeze me so tight so I can't take no more
They're size 28 but I take 34. . . .

I'm on a low budget
I'm a cut price person in a low budget land."

Records come about by curious twists and turns sometimes. The title of an album is usually decided, in our case, when the tracks are played back after they are all recorded and mixed. The stand-out songs are chosen to lead the promotional campaign, and then a decision is made as to which cut will be the single. With *Low Budget* there was no option—one song dominated the style and content of the album almost from the start, although the song itself came about in a curious way.

It started as a bit of a lark. We'd finished our touring campaign to promote *Misfits* and I was putting some ideas together to start writing the next
record for Arista. I thought it might be amusing to go back to the old single
format where I could record songs that fit the time rather than just write
for the album concept. In the early days of the Kinks I had cut my teeth on
writing and recording three to four singles a year, sometimes with totally
different sounds, style, and subject matter. After the profound message of
songs like "Misfits" and "A Rock 'n' Roll Fantasy," this next song could only
be described as a musical and cultural cross-dresser. It was a dance track
conceived and inspired by America, but written and recorded in London.

It originated from a few evenings spent at Studio 54, where Bob Feiden
and Michael Kleffner sometimes took me to see what, in their opinion, was
"happening." I joked with them that I might write a disco song that could be
played there. I understood some of the cultural origins of disco, but I really
was not a fan of pure pop disco music. Yet it was in vogue at the time and
I thought it would be fun to take a stab at it, more for my own amusement
than anything else. Feiden and Kleffner had thrown down the challenge, so
when I got back to England for our next recording session and rehearsals
for the upcoming UK tour I wrote "(Wish I Could Fly Like) Superman" with
a disco beat straight out of *Saturday Night Fever.* The lyrical content, however, was different. The lyrics reflected the political situation in England.
The "winter of discontent," the three-day week, the power strikes, the lorry
strikes—everybody seemed to be on strike. I wrote this song about a world-
weary person who was experiencing this unrest. The only light at the end of
his tunnel was the fact that he imagined he could fly like Superman in an
attempt to liberate himself.

The character I adopted was a downtrodden Londoner, verging on
manic depression. The only time he shows any optimism is when he sings
the chorus, then for the bridge, he reverts to manic mode before returning to
his glum rant for the next verse. Perfect for the times, perfect for the Kinks
audience, and particularly suitable for me to sing.

When the song was recorded I insisted that the rhythm track have a
four-to-the-bar bass-drum beat throughout the record, but because it was
before the days of the Kinks pre-looping using sequencers, I persuaded Mick

Avory to sit in the studio on his drum kit for hours on end playing the same pattern over and over while we constructed the song around it. I even over-dubbed an ARP synthesiser part to give the track extra joke value while Dave's guitar riff kept the track rooted in an R&B feel rather than a pop disco sound. Listening back to the recording I thought what a trouper Mick Avory had been to do take after take on the drums until he got it right. During the recording he obeyed my instructions slavishly while I bobbed around next to him in the studio indicating when to play louder and when to play softer, and to mark the beginnings of verses and choruses. Then halfway through the track I made a gesture that indicated that I wanted to break up the monotony. Mick slipped in a skipped beat, almost like a jazz player, but fell right back into the rhythm so that the listener felt change but was unaware of what happened. Only a drummer from Mick's generation could have done that. There were two rock drummers in the world capable of doing it at that time—one was Mick and the other was Charlie Watts. No one listening to the finished record would be aware of this subtlety except me and Mick, but to me, it validated the whole rhythm track—it showed that the backing track was not robotic but had a human element.

It was only a bit of fun but even so I was astounded when "(Wish I Could Fly Like) Superman" was greeted with great enthusiasm by Clive and his promotion team. When I discovered that they were serious about releasing the track, I was so determined to make it a dance hit that I actually went to clubs in England while we were on tour to test it out in discos. People loved it; they danced to it without knowing who the band was. One night the dancers in the club actually applauded at the end of the record. I didn't think it meant we were "selling out"—the song still had the same Kinks charm and sense of fun, yet it retained a political edge. Clive was ebullient as he pronounced that it would get us on Top 40 radio, and wanted it released immediately. He sent me a telex that said "It is very pertinent to the time, accessible to radio, and it is so you." I am not quite sure what the "you" meant, but I took it as a compliment.

He put it out as a single without an album behind it. The UK Arista office was less than enthusiastic, though. The song was a tongue-in-cheek, politically motivated rock track with an R&B disco edge, but they felt it had nothing to do with the current disco market. There weren't any "shake it ups" or "get downs," on the record, or any other words in the disco vernacular, and the London promotion people thought that radio "would not get it."

The Kinks had been concentrating our time in America focusing on the audiences we had started to build up there. More to the point, our sense of humour was beginning to be understood by the American market. There was continuity, a product flow, in America, whereas in England it was all a bit piecemeal and driven by the somewhat ephemeral taste of British radio.

The Kinks had been part of the original beat revolution that had conquered America, but instead of celebrating that fact by letting us evolve, the media in the UK at that time gave the impression that they wanted us to keep churning out the old hits and did not want us to progress further. However we did have a loyal fan base in the UK who stuck with us through thick and thin, even though it was hard for us to get airplay in our homeland. Another important factor was that geographically America was large enough to absorb more diverse music, which allowed a record to build market to market. If they didn't like a track in Philly or Atlanta, they might love it in Boston, whereas if a UK station decided not to put a record on the playlist, that was it. It was like a death sentence with no chance of a reprieve. There were a few alternative stations dotted around the UK, but if you couldn't get on a couple of key programs the record was over. It was hurtful to me personally because I thought that if anybody would understand our sense of humour, the UK would. In some respects though, this initial rejection went on to inspire the title track of one of the most successful Kinks albums.

CLIVE HAD ORIGINALLY INSISTED that we sign with Arista worldwide, but the problem was that not every territory was controlled by Clive. Each international branch of the label had to bring in its own individual hits and was responsible for its own budget, and these branch offices were not always in agreement with what Clive wanted. "(Wish I Could Fly Like) Superman" was a case in point. The Kinks had a short tour of England planned, which needed financial support from the record label, but I remember that the UK office told me by phone that they could not give us a budget for it. I was fuming with anger and felt a sense of betrayal as we had confirmed the dates on the understanding that there would be tour support to help fund the shows. After this upsetting phone call, my tour manager drove me up to London from Surrey for a recording session at Konk. The hour-long drive gave me time to vent my frustration by scribbling down an angry, bitter lyric about a man who was dispossessed and penniless but still wanted to put on a good show. This was the first draft of the song "Low Budget."

The band was waiting for me in the studio to record a song called "Pressure," which I had recently written. We did "Pressure" in two takes; this actually became the master track that was used on the final *Low Budget* album. Then I suggested that Dave start playing a riff to accompany the "Low Budget" lyrics that I had just come up with in the car. Mick joined in on the drums, and I sang. We put down the track without even realising that we hadn't taught it to bass player Jim Rodford. As we played back the recording I realised that we would be able to play it anywhere. It would go down equally well in an American rock arena or an English seaside vaudeville show at the end of the pier. I knew at that moment that we had the key track on our next album—something I could take to Clive and present as the Top 40 record that would come out within a few months of "(Wish I Could Fly Like) Superman." As soon as the "Low Budget" track was finished, we had it couriered over to Clive, who loved it. The album was on its way and already had its focus. It had an identity, it resonated with the times, and most appropriately the song "Low Budget" had retained the feeling of British humour, even down to the use of Cockney slang and vaudeville slapstick. Now all I had to do was finish writing the rest of the album in New York.

AT THE TIME WE SIGNED WITH ARISTA, Clive Davis lived on Manhattan's Upper West Side. Even though the apartment I rented on the Upper West Side was in the building next to the Dakota, where John Lennon and Yoko Ono were living, most everybody in the neighbourhood led quite normal lives. This was different from seeing America only from the vantage point of a hotel room; I was living and interacting with the "civilian" population. I listened to WPIX or WNEW in the mornings and was inspired by these local radio stations; I wrote songs to fit their format. Chatting with neighbours in the apartment building and assimilating with the local community, I was inspired to write songs like "Catch Me Now I'm Falling" and "A Gallon of Gas." The latter was about the emerging oil crisis in America, where oil and fuel prices had always been dirt cheap. Now there was an oil shortage and citizens were feeling the pinch. At the time, petrol pumps were running out of fuel, but the song was also about the world running out of resources and the fact that such a vast country, built on the automobile, was discovering for the first time how powerless it would be if it ran out of gas. I wouldn't have written that song in the same way if I had been living in London, where oil prices were already too high; the songs had taken on a new American edge. The song " Catch Me Now I'm Falling" even had the lines:

"Now I'm calling all citizens from all over the world
This is Captain America callin'
I bailed you out when you were down on your knees
So will you catch me now I'm falling?"

At least our American audience would relate but just the same, I couldn't have written the song if I hadn't believed in it.

Apart from "Low Budget" and "Superman," the bulk of the tracking was done later in New York in true low-budget style

We recorded at the Power Station on the West Side, near Hell's Kitchen. Other overdubs and tracking were done at a small, cost-effective studio downtown on Greene Street, but the main recording was done at the Power Station. I picked the big room, Studio One, where Bruce Springsteen was recording his album *The River*. We could only afford to record there for between six or seven days so we worked in shifts.

Studio One had one microphone placed high in the soaring, cone-shaped ceiling, which created a more ambient sound. Bruce and I had a brief discussion about the sound we were both after at that time. We discovered that we were both trying to get a more ambient sound on the drums, but went about getting it in different ways. I bumped into him as the Kinks finished the day shift and he was about to embark on his all-night session. He was having a shave in the men's bathroom, getting ready to do some vocals; a true professional getting himself ready for the "moment." I asked him,

"Have you used that big mike in the centre of the room yet?" He replied that his engineer had been trying to capture the live snare sound but it was difficult to bring up the overhead mikes without losing the bass drum. I said I thought we had a way around it and would give him an update before we left town, but our paths never crossed again that trip. I left New York as soon as our recording was finished, but the "quest" for that sound stayed in my head. During this time Jim Rodford was still on bass and Gordon Edwards had been for a short time on keyboards for live shows, but in order to save on travel expenses Ken Jones decided not to bring Gordon to New York. As a result all the keyboard playing was left to me. John Rollo, the Konk Studios engineer, came over to assist the recording at the Power Station where we used Scott Litt as tape operator. In keeping with the projected title of the album, the Kinks had to stay in the cheapest of hotels. The Wellington in Midtown offered the best rates, but it required that the band share rooms. John shared a room with Jim, and Mick shared a room with Ken.

It was during the band's stay at the Wellington that Jim—who must have had severe jetlag or was simply tired and missing home—mistook his roommate John's bedside table for the loo one night. This mishap aside, everything went smoothly and Jim played brilliantly on the record, but after that night's toilet experience we gave Jim his own room to avoid any further mishaps. During a subsequent tour I arrived back at the hotel after a late night with Mick Avory and discovered Jim asleep in the hotel elevator.

My brother Dave was by this time spending more time in Los Angeles while Mick, Jim, and I put the basic tracks down. Dave flew in later in the week for a few days to overdub the guitar parts and backing vocals. This actually worked out well because Dave and I had our own musical radar; whereas with other players it would take sometimes days to arrange and record overdubs, Dave and I could do it in two or three takes. If it took more than that it generally meant trouble, because Dave would become frustrated and we would start to quarrel. The tracks where it did take longer I rerecorded with the whole band so that Dave could lead the track.

On one Power Station session while Dave was held "captive" in the studio, I started vamping a song I'd been writing in the apartment on the Upper West Side. Dave picked up the chords and played along, as he used to do in the old days. Mick joined in. I'd acquired a new Yamaha CS-80 synthesiser from Manny's Music and was experimenting with its multilayered sounds. People in the studio control room stopped what they were doing and listened. The riff was inspired by "All Day and All of the Night," and I was writing it live as we played. It had morphed into another song, called "Destroyer," and it was all done in one take. I shouted the changes down the microphone—"the next chord"; "go to this chord"; "go to this chorus"; "go back to the verse"—and it worked brilliantly.

Blondie was in the next studio during this session; they were in the process of recording *Eat to the Beat* in Studio Two, a smaller, more compact space but adequate for the tight sound that they were producing at the time. By the time we'd finished the track, Debbie Harry and members of her band were assembled outside the control room to hear what they thought would be a Kinks classic. The song would lay the foundation on which we would build a complete Kinks revival in America.

There was an element of magic, fearlessness, and surprise about the whole moment. I still hadn't finished the lyrics, but the groundwork and backtrack of "Destroyer" was already complete. That big central microphone in Studio One was doing its job, and Mick's snare drum sounded powerful, explosive, and dangerous—in keeping with a song about a man who completely ruins his life through feats of self-destruction. The song was almost like an instalment of a serial, and now the Kinks were about to serve up the next part of the epic drama to our fans. We did some other great tracks: a ballad called "Little Bit of Emotion," about the social outcasts I had seen on the streets of New York. Then the first version of "Better Things," although this didn't make the final album, it served as a great entrée to our final recording of the song for the *Give the People What They Want* album recorded a few years later at Konk Studios in London, using the same explosive drum sound that we had started to finesse at the Power Station.

We laid down some other tracks, including "A Gallon of Gas," "Attitude," "National Health," and "In a Space," then it was off to London to complete the recording. The tour to promote our "unfinished" album was already being set up and the record had to be finished very quickly—late summer at the latest—in order to make the release date. After finishing off the mixes and over-dubbing touches at Konk Studios, I was back in New York with the band doing the photo shoot for the album sleeve.

I'd been inspired by a new promotion technique I'd seen on the streets of New York: people spray-painted stencilled names of products or stores on the sidewalk to advertise restaurants and other businesses. It was so cheap and effective that I thought it would be good to give *Low Budget* a similar graphic presentation on the album cover, so we hired Garry Gross, a well-known fashion photographer, who'd put together a glamorous set in his photographic studio. He was disappointed to find that the expensive female model he had hired for the session would be having only her feet photographed for the picture and that the shoot would seem as though it had taken place outdoors. My concept was to photograph her standing over the *Low Budget* logo, which was to be stencilled on the street. During the shoot I received a panicky phone call from Clive himself. "Ray," he shouted. "We can't go ahead with the photo shoot!" I said, "Clive, it's already done." He said that the album is called *Low Budget* but it's going out at full retail price—we had to change the title. I tried to calm him down. "This will not be misleading to the paying public; it is an artistic statement." I explained that the shoot was already paid for and already designed, and we had a few backup shots of the band if the title was changed, so he let us complete the shoot. After a while he accepted my position, and *Low Budget* went out as planned. The marketing of the record would be simplified by using that stencil imagery again and again on T-shirts, posters, and adverts for the gigs. The Kinks were finally learning how to market themselves for America.

The stage sets of most touring bands at this time were typically full of expensive stage effects, with spotlights and pyrotechnics, but for *Low Budget* the Kinks went back to basics: torn drapes and tatty plants hanging from broken flowerpots. Everything looked cheap and tawdry, which was perfect for the album's image. After a brief production-rehearsal period in Dallas, we did our first date using our new keyboard player, Ian Gibbons, at a club in Dallas–Fort Worth. We embarked on a sellout summer tour of the U.S., and *Low Budget* became one of the best-selling Kinks albums. . . . all thanks to the record company in the UK who could not give us a few thousand pounds for tour support. At the end of the tour, in Providence, Rhode Island,

Time-Life Video shot the entire show, documenting the Kinks at their peak on the long climb back to success in America.

WHILE THE SONG "LOW BUDGET" WAS A HEAVY ROCK TUNE mixed with Cockney vaudeville slang, it worked in the States; indeed, the *Low Budget* album pushed us into top-twenty status on the album charts in America. We were back, but it had taken nearly ten years after our tentative Fillmore East return.

All the touring had finally paid off. Ken Jones was still our tour manager, but with Elliot Abbott and Renaissance Management, plus our strong team at Arista, we felt really on top . . . . "But then the rot set in"—as the old cliché goes—or it started to, anyway. My brother, Dave, was becoming frustrated by what he described as playing second fiddle to me, and he began plans to make a solo album to take advantage of the rising tide of Kinks success. I had no problem with that; Dave had done some great solo work since his first hit "Death of a Clown" as well as contributing to the Kinks albums but I had the distinct impression that these efforts were becoming almost adversarial. There was also a revival of the animosity between him and Mick Avory that had started when, as teenagers, they had shared a house together in the heady days of the swinging '60s. Their new phase of bickering was probably an indirect way of getting at me, particularly as Dave gave the impression that he resented my high-profile personal life—specifically, my relationship with Ms. Hynde. I have never been good at taking a photo opportunity, whereas it sometimes seemed that Chris only had to visit the bathroom to find the paparazzi waiting to snap her when she exited. And why not? For a few months in 1980, her band was one of the most-photographed bands in the world. During Dave and Mick's dressing-room spats, Rodford and Gibbons would stay silent. They were careful not to be seen taking sides, and Jonesy did his best to act as mediator.

GIVE THE PEOPLE WHAT THEY WANT, 1980

In the summer of 1980, the Providence concert was released as an RCA VideoDisc called *One for the Road*. The associated concert album of the same name was released on Arista. RCA and Arista would eventually be owned by the same parent company, but it was a hard task at the time to get the two companies to talk to one another and coordinate a proper campaign. The album itself was recorded at various different cities in the States, which proved to be a challenge for the mixing, because I was determined to make the album sound as if it had been recorded at one venue. The cutting and mastering was a particularly difficult undertaking for Bob Ludwig, who cut all our records at Masterdisk on the West Side of Manhattan. One afternoon in New York I was walking along Broadway and saw Bob jogging along the street. Apparently he had started to get in shape physically before he attempted to master *One for the Road*. He had even stopped smoking, in order to get in shape to cut the record.

I always attended the cutting sessions, much to Bob's occasional irritation. The combination of me being in the cutting room and Clive phoning in his ten cents' worth would have given a lesser man a nervous breakdown, but Ludwig who as well as being one of the world's great cutting engineers was also turning into a consummate diplomat as he fielded Clive's calls. He managed to remain in control, and as a result the cut was loud and seamless. Afterward, Bob said, "This is not so much like cutting a record. It's more like taming a lion." Coordinating the mixing, cutting, and artwork was massively challenging, but nevertheless the album—which contained live versions of many hits from the Kinks catalog—was a huge success.

Our gigs improved also. We played the Forum in L.A., the Oakland Arena in San Francisco, and convention centres all over America. We had programs, T-shirts, and other merchandise for sale in the lobby of each venue, which became a big part of our income at this time. In August of 1980, we started the *One for the Road* tour at the Curtis Hixon Convention Hall in Tampa, Florida, after a warm-up date in Fort Lauderdale. I was working closely with Elliot Abbott at this time, plotting and conniving in the back of the limo as we went to gigs. Elliot had this ability to know how many people were at the venue by looking at the garage and the parked cars. "A good house tonight," he would say. "This is going to be capacity crowd, because the garage is full." I mentioned I had this song called "Give the People What They Want," which had been partly inspired by the 1951 film *Quo Vadis*, which I had seen years ago. In the movie, which was about ancient Rome, Nero's wife tells him to throw the Christians to the lions. "Give the people what they want, Nero!" she exclaims. That line stayed with me from childhood. It surfaced again as I witnessed all the excitement around our shows. Performing was becoming more gladiatorial as the audiences pushed us harder and harder to provide entertainment, no matter what the cost. Elliot looked at me with dollar signs in his eyes and then spoke as if he'd had an epiphany. "That's it! That's the title. Give the people what they want."

I went back to London and recorded at Konk. I even had the sound of the record in my head. I wanted it to sound as though the listener were sitting in the fiftieth row at one of our venues. We were playing large arenas at this time, and the front-of-house crew said the sound at row 50 was an incredible combination of punch and echo. We'd get the power from the front of the stage combined with the ambient echo from behind as the sound bounced back from the rear of the hall. I needed to re-create this in the studio, so Konk engineer Ben Fenner and I devised a new way of recording. We put up corrugated metal on walls of the studio so the reflected sound slammed back around the room as it was triggered by the snare drum. This provided the kit with an overwhelming wallop as Mick hit the drums. All the tracks were recorded at Konk, and the album was turned around very quickly. It had to be—the first tour date to promote it had already been booked. This was working under pressure, but we had a goal at the end, a target. This was the first Kinks record on which all the songs were designed to be played live in an arena, and the sold-out arenas were all waiting.

Give the People What They Want would probably be the most bitter, aggressive, dark, riff-laden, and arguably the most successful album we did on Arista to date. The song "Killer's Eyes" was inspired by an assignation attempt on Pope John Paul. "A Little Bit of Abuse" was about a violent relationship. "Art Lover" was a semi-autobiographical song I'd written about a failed battle for child custody after a bitter divorce. The opening track, "Around the Dial," was a celebration of the independent DJ's who were starting to disappear from the airwaves because they were still trying to play records of their own choice rather than submit to the corporate, play-listed stations. The track's powerful opening chords would provide us with the start of our new stage show to promote the album. Strange to think that one of the most optimistic songs on the album, "Better Things," came from a period of extreme insecurity a few years earlier. I was becoming the much-travelled rock singer in one respect, but on the other hand, I was still the wide-eyed nineteen-year-old kid who had yet to embark on world tours. Somehow I hadn't grown up. I hadn't found my identity. Maybe Americana was a delusion or a distraction for me. I was gaining an audience but losing myself in the process.

14

BETTER THINGS

"I know you've got a lot of good things happening up ahead.
The past is gone it's all been said.
So here's to what the future brings,
I know tomorrow you'll find better things."

Sometimes my tunes stay in my head for years. They actually do become the soundtrack of my life, but if I need to I can stop singing them whenever I want. Life, on the other hand, moves on regardless.

Fast-forward to January of 2004. The Tremé district. New Orleans. Outside, it was like a sunny spring day even though it was the beginning of January. That's one of the joys of being in New Orleans that time of year.

After all the dramas of the New Orleans stay so far, I'd crashed on the sofa and slept most of the previous day and night. I was feeling fresh and ready for the new day so I got up bright and early and walked into the French Quarter to buy breakfast and read *The New York Times*. My song "Better Things" went through my head. It's a "breakup" song with an optimistic chorus that looks forward to moving on to a better future, so that day it made me feel good. Sitting in a coffee shop reading the *Times* made it seem like sanity had returned to my life after the past days of madness. The Arts and Leisure section was full of news about upcoming events at Lincoln Center, concerts, and reviews of Broadway shows.

I had already received a few phone calls from the UK from well-wishers congratulating me on my CBE. I had just been named as a commander of the Order of the British Empire; an appointment that had been announced in the Queen's New Year Honours list. I had known about this for a few days but had had so much to deal with that it had slipped my mind. Before now I had been too preoccupied with my personal issues to even contemplate whether or not I should attend the Buckingham Palace ceremony. In fact when my office had originally received the letter from Her Majesty's

Government, they thought it was a tax demand and kept the letter from me for a few days. The news of the CBE made me feel that 2004 would be a year full of optimism, and I was determined to get back and finish mixing my album. Then I would come back to start my marching-band project with John McDonogh High School. The narrow escape from the cliff-top disaster in Ireland at Christmas and the traumatic events of the previous few months faded as I finished my breakfast. England was very far away from my mind as I strolled in the morning sun. But I was feeling patriotic and had even bought an English rugby shirt on my departure from Heathrow and was proudly wearing it, so I must have felt some English pride return after our rugby team had won the World Cup a few months earlier. That lyric popped into my head again.

"Forget what happened yesterday, I know that better things are on the way . . ."

It was Sunday, after New Year's—that in-between time as the holidays wind down, when nobody seems to know what to do. On the way back to the apartment I walked along Rampart Street to see if the launderette was busy. I needed to get some washing done and the launderette had a good wash-and-fold service and a TV on the wall, as well as a fair-to-middling jukebox for anyone to listen to if they wanted to sit and wait. It was a little crowded so I thought I would come back in the evening. There was a college football game on in town that night and the streets would be less crowded. As I left the launderette I noticed a plaque on the wall by the entrance. The sign stated that the building had once been a recording studio owned by Cosimo Matassa. Another sign stated that many of the greats had recorded there including Fats Domino and Little Richard. Now, somewhat sadly the building was a launderette.

When I arrived back at the apartment I started to take care of most of the chores that had been put to one side after the dramas of the last few days. I tidied up my case after Rory had unpacked it for me a few days before. I was pleased to discover that she had taken the bra and panties she'd found there. I thought about if she had still been with me, we would have gone up to the

New Orleans Health club for a game of racquetball and a swim but I had to put these thoughts out of my mind. I felt that I needed to be ready to leave as soon as I had been to the marching band rehearsal the next day. A flight was held but I thought I'd wait to see the outcome of the meeting at John McDonogh.

I sang as I rummaged through my clothes and repacked my case. "*I hope tomorrow you'll find better things . . .* " I walked into the kitchen to make a cup of coffee and saw an envelope with my name on it propped up against an empty wine bottle. I hadn't seen it before now. In fact I hadn't been in the kitchen at all since Rory left but recognised the writing as being hers so I opened the letter with a certain amount of trepidation.

Inside was a congratulations card with a very short handwritten message. "Well done on your award. I'm sorry things could not work out. I've taken that job in Asia. Have a good life. Then she'd written something in Swedish that I could just about recognise. "*Jag älskar dig!* (I love you!)" I sat and thought about the good times. I put WOZ on the beaten-up radio the previous occupant had left in the apartment. I wondered how anyone could take off like that and still leave behind a note that said they loved you. Maybe that was the message. She loved me but couldn't be with me. But that was that, we'd finally broken up and I would never see her again. I thought about what Travis would probably say. "I've heard that beat before."

I didn't want to spend the rest of the day alone so I called up Travis, whose line was dead. I tried Alex Chilton but the answering machine came on and I left a message. Alex was known to be a recluse, but even though he was probably at home, he had a habit of screening his calls by listening to who was leaving the message before bothering to answer. He was probably engrossed in his Thackeray book or he simply didn't want to speak to me because he wouldn't know what to say. As a final resort I called J.J., who said she'd come to keep me company. I didn't want to send any false signals and didn't even greet her with a polite welcoming kiss when she arrived. She had got dressed up to meet and was wearing a retro outfit complete with mini skirt and tight, white, plastic–looking, almost kinky, knee-high boots. She said she would hang out with me until I left the city. We talked for a while about nothing specific and she proved to be friendly and better company than I'd imagined. Then after I tidied up, we decided to go for an early dinner to avoid getting caught in the crowds heading to the Louisiana Superdome later. The Sugar Bowl, the big college football event of the year, kicked off at eight that night and even though it was a while before the start of the game the streets were empty. New Orleans is a small city, so it can be virtually closed up by a big ball game or parade. J.J. had to work the next day, and I had the school marching-band rehearsal to attend in the morning. I decided to smarten myself up as if we were going out on our first date. I even wore a jacket and tie.

We decided to go for a walk in the Quarter to look for a restaurant. At first I wanted to go to a little African joint on Decatur Street, but then we both remembered a little Japanese restaurant in the Marigny area called Wasabi, so we made our way there.

We had a relaxing meal and shared some sake before I paid the bill. Over dinner, J.J. opened up more about her own personal life that showed her in a completely new light. I deduced that she was a loving, caring person and not so much of a caution some people had made her out to be. She was a totally different person than the woman I'd thought she was. I wanted to get a cab back to the apartment, as it would be getting dark soon, but we thought it would be better to walk back to get the last of the sun. During the meal I talked about my days on the road, when Tony and Big Bob accompanied me everywhere; I said that he would be eating with us had he been alive. I explained that Bob had once shown me a bullet wound he'd sustained to his leg while he was working in Chicago as a cop.

I decided to forget about getting a cab and to escort J.J. back to her apartment. We walked back along Burgundy Street and talked about returning to New Orleans once my record was finished. The street was empty; the whole world seemed to be at the Superdome or watching the Sugar Bowl on TV. A solitary black guy walked toward us in the distance, wearing a baseball hat and large pants that crumpled up around his ankles. I was about to comment about how unusual it was too see a solitary figure swaggering down this quiet neighbourhood dressed like a rapper. His strange, shuffling walk, full of urban attitude, seemed out of place. I was about to tell J.J. that we should take a detour when I brushed against a thorny tropical hedge. One of its spines stuck into my right leg like a knitting needle. We stopped briefly while I untangled myself from the plant, then we crossed to a side street off Burgundy.

In all my travels across America I have tried to remain streetwise. Follow the rules. Stay aware; look confident; look like you know where you are going and show you are mindful of everything going on around you. Most of all you must try not to look like a tourist. My guard was down. I was beginning to feel relaxed enough to walk home. J.J. was carrying this conspicuous-looking crescent-shaped '60s handbag that was swinging off her arm like a big black leather half-moon. In retrospect, it was a perfect target for a mugger, impossible to ignore; it was almost as if it said, "Please steal me." She had everything worth keeping in her handbag. Normally my valuables would be left in a hotel safe or in a hotel room, but the alarm had not been fitted at the apartment and a few of the window shutters were broken, so I decided to take all my valuables with me in J.J.'s handbag, including my wallet, cash, and credit cards. Wrong.

It was not supposed to happen this way. I swear I thought it was a zombie walking toward me. I would have been more on my guard if I had been in London's Turnpike Lane or Wood Green, but on a relatively quiet street in a safe part of New Orleans? Never. He was like a dead person, only air keeping him alive, like so many of the lost souls down there. I thought the guy was stoned at first by the way he was swaggering along. Then he veered across the pavement and bumped into me really hard. I remember our faces were inches apart, his desperate eyes staring at me with a tinge of fear in his pupils—aggressive but totally unconfident and afraid at the same time.

"Not now, no!" I shouted, almost as though now was not a convenient time.

"Hey, who you pushing, motherfucker? You pushing me?"

"No!" I shouted firmly. I didn't like the way my "no" sounded. It was too confrontational. What I really wanted to say was, "No: I really cannot let you do this. Try some other time. I've had a bad few days."

This fellow was not ready to listen to any reasoning Englishman. I instinctively threw my arm in front of J.J. I even shouted out for her to run while I held him off, but before I could act, I felt myself being punched and then pushed to the ground. I landed a few yards away and saw the mugger threaten her with a gun. I may have even heard a shot, but it sounded distant, like a firecracker. From where I was standing I saw that she had fallen and was on one knee, and the guy was shouting. He fired a shot from his shiny silver gun into the sidewalk as he spoke.

"Give me the fucking bag, you bitch."

A thought went through my mind: "What reason does he have for calling her a bitch? He has no right. She is a good person. He has no cause." Then again, he was not going to say, "Please put the bag down, madam."

I suddenly remembered the article about the fatal shooting of the New Orleans man whose wife miraculously escaped being shot, too, after they were held up at their home a year earlier. There had been no need to kill the husband, but the robbers had murdered him anyway. They had the money, but taking the man's life was a freebie. Somehow this incident stuck in my mind. A sense of panic and anger came over me, and all at once I seemed to lose control. The husband thought that if the robbers got what they wanted they would simply go away, but they still killed him.

J.J. was doing the smart thing. She threw the bag away in the hope the mugger would chase it and leave us alone. But it was not a simple case of fight or flight. It was just as easy for him to kill us both. The street was empty, and there were no witnesses, so what was to stop him from doing us both? All the police were at the ball game or dealing with the traffic. Why not kill us? I chose to fight back.

"Fuck this," I shouted in my thickest London accent, which echoed around the quiet street.

All the frustration and repressed anger I'd tried to control over the past months seemed to boil over. I realised that we all have a button that can be pushed when years of anger are channelled into one moment. I'd hit that moment. My breaking point. I ran after the guy. I wanted to catch him and beat the shit out of him. Wrong decision again. The mugger ran after the bag and grabbed it. By then I was too angry to think straight, so I decided to chase him down the street. This all happened in a moment, but I had no chance to think about it; it was instinctive. At that point his accomplice's car had pulled up, and he ran across to get in. I foolishly kept running after him, but when I was within ten or fifteen yards of the car, the mugger stopped by the passenger door, took up the classic two-handed shooting position, took aim, and fired his gun. It was already dusk, so the flash from the gun seemed to light up the street. Just as I saw the bright-coloured light come out of the gun, I dived to my left, away from the direction of the bullet. I fell to my left and felt a heavy thump as the bullet hit me. It was as though the whole right side of my body had suddenly gone dead. It was fortunate that I decided to fall to the left at the very moment he pulled the trigger, otherwise the bullet might have hit me in the chest or stomach. The gravel felt cold and rubbed against my face. Thoughts went back and forth. I was only just talking about my old security guard Big Bob in the Japanese restaurant minutes earlier. Now I was in perilous situation and I hated myself for it. Images of Bobby and my old "minder" Big Tony flashed before me. I imagined them scolding me for my reckless behaviour.

"That's a fine mess you've got yourself into, my lad."

Then I remembered Bobby saying to me, "What's scary about guys like you is that as big and strong as I am, you'd still keep coming at me. It's like you got nothin' to lose."

I rubbed my face in the gravel to repress some of the pain that was starting to shoot through my body. If I'd had one of the Big Guys with me, maybe this wouldn't have happened.

"Everybody's afraid of the Big Guy called the 'Gorilla,' wish you
    could be here today, now I am laying in the gutter.
Though the cop cars surround me I feel afraid,
Now I'm laying here staring at the pearly gates.
Tony, Tony you gave me security, you were a minder extraordinaire,
    and I miss you now that you're not there
Terrified and in a fret, like a child whose lost his mother
Shivering a cold, cold sweat with my face in the gutter.
Bobby, Bobby you gave me security, and Tony, Tony you did the same
    for me,
Now you're both sadly demised, I can't believe I'm still alive.
Bobby came out of Chicago to give me a helping hand, sat me down
    when I acted so stroppy and he did the same for my whole band.

Tony came from South London, he was a Cockney boy
He saved my arse back in '79 when I acted such a silly boy,
'Come on man, don't be a fool, come on man you're gonna crawl, one
*   day your gonna fall.'*
Everybody's afraid of the Big Guy called the 'Gorilla' but he was never
*   heavy out of hand—*
In fact he was a gentle as a lamb.
Tony, Tony you gave me security, you know, Tony, Tony you gave me
*   security*
Minder extraordinaire, I miss you now that you're not there, I miss you
*   now that you're not there.*
No you're never alone as long as the Big Guy's there."

LYING IN THE GRAVEL STREET, I started to do the "shock" dance. I had seen this performed recently outside Alex Chilton's house on Prieur Street a few months earlier. I had been visiting Alex one evening, and he had been reading aloud from a book by Thackeray. When he came to a certain punctuated moment in the text we heard a gunshot outside his house. We ran out and saw the victim lying flat on his face in the gutter a block away. His head was turned to one side, and blood was coming from his neck. He was banging his hands on the gravel, and his legs were twitching in shock, almost as if he were dancing.

We walked over to him, but we were told by a woman onlooker not to touch him until the paramedics and the police came, which they did a few minutes later. By the time the paramedics arrived we thought the man must have died, because they covered him up and took him away in an ambulance. Now I was in the same situation, only on a different street; I was in the gutter, my hands were in front of me beating against the gravel, doing the "shock" dance, and my whole body was shaking except for my right leg, which did not move. After the gunman had shot me, I waited a split second for him to come over to finish me off, but luckily he got into the car and sped off down the road. I shouted out with pain and frustration. By now a few onlookers had gathered around me; J.J. got the license number of the getaway car. A stranger's voice said it would be okay. A neighbour called the police, then the paramedics arrived and dragged me to another part of the road, where they proceeded to cut my trousers so that they can get to the wound. I shouted at them, "These are new pants!"

They politely replied, "We don't give a shit, sir; we want to save your life."

They got on the radio to the hospital. Suddenly they started referring to me as a male Caucasian, a victim. They scraped up my body onto a stretcher and put me into the ambulance, seeming very concerned about my heart rate, which was down into the low twenties.

"It's okay," I said. "I'm a runner; I have a slow heartbeat."

"Not this slow—this is dangerously slow. He's going into shock," they said over the radio. "We might need an emergency room when we get there."

"Where?" I asked.

"Charity Hospital."

They injected me with something to take away the pain and the trauma, but the shock dance didn't stop, and my heart rate got slower and slower.

15

UNKNOWN PURPLE

"I just had a really bad fall
And this time it was harder to get up than before.
I shouted to the heavens and a vision appeared,
I cried out 'Can you help?'
It replied 'Not at all.'

After the fall is over
You will be on your own."

Charity Hospital. Entrance. Evening.

I was flat on my back in the ambulance . . . . a policeman standing at my shoulder . . . faces stared in at me through the ambulance windows as we entered the hospital facility. A combination of emotions. Smiles. Concern. Confusion. I was aware of some activity in the background as they wheeled me out of the ambulance. A small crowd gathered outside the hospital. Not sure who they were, though. As I was taken into the hospital, an orderly tied a wristband to my arm. They had a load of wristbands ready to put on patients being wheeled in through emergency. I still knew who I was. I was still conscious, but many others on stretchers were not. To the world they appeared to be just anonymous bodies. Unidentified human debris. I looked at the name on my wristband. My new identity was "Unknown Purple."

I could have pondered for years about what to call myself if ever I were to change my identity. Struggled endlessly with variations on my own name. I could have labored for hours over intricate wordplay and smart synonyms. Now I was saved the trouble. "Unknown Purple" was on my wristband and in the files of Charity Hospital, that was who I would be. I complained that I felt freezing cold. An orderly explained that it was probably shock.

They wheeled me into what must have been the trauma room. Surrounded by more faces I could not recognise.

"How tall are you? Date of birth? How much do you weigh?"

I explained that I weighed eleven and a half stone. They only dealt with pounds. I asked them to work it out.

"You know, sixteen ounces, one pound, etc."

An orderly got out pencil and paper and started working out my weight. A trickle of laughter spread around the room.

A senior doctor looked over and looked into my eyes.

"What's your first name?"

"Ray," I replied.

"Well, Ray, we are going to take care of the pain, and then we are going to move you over onto your left side for an X-ray."

I was in no position to refuse. Less than a few hours earlier I had been in a Japanese restaurant fussing over my order. Whether to have the bean curd or the mixed vegetables. A few hours ago I was examining every detail of my life and my career and every other self-indulgent issue known to Western civilisation. A few hours later, here I was letting these people do what they had to do to save my life.

Procedure followed procedure. My right leg felt like a dead weight. Again, the senior doctor looked into my face. He was smiling now.

"Well, Ray, you are almost done here. Oh: have you always had a slow heartbeat?"

Before I could launch into my speech about being a runner and always having a slow heartbeat, someone in the background shouted.

"The entry and exits are clean—no fracture. No arterial damage."

I sensed a feeling of euphoria spread though the room. As they started the process of moving me through to the treatment area, someone asked if I got a good look at the guy who shot me.

"Yeah. Something about his eyes. Like he'd been in a fight. Yes, the eyes—a sort of Mike Tyson vibe."

The pretty black nurse wheeling my gurney burst out laughing. "You say he looked like Mike Tyson? Hell, all black criminals look like Mike Tyson. Don't you know that, mister?"

I was in too much pain to try explaining myself. It was just beginning to sink in. I had been shot, and there was a hole through my leg to prove it.

The crossover between fantasy and reality had just been defined for me. Any doubts I may or may not have had could be put to rest. It was almost a relief to know that I was in the real world. The truth was all around me, and it was absolute. I was not imagining all this. It was not a mood or a whim. This was not one of my ideas for a song or script that had been cobbled together in my subconscious. This was fact. As they wheeled me from one part of the emergency room to another, I saw my reflection briefly on one of the metal surrounds above the lights on the ceiling. I gazed at my reflection and wondered if that distorted shape was really me.

The nurse slid my gurney into a small cubicle. I was separated from the patient next to me by a thin curtain. I could hear this guy groaning. I looked down at his feet, which stuck out from behind the curtain. He was wearing orange coveralls from the Louisiana State Penitentiary. The prisoner was shackled to his gurney and swearing at the nurses who were trying their best to treat him.

"Hey, stop your cussing. We're trying to help you, boy, don't you know that?"

The prisoner relaxed as his pain started to subside. A nurse stood over at the foot of his bed, looked at him, and smiled. "This one is ready for the recovery room."

It wasn't until they wheeled him out that I saw the slightly comic sight of another convict still manacled to the one lying on the gurney. It all seemed surreal, particularly as he was unharmed and passively drinking a can of diet soda while manacled to the injured prisoner.

Then more doctors swarmed around me. Their eyes were not blinking. Don't know why, but I'd always associated that look with someone who is in a state of panic.

The real drama was not about my leg. They said that it was a clean hit. The real concern was about my heart. "Oh, me bleeding heart," I thought.

Then I heard the voices of my two friends, Bob and Jeanne. J.J. had gone down to the police station to give a statement. Bob put his head around the curtain and gave me a broad grin.

"You look great."

Bob had this way of delivering a simple line, speaking it with such belief, that it was impossible to imagine it being anything other than the proclamation of an undeniable fact. "You have just been shot. . . . You are in the ER. . . . You are full of needles and drips coming out of your arm. . . . But it is true: YOU LOOK . . . GREAT!" I actually believed him.

A young white nurse walked over to my side and grabbed my injured leg. She started prodding and poking. She had the soft voice of an angel, with an elegant profile befitting a ballet dancer rather than someone who is used to working on human wreckage, but there was almost a maniacal sense of purpose about her.

"The less you move, the less this will hurt."

I couldn't wait for it to be over. She proceeded to take what can only be described as a glorified bicycle pump and started drawing off fluid from the gunshot wounds in my leg.

"We have to remove the pieces of bullet and clothing in your leg to stop infection."

I smiled and tried not to move.

The angelic nurse continued to pump away at me. After what seemed an eternity, she shouted out to someone in the next cubicle, "Okay, Unknown Purple clean!" I tried to say thanks but she walked straight out. Another doctor was saying under his breath, "Does he have insurance?" I had to get out of there. I heard Bob and Jeanne talking in the background and tried to get their attention. In my deluded state, I actually thought that I could still be okay to meet the principal at John McDonogh High School the next day. "Someone help me. I've got an important meeting tomorrow." The pretty black nurse looked me right in the face and shook her head. "Mr. Ray Purple, you ain't gonna be taking meetings for a while. Now just relax." Her words were reassuring. If nobody knew who I was, then I fantasized about leaving the hospital with a new identity and starting a fresh life. Even though I was in a life-threatening situation, I enjoyed being Mr. Unknown Purple. Then as I was being wheeled away on the gurney, someone asked me, "Would you sign this for me? I'm a fan." Damn.

It was actually a copy of my X-ray. Word was spreading; I wouldn't be Unknown Purple for much longer. Drugs were pumped into my body— pain-heart-sleep and morphine for Mr. Unknown Purple, but even though my name was about to be restored, I still had doubts about my inner self. I liked being someone else. Being myself had often gotten me into trouble.

ON OCTOBER 5, 1980, I was actually arrested for impersonating myself. Vancouver, Canada, is less than an hour's flight from Portland, Oregon. Just a few hundred miles apart, but with different borders, laws, cultures, and mind-sets. We were due to play the Memorial Coliseum in Portland that night, and everybody had tied one on and got really drunk the night before in Vancouver, so we used the short flight as a chance to sober up. Just after we landed, a U.S. Customs officer came onto the plane wearing a Mountie-style hat.

"Is Ray Davies on this plane?" I was slouched in my seat in the front row and pushed my sunglasses down over my nose as I held up my left hand without thinking.

I said, "That's me," and before I knew it the man had pulled me to my feet, slapped some handcuffs on me, and put them behind my back. "I'd like you to come with me, sir; we have some questions to ask you." I immediately thought back to the noise we'd been making in the hotel the night before; there'd been a bit of drinking, but nothing else untoward. The first thing that went through my mind was to make sure that my small carry-on bag was secure. "I want to make sure I can see that bag at all times so nobody puts anything in it," I said to the man. I had heard of instances in which small amounts of drugs were planted by investigators just so they could hold and question suspects in the hope that it would open up a larger inquiry. Customs officials at the border between Canada and the U.S. were noted for being very tough on ordinary people, not to mention suspects. Before I knew it I was frog-marched off the plane and taken into a holding area inside the customs hall, still with my hands cuffed behind my back. My tour entourage had protested that they needed to see me, that we had a sold-out show that night, but in situations like this the authorities go deaf and dumb. I sat there for about an hour before being offered a cup of water, and I tried to quiz the customs people in a respectful manner, as I didn't want to piss them off. "Has anybody got any idea why I'm being held here?" I asked a large overweight customs lady. "Your situation is being assessed now, sir. Somebody will be in to see you shortly," she said. After a while some officers came in and took the handcuffs off and took a snapshot of me. I made some corny joke about letting them have autographed pictures at the show that night, but they didn't react at all. Then a plainclothes officer came in and went through my details: where I was born, passport, visa, etc.

"Do you spend a lot of time in California, Mr. Davies?"

"Only when I play there."

"You never signed any cheques when you were there?"

"I don't sign cheques on the road; tour managers look after that."

"The thing is, Mr. Davies, is that you're wanted for forgery, which is a serious offence in the state of California."

I was, to say the least, shocked by the accusation, but I was also amused. I demanded an explanation.

"We have your picture, Mr. Davies, and we're in communication with Washington now, and the Bureau is getting the details. We're moving you over to a holding facility shortly."

I half expected the customs guy to take off a mask and expose this as being a joke set up by my tour personnel.

After another hour had passed, I hadn't seen anybody or had any access to legal help. They took my prints and my picture, and I just sat there. That night, thousands of fans would be going to the auditorium in Portland to see their favourite band play all their well-known songs, and autograph hunters would be getting their memorabilia ready to sign, but one of the band probably wouldn't make the show. Suddenly a new bunch of people came in and asked me the same questions all over again—there must've been a change in the shift. They repeated that I'd be taken to the holding facility shortly. My interpretation of that meant jail. After another anxious wait, the first plainclothes officer came back. His face looked less confident, and he seemed much more conciliatory.

"You are Mr. Davies, yes? Mr. Ray Davies?"

"I am . . . at least that's who I was last night and quite sure who I am today and plan to be tomorrow. You must have the wrong person."

I knew I was being too cocky, and I could sense that the officer was trying to think of an excuse to keep me in custody. He decided to ignore my smart-ass reply. "Then if you're Ray Davies, who is this guy?" He took out a picture of someone who, apart from having two eyes, a nose, and a mouth, looked nothing like me.

The officer continued, "Doesn't it look vaguely familiar to you?"

I started to feel more confident and got into cheeky-chappy mode. "Well, he's not my identical twin."

The officer's reply overlapped mine. "This is the Ray Davies who's wanted for forgery; he's been signing cheques using your name, and he says he's a musician."

The officer took out a piece of paper with the signature on it that he'd been forging, and it looked very similar to the sort of signature I sign when I'm in a hurry after a gig. He must have used that and copied it to forge the cheques. The questioning continued.

"It appears that this has been a mistake. Those scars on your face—how long have you had those?"

"Since I was fourteen years old. I had an accident and had to have surgery."

"How come you never got your teeth fixed? Aren't they pretty awful teeth for a rock singer?"

I told him that as far as my teeth were concerned, I was born that way, with a gap between my front two teeth.

I really hadn't wanted to go into detail about my teeth or my scars, but apparently they'd saved me. The FBI files showed that I had these distinguishing marks that the forger didn't have, and I was identified by the Portland police department as the genuine article. An apologetic air spread through the room, and the officers started to look embarrassed. The fat-lady police officer gave me a cynical smile. "So you're playing tonight? Got any free tickets?"

By now my tour manager Jonesy had arrived with Big Tony, and I passed over the ticket request to him.

Later that night I arrived at the venue, and as I got out of the car and headed for the stage door, some fans ran over and asked for my autograph so

I signed a couple, as I normally do without even thinking. Then a guy walked up who was roughly the same height and build as me. I looked him in the eyes and thought about my experience earlier that afternoon. Even though it is my instinct to try to please everybody, I said I'd do it later and walked straight past him without signing. As the stage door closed behind me, I'm convinced I heard him say in a broad American accent, "That Ray Davies? He wouldn't sign my album. What an asshole."

16

THE MORNING AFTER

"Things have gotta change
This is the morning after
When reality bites the morality sets in
To those damaged limitations."

CHARITY HOSPITAL, JANUARY 5, 2004

Now reality had well and truly set in. Back when I was Unknown Purple, I did not have a clue where I was. Later I realised I was in a large emergency recovery room with five other patients. The local TV station was showing a James Bond film marathon on a TV that hung from the ceiling above my bed. People in the movie kept getting shot. I felt like shouting, "Don't these people know that getting shot really hurts?"

Nurses and doctors began asking me questions. "Who are you? What do you do? Where do you live? Next of kin? DO YOU HAVE INSURANCE?" A nurse said lots of phone calls are coming in.

"Are you a musician?

"I'm not a musician, I'm a writer. Okay, I'm a musician-writer."

Then suddenly J.J. came into the room. She was putting on a brave face as she spoke. "You see, I said I'd keep you company until you left town and that's what I'm going to do."

I tried to sound cool, and spoke to J.J. in a confident way. "Thanks darlin'."

I saw her looking away from the cardiac machine I was hooked up to, probably because she was afraid of what she might see. She didn't need to ask what was wrong, because the slow *plod, plod, plod* of my heartbeat—which was still struggling to stay above 50 beats per minute—bleeped from a speaker attached to the machine. It was obvious that the focus had completely shifted from my gunshot wound to my cardio problem. There was a sense of concern among the staff; I saw it on their faces and in their eyes. A doctor proclaimed that I was "all over the news"; it sounded as if he thought being shot was worth it for the publicity. J.J. looked exhausted, so I told her to go home to try to get some rest.

Then a nurse told me I needed to urinate and gave me a bedpan. Not only could I not cope with the demands of peeing on cue, I couldn't even move without help. They gave me more morphine, which put me into a trancelike state.

I kept drifting in and out of sleep. The sound of the machine bleeping confirmed that I was still alive. It's a fact that computer tempo presets start at 120 beats per minute and often get faster on most dance records, but not on mine. There are not many dance songs that are set at 50 bpm, but in my blurred, medicated state I imagined the hospital staff dancing to slow disco tracks around my bed in a bizarre music video.

"Me: Listen to my heartbeat.
Hospital Staff: Yeah, all fall down help this poor man off the ground.
Me: Listen to my heartbeat.
Hospital Staff: Yeah, all fall down.
Me: Someone help me off the ground."

My medicated haze focused into reality when I opened my eyes and saw my nurse, a large black woman, standing over me, staring at my abdomen. She had a stern look and was so tough-looking that I imagined her pulling a riverboat down the Mississippi single-handedly. Her gaze stayed down at my waist and then drifted up to her clipboard. Her voice was deep, clear, and very relaxed.

"Have you passed water yet, Mr. Ray?"

"Pardon, nurse?"

"Passed water, baby. Ya know, honey. Urinated."

She wrote something on her notes and looked me in the eyes for the first time. She held up a plastic bedpan.

"Now, baby, you gotta pee for me. Try using this. If it don't work by the next time I see you, I gotta take another recourse. Know what I mean?"

I didn't quite know what she meant, as I was lying on my back, but I nodded anyway.

With the help of the nurse, I attempted to stand and pee into the bottle provided, but a vivid, all-consuming pain shot down my right side. I felt a sharp, penetrating ache down my right leg. The pain was awesome.

"Please give me some more morphine."

My body felt numb, but inside I was beginning to panic. I asked an orderly for a notepad and pen so that I could write a message asking for help from the outside world.

BY THEN I HAD BECOME A MINOR CELEBRITY in the recovery room. I was still on morphine, but conscious enough to realise that people had figured out that I was not just "Unknown Purple." One of these people was a orderly called Beauford, who played air guitar and winked at me as he walked past my bed. His coworker, another orderly, had seen me play my solo show *Storyteller* in Atlanta and had told Beauford who I was.

"Hey, man, I'm a rock 'n' roller, too, but I've got ten grandkids. I can relate to your music." As Beauford strolled away, I saw that on the back of his head was a perfect mullet.

Later he introduced me to his wife, a pretty, plump woman named Jen, who was a nurse on the ward. "Be polite to Jen; she gives you the medication." Beauford explained that Jen was his third wife. He said that the orderly who saw my *Storyteller* show went hunting with him on weekends and was interested in finding out what type of gun was used to shoot me. Then Jen interrupted and gave me some meds.

Soon after, I looked around the room to see who my current neighbours were. Everyone in the room was black except me. In the bed opposite was a woman of about forty. Her kids came in for a visit. She had cardiac problems and was hardly able to speak. Her heart rate was well over one hundred. I tried to communicate with her using basic facial and hand gestures, but she didn't seem to have the energy to respond except for the occasional smile. To her right was a young guy in his early twenties. They had put him in restraints during the night. He had a large tube up his nose, which emitted a high, wheezing whistle every time he breathed. His face had a look of fear the whole time. During the night I heard him screaming. Must have been some sort of drug problem. It sounded as though he was in terrible pain, both mentally and physically.

To my right was an old guy they must have brought in during the night. He was still fully clothed and wearing his baseball hat. He didn't move. I asked a nurse what was wrong with him.

"Only God can decide on the fate of some poor souls." She shook her head slowly and sadly.

I took this to mean he was terminally ill. Another nurse gently pulled the curtain around his bed.

The kid to my left was being wheeled out. He protested in a squeaky voice. He was also strapped to his bed with restraints.

He was replaced by a middle-aged white woman named Brenda. She had long salt-and-pepper hair and a trim figure under her hospital gown. She lay motionless on her side. Her thin body protruded through the blanket, and her hips were delicately poised under the sheets in a way that made it seem as though her whole body were resting on her pelvis. There was something sensual about her shape. Her head was arched back, and her mouth was agape. It looked beautiful—good enough to kiss. Her lips were dry and soft-looking. She regained consciousness and desperately begged a nurse to give her some morphine. Her face was beaten-up, and there was a fresh cut across her cheek. One eye was bruised. She looked like J.J. She could have, in fact, been a dead ringer for J.J., apart from the salt-and-pepper hair.

Later she whispered across the room that she had overheard a doctor saying that I might be moved to University Hospital.

"You'll be okay there. They give you morphine." We both fell asleep. When I awoke, I looked over at my morphine companion. She was staring at the ceiling. Her pulse rate was soaring, and her heartbeat was faster than mine. I was still only around 55 bpm—still too slow for a dance track. Why had I even been thinking about her erotic shape? The drugs they administered must have turned me into some kind of sicko. Perhaps I was developing a crush on J.J. The woman in the bed opposite was probably dying, and for all I knew my heart could have stopped beating at any moment. So why, then, did I have time to think about such stuff?

What is sexy? What drives people? Had the guy who shot me spent all my money yet? What had he done with J.J.'s handbag?

Where were the clothes I was wearing when I got shot? I needed to finish my record before I died.

I began to panic, yet my heartbeat remained leisurely. What should I do? I looked at the notepad the orderly had brought me. "What will I do? I'll do what I do." I started to write down a lyric to a song based on the characters assembled in the emergency room:

"Listen to my heartbeat
Yeah, all fall down.
Someone help me off of the ground.

Beauford and Jen
He's got ten grandkids, she's the third missus.
He grooves around intensive care strutting his stuff
He's got a perfect mullet hanging down his back.
And Jen walks in, gives a little wiggle
Makes old Beauford grin.
He tucks me in, touches my feet
'Hey buddy, you know you got a slow heartbeat.'

Listen to my heartbeat
Yeah listen to my heartbeat.
And the marching band plays along,
Plays the morphine song on the Charity ward,
Yeah the marching band plays its song. . .

And opposite me Brenda the alkie coughs so deep,
It's the drugs and the drink,
It could happen to anyone
Sure makes me think . . .
And the bed beside her is full of cables and leads
Nobody visits, nobody grieves.

Hey listen to my heartbeat,
Yeah listen to my heartbeat. . . .

Jen takes some blood out of my arm
Rolls me over just like that.
Listen to my heartbeat,
Slow but clean.
While Brenda the alkie looks so mean
They wheel her out, she starts to cry,
'If I don't get better, I'm gonna die.'
I'll go cold turkey till I'm clean
She'll go to jail, but I'll get the morphine.

Listen to my heartbeat . . .
Yeah all fall down.
Someone help me off of the ground."

THE NEXT MORNING THERE WAS A BRIEF MEETING with a woman who ran the PR department at Charity. She was becoming slightly overwhelmed by the number of inquiries she was getting about "the English rock singer who is recovering in intensive care." I suggested that they issue a statement to the press saying that I had only received a "flesh wound" and that I had been discharged and sent back to the UK. That way the heat would be off the hospital and I would be able to recover away from media attention.

In the TV marathon above my head, James Bond shot a would-be assassin with a gun that had a silencer. It might be a quieter death, but it still must have hurt. I fell in and out of sleep. Suddenly I felt a presence. I looked up. It seemed as though I hadn't spoken in days. My voice had gone croaky, and I could hardly get the words out. "Travis Davis." He was wearing a sharp black suit and tie, like a blues brother. His smile was almost broader than my own.

"How you doing?"

"Why are you here?" I asked.

"Well, people in these parts get a little touchy when a visitor comes to town and gets all shot up for no good reason. But then again, it may have not been such a random mugging. Speculation on the grapevine is that someone arranged a hit."

"I tried calling you the other day but your line was dead," I said.

"Oh yeah, I had some trouble with my land line."

As he spoke, he looked around the small ward and shook his head disapprovingly. "You know, you really should ask them to do something about the security here. I mean, anybody could come in. They might even come in and finish the job when they hear you're going to press charges."

Travis was right. I still hadn't really spoken to the cops at any great length, but we had gotten the license-plate number of the getaway car and the police thought they had the identity of the shooter. Travis glanced up at the machine measuring my heart rate. Then we heard the sound of a gurney being wheeled down the corridor.

"You're going to have to take it easy, my friend. I've got to go."

Travis took out a packet of matches and put them on my bedside table.

"If there is anything at all I can do, just call. I can always be reached on my cell number; it's written on the back."

He patted me gently on the shoulder and shook my hand. As he left he made a parting gesture. He stopped and gave me a smile. Then he pointed at me with his index finger.

"You're protected from here on, fella. You've got a ring of luck around you right now, but you either stay in this town and roll with it or you get the hell out. If you decide to stay, I'd love to arrange for you to play my club sometime. It may be a hole in the wall, but it's the best music bar in the world. See you, kid."

I blinked and he was gone. On the television above my bed, James Bond unscrewed the silencer from his gun.

THE RECOVERY ROOM WAS BARE-BONES and had no frills: just the basic necessities. Only one thing that seemed plentiful: ice water. I could be crying out in pain, going into convulsions, in cardiac arrest—but the only sure thing, the one certainty, would be that the ice-water jug would be topped up as regularly as clockwork.

As Brenda the alkie had mentioned, the hospital staff had been discussing the possibility of moving me down the road a few blocks to University Hospital, a sister hospital to Charity Hospital that had a more sophisticated trauma centre.

Bob and Jeanne were giving me moral support as usual, but the problem was that my insurance coverage had still not been clarified. However, there had been some calls to people in my office in London, who told the hospital that the insurance was in the process of coming through. It was generally agreed by all to waive protocol and move me to University Hospital in the interim. The short move, via stretcher and ambulance, would be "on the house" until my insurance was resolved. I remembered that the first time I came down to stay in New Orleans I had accidentally videotaped University Hospital on my video camera. I started to think about the narration I was writing for my home movie.

"University Hospital is one of the first buildings you see as you emerge from a series of tentacle-like winding freeways that unravel just before the city appears. The hospital rises like a white sentinel, ushering the traveller on, like a signpost to the city. The interior reminded me very much of an old English secondary modern school from the 1960s. It was utilitarian in design—basic, intended to meet fundamental needs—and in its day it might have seemed state of the art. But now it gave the impression that its time had passed. Time and a climate of extremes—blazing-hot days along with damp, tropical nights—tested the resilience of any building and contributed to the overriding sense of decay, which in a way added to the decadent splendour of the city. Now the cracks were beginning to show on the once immaculate stucco walls."

By the time I had finished my imaginary monologue, they had moved me—complete with my bed and all the IVs monitoring my vital signs—from the recovery room at Charity to the slightly more refined space at University. The move was swift, and as we entered University and they began wheeling me down the halls, I could see thick black dirt marks stuck to the metallic window frames. The tiles on the floors were bumpy and uneven and made the clattering journey to my new resting place seem like a ride at the fairground. They disconnected my heart monitor, as my rhythm was slightly more stable, but even so it was still the main concern. On the wall opposite my bed was a sign that asked you to rate your level of pain on a scale of one to ten. The nurses came in to check my charts and "vital signs," but the name game continued. For some reason they still had a problem with my "sir" name and settled for Mr. Ray whenever the hospital staff spoke to me. At first the surroundings at University seemed luxurious in comparison. Bob and Jeanne stopped by with some homemade gumbo, which, as great as it was, did not improve my heart rate, which was still too slow. One of the hospital cardiology specialists, whom I will call Dr. Tracy, arrived with a bunch of young student doctors. Tracy seemed to be in her late fifties— a large woman with a commanding presence and a thick southern drawl. They took turns asking questions about my heart, about my medical history, and, yes, about my insurance. They said they would review my situation the following morning.

That night I decided the time had come to either pass water or undergo extreme medical procedures too horrendous to even consider. I was helped to a standing position by a nurse. She was in her forties and had short black hair.

I had just had some morphine, so the pain was reduced. Even so, I could not put any weight on my right leg. I had her supporting me on my right arm while I held the bottle in my left hand. I asked her to talk to me about her life.

"I was married at twenty . . . divorced at thirty. Have a lovely daughter who married too young and divorced. I have a beautiful grandchild, though. . . . My daughter's ex managed to cheat her out of any alimony. . . ."

My leg was giving me terrible pain at this point. I still couldn't pass water, but I continued to listen to her story.

" . . . He came from California. . . . Has smart rich attorneys; now they have custody. . . ."

I managed a drip. A trickle. "Oh, God, please let me pee." She looked straight ahead as she spoke.

" . . . My daughter disappeared. . . . I haven't heard a word from her in two years."

I was moved by the nurse's story.

"That's the saddest thing I ever heard." I said.

Then the trickle became a little pee.

She casually looked down and then glanced out the window at the evening sky before continuing the story of her life.

"I know it's a sad story, honey. I try not to think about it too much. I think I might go mad if I did."

Then the water flowed a little more. I apologised, but she was laid-back.

"Yep . . . it's not until you hear about other people's lives that you really know how sad the world is . . . . Don't worry, honey. It's not you. It's IV pee. It's not your own liquid. Just pure chemicals, baby."

My embarrassment subsided a little. Then I relaxed, and two days of intravenous drip started to shoot out of me. Thank God.

She was still concerned by the amount of pain I had in my leg when I tried to stand.

"You shouldn't be in that much pain, honey." She made some notes on her report sheet before she went off duty for the night.

I was still plugged into the machine that measured my heart rate. It was still running low, but it was about right for me. I thought about the sad personal tale the nurse told me while I was trying to pass water. About how so many people have tragic lives. About how professionally she behaved. About how we are all casualties in one way or another. I wondered if she drank a lot.

I looked over at the sign on the wall opposite my bed.

"What is the level of pain on a scale of one to ten?"

Everyone who came to examine me asked me that. I wondered if they assessed their own pain.

As NIGHT CAME, MY VITAL SIGNS WERE TAKEN, my meds were assessed and administered, and after an extra-strong dose of Ambien I went into a comatose state. Before nodding off I overheard hospital staff discussing the fact that my "shooter" had still not been captured. They mentioned that on other occasions, witnesses at a crime scene had had been killed by the original assailant, who would return to finish them off. I thought about what Travis had said and wondered whether there was any security at the doors of the hospital—whether anyone could just walk in. Because of this my sleep was troubled and uneasy.

In the pitch dark I heard a noise at my door and voices speaking in hushed tones. Then the door creaked open and I saw a shadow of a man silhouetted in the half-light from the hallway. This person was soon joined by a second figure, and together they crept in and stood ominously at the side of my bed. One of the men lifted up his arm and then reached into his pocket for what I assumed was a revolver.

"This is it?" I thought. "That's the end of me."

A voice whispered.

"Mr. Davies."

He knew how to pronounce my name. The voice sounded educated, like some kind of Ivy League graduate. The volume of his voice went up slightly once he knew I was awake.

"Mr. Davies. We work in the radiology department, and we have discovered something about your injury."

I wondered what was going to happen next.

"We think you may have a fractured femur and will inform your doctors tomorrow. We just thought we'd give you a heads-up."

I responded with a polite whimper. I told them to send a report in the morning. I was concerned, but still half asleep. I took a deep breath, thinking they had left. Then they came back with a request.

"Meanwhile, we wondered if you would please autograph your X-ray for us. We are both major fans, and we saw you in concert when you played in Massachusetts a few years back."

I couldn't believe the audaciousness of these guys. They seemed to have no respect for my privacy and had completely bypassed what little semblance there was of hospital security.

I signed the X-ray with a felt-tip pen and then attempted to go back to sleep. I rolled over, and the pain shot up my leg. If these guys were right, I would have to find another way to get to the bathroom. Oh, brother, what a mess. I would have flown back to the UK if I could have, but I had no choice but to stay put.

The next morning, an orthopedic consultant whom we can call Dr. Lander entered my room with a few of her attendants. She was in her early forties, articulate and elegant, and would not seem out of place in a smart private clinic on the East Side of Manhattan. She smiled in a reassuring way and turned on her bedside manner before going on to make the following announcement.

"Without wishing to sound like a maître d', I'd like to let you know that we think we have an opening for you in another cubicle. There'll be more privacy there for you, and given the fact that you're all over CNN and becoming a celebrity in the hospital, it might be for the best. Then we can start some physio and get you home." I couldn't help noticing a hint of facial hair above her top lip as she spoke.

I mentioned that some radiologists thought I had a broken leg, and she said she would look into it. Later I was wheeled into my own separate room on the fifth floor. The view from my window was of that same biomorphic freeway that runs in and out of New Orleans. I could see that beyond the Superdome the sun was setting and the rush-hour traffic was in full flow. The meds were having a pleasant effect on me as I drifted in and out of reality. As evening fell, the hospital staff started to put the patients down for the night. I still hadn't heard from my office at home about whether my insurance coverage had been confirmed. I'd heard horror stories about hospital bills in America and felt particularly insecure, as everything I had—including all my identification and the credit cards in my wallet—had been stolen.

After breakfast the following morning, a large orderly swaggered into my room and announced that he was to give me some light physiotherapy on my leg. I wanted to explain about the pain I was having, but he said some light physio would take care of it. I had only been in the hospital three days, but already I was becoming institutionalised enough to go along with whatever the doctors deemed appropriate. He started giving both my legs a mild massage and was about to stand me up for some leg stretches when one of my nurses came rushing into the room, waving her arms frantically.

"Stop!" she shouted. "Put Mr. Ray back in bed. There is a break in his leg!"

The tall physiotherapist froze where he stood, then gently laid me down on the bed. When he had made me comfortable, he quietly backed out of the room.

After a while I received another visit from the eloquent Dr. Lander. Again she flowed into the room like a ballet dancer, followed by her two assistants. Her entrance reminded me of *Swan Lake*.

The doctor had some disturbing news.

"Last night, one of the cardiology team heard about the pain you were having when you tried to stand. In short, this person decided to digitalise your X-ray and blow it up. In doing so he discovered that you have what we call a displaced fracture of the right femur—like an eggshell that is cracked but not broken. It's something that could not be seen on a regular X-ray. This will require an operation. We will insert a titanium rod into your right thigh." I was beginning to wimp out at this point.

"Couldn't I rest and we just let the crack fix itself?" The words sounded ridiculous as soon as they came out of my mouth.

Lander continued in her analytical way.

"The danger would be that if we let this go unattended, you would be walking out of the hospital and your leg would just snap." It was quite probable that the leg had actually snapped while I was trying to walk to the bathroom.

"However, we cannot operate until the cardiology department has cleared you. Meanwhile, we will send you down for some more X-rays."

Images of hip replacements came into my head. Then the cardiology people arrived for another consultation. Dr. Tracy led the way, with even more students in tow. The room was filled to capacity, as though I were holding a meeting. I was terrified. I imagined pacemakers, bypass surgery, transplants, and the like. But I put on a bold front.

"Come in, ladies and gentlemen. Sorry, but I have no refreshments to offer you."

The younger students laughed. Dr. Tracy continued in a businesslike manner.

"Have you ever had a stress test on your heart?"

I told her that I had once had some fancy cardiac tests done up north, in New York City. Dr. Tracy obviously felt a little peeved at my mention of the North-South divide. Some people down here still remembered Robert E. Lee.

"Well, those high-striding doctors up north can fill you up with all sorts of dyes and fluids . . . while down here, we just cure ya or shoot ya." Tracy bellowed out a laugh at her own wisecrack.

Nervous laughter fluttered around the room as Tracy became serious. "Well, the only way we can be sure you are up to the operation is to give you a stress test. That, without doubt, is the only way to be conclusive."

"What next?" I wondered out loud. Tracy continued enthusiastically.

"We have to find out if your heart rate can go above one sixty-five to see if you can make it through the operation. It's a simple procedure. You can't go on the treadmill because of the fracture in your leg, so we will pump you up with a machine that controls your heart rate. You won't have to do a thing. Just lie there, and we'll do all the work."

"What if the machine goes too fast—will I have a heart attack?"

"We can deal with that scenario."

Dr. Tracy gave me a pat on the shoulder and a reassuring smile before leaving the room with her entourage of students.

A new, younger doctor appeared. He came straight out with the fact that he knew who I was. He was on an early shift in the ER the night I was admitted, and he said that somebody must have gotten a tip-off that there was a broken bone somewhere.

"You had shrapnel show up on your X-ray, and where there is shrapnel in a wound there has to be a break."

He went on to say that he was writing film scripts for Hollywood and had had some good feedback on his last one. Told me I should write down my experiences in the hospital.

"You've met a great bunch of characters down here, and your situation would be hilarious if it were not so scary."

He said he would buy me the Robert McKee book on screenwriting for me to read while I recovered and would pop in to see how I was doing from time to time. I thought about what he'd said and started trying to make notes on my pad, but I kept thinking about the songs that were waiting to be mixed in London and about the fact that all my recent experiences had been predicted in the lyrics.

I WAS JOTTING DOWN SOME NOTES on my pad when I sensed that there was somebody in the room with me. I raised my eyes to see an elderly black gentleman standing by the door. He was almost like a character from central casting: white beard, white hair, beautiful features, wearing a three-piece business suit.

"I'm here to see if you're well . . . spiritually well. I'm the hospital chaplain, and I wondered if I could help you." The whole moment seemed staged and slightly clichéd. The gentleman continued. "Are you Baptist? Or what are you?"

"I'm Church of England, old boy; don't know what that equates to over here, but I went to a church school." I felt proud for saying that, as if it gave me some brownie points. He continued to quiz me. "Do you have any idea why you were shot?"

"Must've been a random thing. I understand from the hospital staff it happens quite a lot around here." His smile was like that of a benevolent cartoon character: the whole bottom half of his mouth seemed fixed in a large grin, and he had gleaming, spotless teeth. I was just wondering what brand of dental floss he used when he spoke again.

"D'you think you'd recognise this person if you saw him again?"

"'Course I'd recognise him—he was one inch away from me. But I can tell you something; he looked scared."

"Why d'you think he looked scared?"

"Because he looked like he had second thoughts at the last moment, but it was too late to turn around and walk away. I was already pissed off at him."

The chaplain looked at me calmly while I continued. "Yeah—he looked lost and confused." Suddenly I realised that with all my bravado I wasn't telling the truth. I was imposing my own predicament on a person who was probably just attacking a random victim. The word "lost" had opened me up, and I became soft-spoken and emotional.

"You were lost?" he asked.

"Yes; I have been for a long time. You see, I tour a lot. I guess I'm trying to find my way home."

I went on to explain that in reality I had no home. I had a house to live in, a car in the garage, but I was completely lost. The clergyman said a prayer with me and then said good-bye. I thought about that man and whether or not I had imagined him. The next day I asked if he had been around, but nobody in the building could be found to match the man's description— although he was real enough to me.

SPIRITUALITY DRIVES THIS CITY; there are Baptist churches on nearly every street, even if some of them are only poorly renovated shacks. In certain neighbourhoods gospel music can dominate the sound-scape before it becomes absorbed within the drone of the city. Belief in God is important for people who have nothing else, in a town where so many are poor and out of work. The projects in New Orleans appear to be more dangerous than any UK council estate or shantytown. One of the apartments where I stayed in New Orleans was near to what was suspected to be a crack house, but there were no flashy criminals wearing medallions or big fedoras living there; the residents were ordinary inhabitants who have to deal with a drug culture every day as their norm. You could hear the occasional gunshot and fight or quarrel, and I felt that some of the kids playing outside these houses were just waiting, dreading the day they would be old enough to get on the same treadmill. Ambition was in short supply, and that's why I thought music and marching bands were so important: they offered some alternative.

Some of the workers who performed menial tasks in the hospital were so sickly that they could almost have been patients themselves. The woman who delivered my meals was short and had what I can only describe as slightly disorganised features. One eye seemed lower than the other and was slightly smaller; as she took the lid off the top of my plate she said apologetically, in a whisper, "Well, Mr. Ray, it's pork chops today, but you can skirt around the gravy and the meat because there's some nice beans and rice." If I'd been in the safety of a plush London private hospital, I would've been treated to a special vegetarian menu and high-quality wine. Here, you just got what was already going. She could see I was feeling sorry for myself, and I longed for a nut cutlet and a glass of Cabernet. I negotiated the plate cautiously with my fork and prodded the occasional bean. Then I heard the woman begin to sing in a quiet but very distinctive voice, a Mahalia Jackson song I'd heard many years ago. The woman explained that she sang in her Baptist church sometimes and it meant a lot to her to help people like me. As she sang she moved close to me . . . almost singing in my face, but her breath didn't smell at all, and the beauty of the moment surpassed any trepidation I might have had. The small performance became a regular event at mealtime, when she would quietly serenade me. One night I saw her leave after she finished work. She had a scruffy overcoat wrapped around her as she walked with a slight limp, showing early signs of arthritis. Her body was old, but her face was young, and her voice was like that of an innocent child.

THE TIME CAME FOR MY STRESS TEST. Two men walked in; one of them had large, bulging eyes that did not blink and got larger when he spoke. "Mr. DavEEZ. We are just going to strap this around your left arm and get those veins nice and big. Then we will put this needle in, which in turn will control your heart rate." I was less than reassured. He punched some data into a computer while his assistant pumped up my arm. The assistant was a fan. Saw me play once in New York. Mr. Big Eyes continued.

"Mr. Daveez. Is that how you spell it?"

"That'll do. Ouch!"

A large needle with a speedometer-like instrument attached to it was inserted into my arm.

"Good. Mr. Daveez, we are going to take your heart rate up to around one sixty-five from where it is right now. It's only fifty-five at the moment so we'll have to do better than that."

By now I was in a state of panic.

"What if my heart can't take it?"

"That's the whole point. We are actually trying to establish whether you are prone to having a heart attack. Better to have it here than during the operation. We can deal with it better. Don't worry. You're in a hospital."

I wanted to faint. It was like a sketch from *Saturday Night Live*. Mr. Big Eyes was totally focused on the computer screen. He twiddled some knobs. I actually felt my heart going faster. He called out the speed like a sports commentator. "Seventy . . . Seventy-five . . . Eighty . . . Ninety."

I felt pain in my head. I clenched my jaw.

"Let's try to go over one hundred!"

His eyes grew bigger. Still no blinking. "We're nearly there, Mr. David."

"Davies!" I could hardly speak.

The screen was bleeping, the lights were flashing, and my heart was pumping. Mr. Big Eyes' eyes had maxed out. Surely those eyes couldn't get any bigger. He tore off the computer printout.

"That's it. You're ready for the operation."

The process began. More X-rays, which entailed waiting around in cubicles. One of Lander's car mechanics came to measure my leg for the titanium rod. A nurse administered my pre-surgery medications and morphine. I was pricked and swabbed clean, all ready to be wheeled down to the operating theatre in the basement.

I began to panic.

By now I was on verge of hysteria. Thankfully, in the hallway outside the operating theatre itself, there was my anesthesiologist who was already waiting in professional mode, focused, reassuring, although in my premedicated state he looked to me like Raymond Burr in Hitchcock's *Rear Window*. His would be the last face I would see before going under. Thankfully, the laughing gas was administered; as Raymond Burr's eyes stared into my own, unblinking and unemotional, the wavy special effects distorted my vision and I passed away into memory.

. . . and then the phone rang.

17

STATE OF CONFUSION

"Woke up in a panic
Like somebody fired a gun
I wish I could be dreaming
But the nightmare's just begun. . . .
My girlfriend's packed her bags
And moved to another town
She couldn't stand the boredom
When the video broke down. . . .
I'm in a state—state—of confusion . . ."

I was enjoying a rare opportunity for some downtime amid the tranquillity of an early summer evening in the splendour of the Green Belt area of suburban Surrey. The soft breeze rustled through the large oak tree near where I was sitting on the lawn. It was a luxury to be away from the hectic lifestyle of rock tours and to be able to take stock of my life in the relaxed serenity of middle England. A deer foraged around in the undergrowth nearby. Baby rabbits scampered around and sprung up and down on the gravel drive while their watchful parents nibbled away at the weeds that had sprouted up between the rocks on the driveway. Then the air of sultry calm was broken by the sound of the phone ringing. The main house phone was barely audible in the garden, so a large bell had been installed at the side of the house to attract the attention of anyone who was out of earshot. The simple sound of a phone ringing was like an alarm bell signalling as it echoed around. This made the deer flee into the nearby woodland and the rabbits scurry back to the safety of their warren. I picked up the receiver, and through the crackle of the transatlantic connection a deep, threatening voice hollered down the line. It sounded ruthless, uncompromising, yet charismatic.

"I want you to come to America to play at the US Festival in California."

There was only one voice I knew that was authoritative enough to make such an audacious demand, and it belonged to legendary American concert promoter Bill Graham.

"You want me to what?"

There were no pleasantries or cordiality in his response. "I want you to come to America in the summer, to San Bernardino, to play in front of a couple hundred thousand people at the US Festival."

I paused to think and considered joining the garden moles in the safety of their underground burrow. This was not a good time to uproot myself and jump on a plane to the United States. The Kinks were in the middle of making an album; the whole tour entourage was resting for the summer, and most of the crew had taken on work elsewhere. I'm sure I heard him bang the phone on his desk at the other end.

"Is this a bad connection? Did you hear what I said? I want you to come to San Bernardino and play in front of maybe three or four hundred thousand people. This will be the biggest show of your career."

I was not sure whether my ears were deceiving me, but the potential attendance had doubled within a few seconds. I tried to respond, but I couldn't think of anything to say. Then I spoke, knowing that it would make him more irritated. Nevertheless, I said what I said.

"Today? Tomorrow? I'm kind of busy at the moment." But the relentless promoter wasn't ready to listen.

"I've spoken to your manager and agent. Steve Wozniak is guaranteeing the fee, which is bigger than anything you'll ever make, and logistically the travel routing is doable, according to your tour manager."

I was a little bit irritated by his sudden request, and my second instinct, after the urge to join the moles underground, was to hang up the telephone. Bill Graham was a hero of mine—to me, the greatest rock promoter of that time—and he had turned the American music industry upside down after the British Invasion was quelled. More than anyone else, he was responsible for putting American music back on the map. I should have felt honoured he'd called me personally but as great as he was, he was beginning to piss me off. I'm sure the feeling was mutual, but I couldn't tell him that. In a diplomatic voice I tried to explain that the band was off the road and that I was completing my next album. I explained it'd be quite costly to get to

San Bernardino with the regular tour entourage plus the crew from Dallas. I explained that I wanted to see my kids. That I had booked a summer holiday. I explained and I explained, but Bill was unrelenting.

"You could do a couple of warm-up dates in the South, take a day off while the crew drives across the desert, and you can be in San Bernardino in time for the gig."

He made it sound quite feasible; still, I scoured my deepest imagination for an excuse. I racked my brains for all the excuses I used as a schoolboy when I wanted to take a day off and miss my exams. The only way I could get out of the situation was to make what I suspected would be an unreasonable request so that he would have to say, "Fuck off and forget it." I took a deep breath and went ahead.

"I'll do it on the condition that the Kinks go on at dusk and be the first band to use lights."

I knew what a traffic jam these events were and that everyone would be fighting for stage space. In similar situations, with such a massive list of performers, I always found that when the Kinks went on and were the first to use lights, we created a sensation and were usually impossible to follow. Surely Bill would not agree to this request. The US Festival was an enormous event sponsored by the cofounder of Apple; it was anticipated to be one of the biggest festivals in the world. So the opportunity was too good to miss. Nevertheless, I played hard to get. Bill paused at the other end while he thought it through. He had been the first promoter to take what he described at the time as a "risk" when he brought the Kinks back to New York after our long ban. I could almost hear the wheels in his head turning as he shuffled around his options.

"The first band to use lights? I can pinpoint that time exactly if you give me a moment." With a shout, he asked someone on his end to look at his calendar, and I heard someone shout back the time 7:15 p.m.

Bill confirmed the time to me over the phone.

"Is that a deal?"

I thought about my alternatives and tried to stall.

"I'll have to run it past my manager and my agent, but if it's all right with them it's a deal—provided we go on at that time."

Bill was all ready with his response.

"I told you I already checked it with your agent and manger. They're happy with whatever stipulations you want to make."

"So we go on at that time and are the first band to use lights?"

My attempt to reconfirm met with an affirmation of my request.

"That's the time, and I'll put it in writing."

It felt like an insult.

"That's okay. Your word is enough."

"A deal, then."

"A deal."

I tried to add a "nice to talk with you." Bill had already hung up.

US FESTIVAL, SAN BERNARDINO, CALIFORNIA

SEPTEMBER 4, 1982

I pushed back all my recording dates in the UK, which meant that the recording schedule would be even more hectic if we were to get the album out on time. Then, after a few rehearsals with the band, I found myself travelling to Dallas, Texas, for full production rehearsals with the band and road crew. We did a few warm-up dates to pay for the travel and to earn a small profit before flying to Los Angeles, where our manager, Elliot Abbott would meet us at the airport.

When we disembarked, Elliot was waiting in his bright, shiny new Jaguar, which in Los Angeles music circles was even more prestigious than a Rolls or a Bentley. Elliot spoke calmly, but he looked like he hadn't slept for days. He had a strained look in his eyes. When I asked if there was something wrong, he mumbled, "Bill Graham has moved your showtime, so you have to go on an hour earlier."

I was devastated, to say the least. "Why didn't you tell him I had his word? That we had a deal?" I shouted. "I think it may be mentioned in the contract!" Elliot appeared to be on the breaking point.

"Bill Graham is Bill Graham, and he does what he wants."

My temper was short after the long, draining flight.

"I'll talk to him and remind him that he made a verbal agreement with me." Elliot was doubtful that this would do any good.

"Everybody's tried . . . but Bill won't listen. He's digging in his heels on this one. He said he's had the running order for the festival set for a while and cannot change it now."

Then came the repercussions probably laid on thick to poor Elliot by music-biz insiders. "The word is that if you make a fuss about this, Bill will do everything in his power to make it difficult for you. He more or less has a monopoly in San Francisco—and in the whole Bay Area, for that matter."

I sat and listened while I was reminded of the ramifications of not doing as I was told. It was known that promoters like Bill could block out venues or take a hold on a theatre just to stop certain acts from playing. We would have tried to book a tour only to find that venues were suddenly not available. Then if we did get a venue, a vindictive promoter could put a major act in another venue to compete with ticket sales on that night. The consequences were slightly scary the more I thought about it, so I tried to put it out of my mind. I tried to understand my adviser's point of view. Why not eat humble pie and go on, take the money, and get out of town?

But my entire schedule had been set aside for this date. I imagined Bill doing this to other acts and getting away with it. One thing kept playing over and over in my mind: *We had a deal.* I knew that honour was not prevalent in the music industry, but I thought that Bill might be an exception to the rule. I thought about how mercenary the industry was, and how Bill Graham had fought his way to the top from humble beginnings. How he worked his way up to become the greatest promoter in the business—rising from nothing to achieve great success and respect from his peers. More than anything else, people knew that you didn't fuck with Bill Graham. To most, I would be considered an upstart Limey rock and roller with an attitude problem. I'd fought the "establishment" before, and I hadn't come off too well. Still, I wasn't going to play the game. Maybe Bill was punishing me for asking for the time stipulation in the first place, making an example of me for putting forth such an extravagant request. Maybe he felt that I had to be put in my place. But for me, it was worth the risk of alienating him because of that telephone conversation we had; it had become a matter of honour. Bill was a legend, but I couldn't let that stop me. I would stand by my original condition for playing. Perhaps it was time for artists to stand up for themselves whatever the risk. My decision was made.

We stayed overnight in L.A. at the Hyatt House on Sunset. I had a surprisingly good night's sleep and woke up refreshed for the drive down to San Bernardino. Despite the protestations of my tour manager, Ken Jones, and despite the memories of our four-year ban from the States—partly the result of a dispute involving a promoter—I would not change my mind. Someone had probably weighed this up and figured that I would play ball because I could not risk another dispute that might affect the Kinks' career.

It was a blisteringly hot day, even for California—more suitable for sunbathing at the beach than for playing a rock concert in front of what was estimated to be more than two hundred thousand people in a desert where the temperature was predicted to reach one hundred degrees. Because of the large landmass taken up by the festival, each band was kept in a "holding" hotel a few miles from the site. When we were deposited in the hotel, I made a call to each member of the band: "When they knock at your door, don't go; stay in your rooms until I tell you." Four o'clock came—knock at the door, no one left. Four thirty came, and still nobody left. Finally, I summoned my "troops" and we left in waiting limousines. To ensure that we didn't get there too early, I told the driver to take the slow, scenic route. Our little motorcade reached the brow of a hill, and below us we saw the masses assembled at the US Festival. Proceedings were in full flow; the gigantic audience was jumping, and the dust was rising in the hot California desert.

The sun was just starting to go down as we pulled in back stage. An irritated-looking Bill Graham came storming over to the limo and started thumping on the car window nearest me. I lowered the window using the electronic control only to have a hail of abuse hurled at me. Bill was so infuriated he could barely blurt out his words, which came out in a torrent of spit. He put his face right up to mine. "Call yourself a fucking blah blah blah!" Even great men can appear to be undignified in certain situations. I was personally so embarrassed I didn't know how to react, but in my opinion we had a deal, and I always considered Bill's word to be better than anything written in a contract. He wouldn't stop shouting through the open window, and eventually I had to push the down button to close the window in his face. This mischievous act caused more than a little amusement amongst my small entourage, while the experienced insiders held their heads in their hands, knowing that this would only serve to provoke Bill even more. Bill kicked the car as we drove off and even threatened to have us thrown off site before we had a chance to play. It was not pleasant back stage—Bill was shouting, and his normally polite, professional assistants had turned into irritated henchmen, making life uncomfortable for the band. I continued to wait until it was near our "contracted" time. At that point, we walked toward the side of the stage and politely waited to be told to go on. The crowd was shouting and chanting. Bill approached me in an intimidating way and hurled more abuse at me, but by then I was numb to anything he could say. I entered a Zen-like state of calmness even though I was terrified underneath. Bill was a handsome, swarthy, and strong-looking man with great charisma, and he had an incredibly powerful presence, but I was past caring about my own personal safety and future career. He brushed past me like a prize-fighter. I was in too deep at this point, so I turned to him and said in my best English accent, "You have no dignity."

Bill pulled back the curtain at the side of the stage as he snorted back at me. "What about their dignity?"

I looked at the crowd—they were jumping around and having a great time.

"They are going to get a fucking great show, and I am going to work my ass off for them."

I assured Bill that I'd give it my very best shot and that the band would be great. He stormed off, and the Kinks went onstage. The show went beautifully, and everyone in our crew was more relaxed now that we were past the politics and giving it large onstage. We were due to play for ninety minutes, but after forty-five I glanced over to the side of the stage, where I could see some of the crew looking concerned. During one of my brother's guitar solos, I shouted to one of our security guards and asked him what the matter was. He said, "Bill says that your time is up and you've got to come off now; otherwise he'll pull your plug." We were just reaching the peak of our performance, but I stopped the song dead at the end of Dave's guitar solo. The crowd started jeering; I took centre stage and spoke to the audience. "Sorry about this, but we've got to stop playing because the promoter said he's going to pull our cables out." We started to walk off, leaving the crowd in an uproar. Then we launched into "All Day and All of the Night"—one of our big rock anthems at that time. It was as though the whole desert had erupted, echoing the fury in our performance and sending more of the dust beneath the audience's feet rising into the night air.

It's times like this when a good band becomes a great band, and the crowd was not disappointed. The song ended in a tumultuous crescendo, and we walked offstage. The audience sensed that they'd been short changed and kept shouting and chanting for us to come back on, but we just stood calmly and casually back stage whilst Bill went out to make an announcement. By now his voice was hoarse and weary, but he bellowed down the microphone, "Let's see if we can persuade Ray Davies and the Kinks to come back on." He knew his position had been weakened and that we would go on to do the remainder of our set. I had made my point. The show was a triumph. Afterward we waited in the dressing room, and even though the backstage crew members might have been under instructions to treat us coldly, they somehow conveyed to us that we'd done a fantastic show. I did a few interviews and then got ready to leave. I was looking around for Elliot Abbott, but when I asked where he was, someone told me he had to leave early because Bill Graham was threatening to have his brand-new Jaguar picked up by a forklift and dumped onto the nearest freeway. I was amazed that we had been allowed to get away relatively unscathed. As for poor Elliot, it would have been a long walk home across the San Bernardino desert if his Jaguar had actually been dumped on the freeway.

FOR THE WEST COAST SEGMENT OF OUR NEXT TOUR, it was decided that it was not in our best interests to use Bill as the promoter when we played San Francisco. Normally this action would be regarded as unthinkable, as San Francisco was Bill Graham territory, but this seemingly reckless decision proved to be an indication of how popular the band was at the time. Instead, we used another promoter to book the dates and sold out two nights at the Cow Palace, the very arena that had figured so prominently when we had been banned more than a decade earlier. As I left the stage after the Cow Palace show, I was given a telegram from Bill Graham, which said, "Despite your deplorable behaviour in San Bernardino last year, it would be my privilege to promote your show if ever you come back to the Bay Area." The next time we went to San Francisco to play, Bill promoted the show. We all saved face, and even though in his own memoir he suggests otherwise, the Kinks kept their side of the bargain at the US Festival: we honoured our word and, more than anything else, delivered a knockout show, which was all that mattered at the end of the day. We'd lived up to our album title: *Give the People What They Want.*

COME DANCING, 1982–83

The early 1980s were the great days of the Kinks and Arista in North America. The night we finally made it back to play Madison Square Garden, on October 3, 1981, Clive Davis stood at the side of the stage smiling proudly. Some say he had tears in his eyes. This was not fake; it was genuine pride, because in some way he seemed to understand the monumental obstacle we had overcome after the ban in the '60s. It was regarded as a minor miracle in a business where, generally speaking, if you blow it once, you don't come back.

Gold albums, arena status, Madison Square Garden, Top 40 airplay . . . but then, somewhat inevitably, things started to backfire. In the years we spent rebuilding our career with Arista, my brother, Dave, had been trying to focus on his own solo career, which kept him content while he toured with the Kinks. Dave now had a solo deal and was becoming completely isolated from the rest of the group when we weren't on tour. When we did go on the road, he would bring his new family with him, along with all the other paraphernalia of family life. He spent more and more of his time in Los Angeles and would only come to the UK to record his parts on the albums. Then he would turn back and go home. This pattern continued with our next few albums.

Back in spring 1982, Dave had been in Los Angeles while I was making demos with the band at the Konk studio in London. My older sister Gwen had shown me a photograph of herself taken when she went to the Palais Ballroom, near where my family lived. The old black-and-white photograph, taken in the heyday of the '50s big band era, had inspired me so much that I wanted to recapture that time on record. I demoed the instrumental idea with Mick, Jim, and Ian late on a Friday night, and by Saturday lunchtime I had the lyrics typed out. Jim described the song as "innocent" when I played the completed demo back to the band in the studio. It had none of the heaviness of our previous album, *Give the People What They Want*, and it was the most English-sounding track we had done for a long time. When Dave came back from the States in October, I played the demo for him. It was as though I were auditioning the song; he sat there unemotionally, making no comment at the end. We went into the studio the following weekend to put the track down, and Dave played some power chords over the middle section, which added some aggression that had been missing on the demo. Victoria—the same daughter I'd played "Lola" and "Celluloid Heroes" for as a toddler—was now a teenager, and she had stopped by the studio with a friend as we played the finished track. This made me feel as though her presence had given the track the right karma. I'd devised a key change for the outro that went to E flat, which is not generally regarded as a great chord for the ending of a rock-and-roll record. The band didn't seem to understand until I brought the horn section in for the outro—which gelled to provide the perfect end to the song.

The song "Come Dancing," on our 1983 album, *State of Confusion*, gave us our biggest U.S. single hit in years, even though Clive Davis was initially reluctant to put it out. Its content, in his opinion, was too London-centric. Instead, Clive had wanted us to release a song called "Don't Forget to Dance," a ballad with hooks and riffs. He would ask for, and at times demand, mix after mix so that the record was, in his opinion, just right for the U.S. market. Eventually, though, he opted for "Come Dancing," partly because of its compelling, skipping, ska-cum-Latin rhythm and its polka-like big band ending, but mainly because we had made a video that went into major airplay rotation in the early years of MTV. "It's not my first choice, but I can't keep the video off the television," Clive said, almost in frustration. The rebound effect also meant that "Come Dancing" became a hit in the UK and, eventually, a hit worldwide. We had not only conquered America, but it had set us back on the road to success in the rest of the world—including, most important, in our own country.

Unbelievable as it may seem, Clive's concern was that he'd signed the Kinks as an AOR (album-oriented rock) crossover act and somewhat to my surprise our record had become too popular for that genre. In some ways he would have preferred to have singles that would be played on Top 40 radio stations rather than on pop-single radio stations, but "Come Dancing" did attract an entirely new, younger audience who didn't necessarily buy albums. It was almost as though I had committed a sin by making a pop hit.

Also, we had worked with the director Julien Temple and utilized the medium of rock video, which in some ways had taken power out of record companies' hands. It was thought by a few somewhat cynical insiders that Arista did not want us to be more successful than we already were. Our deal was up for renegotiation at a time when we were in a good bargaining position because we were selling more records, something that might have been on the minds of business affairs in the increasingly corporate ethos of Arista at that time.

MERCHANDISING BECAME A MAJOR FACTOR once we started playing larger arenas. Each album and each tour had its own identity, and merchandising became a way of promotion as well as a source of income at concerts. Merchandising stands were set up everywhere we played from 1980 onward, selling T-shirts, baseball hats, and programmes as well as other mementos. This taught me something about America—the country that had invented consumerism. In the "big arenas," audiences love to be sold something extra, otherwise they feel short changed. They need to have a souvenir to take away with them. Audiences feel comforted knowing that this side of an event is well organised. Merchandising is an integral part of the concert experience. This helped us fit in with the fabric of the American touring landscape; radio stations and promoters were almost reassured by the fact that we played the game. We showed them that we understood our role in the system. It made me realise that it was not all about music. A record had to be more than full of great songs and well produced; it had to have a well-organised campaign. The post–*Low Budget* years and the subsequent albums *Give the People What They Want*, *One for the Road*, and *State of Confusion* all helped to improve our general status in America. When we first signed with Arista, our popularity abroad—particularly in the UK—took a severe knock, but it had been revived by "Come Dancing."

ON THE SURFACE I SEEMED TO HAVE IT ALL. But at the end of 1983, things were reaching a difficult point in my relationship with Chrissie Hynde, particularly after her band had opened for the Kinks at a concert in Denver, where the rest of the Pretenders complained that they didn't have enough stage space and that they didn't get an adequate sound check. Matters turned sourer when Chris came on to sing a song with my band during one of our encores. My brother Dave and Chris liked one another, but I suspect there was more rivalry between her band and mine than I'd first thought. Perhaps I would have felt equally miffed if Dave's girlfriend had come on to do a song or two with the Kinks. This came to a head when the Kinks played JFK Stadium in Philadelphia on June 19, 1982. We'd done an incredible show, and I invited Chris on to do an encore with us. This resulted in a backstage eruption afterward and ended with Dave storming off in his own car. As Elliot rightly said later, it was a "close call" on my part, bearing in mind my brother's sensitivity on a professional level to my relationship with Chris. Perhaps I was wrong to invite her onstage. Perhaps I was and still am wrong in judging many things having to do with my brother, but I never did anything to intentionally harm him. Perhaps he was dealing with his own issues.

There was obviously more that was contributing to the uneasy relationship in my personal life caused by the continual separations and demands of two careers. Where there is touring, there are always rumours, and even if they are not true it erodes trust over time—particularly in the madcap world of touring with rock bands.

Nonetheless, on occasions when we were left alone, without the pressures we both had, it was a walk in Central Park holding hands on a bright summer's day. As I subsequently wrote in a song:

"On reflection, it was not all wine on the wall. . . .
On reflection, it was not all crash and bang.
Broken bottles and abuse
Sometimes there were sunsets on the sands.
Holding on to caring hands
But there were vampire fangs as the angels sang.
It was yin and yang. . . .
True love is really animal."

RETURN TO WATERLOO, 1983–84

D ave's solo albums obviously gave him some kind of artistic freedom, but now I was on the verge of doing a side project of my own and had written a couple of TV scripts. One was a show that I had originally written to accompany the *Give the People What They Want* album—then later abandoned—and the other was a new piece about commuters on a suburban railway line in the south of England, *Return to Waterloo*.

"Not very rock and roll," Dave rightly said, but I had pitched the idea to Channel 4, a new and experimental London TV station, and they thought it pretentious enough to commission it. I would write a script with new songs and put the two together in a new format inspired partly by the arrival of MTV. I saw such a project as a natural extension of the Kinks' career in the early days of long-form video and something that could stand alone as a piece of musical drama on television.

I was beginning preproduction of *Return to Waterloo*, which marked my debut as a television director, when Dave expressed his unwillingness to participate in the recorded soundtrack of the TV show. Perhaps Dave was savvy enough to come to the conclusion that *Return to Waterloo* was an "art piece" and would not enhance our rock credentials. I don't know exactly why he refused to play, but he later agreed to let some of the *Return to Waterloo* tracks appear on the next Kinks album even though he wasn't playing on them.

One poignant moment occurred as I was setting up my first shot on location for *Return to Waterloo*. My assistant director handed me a badly wrapped gift—a pen with a digital clock built into the side of it. I was surprised to discover that it was a good luck gift from Chris and our baby daughter, Natalie. This was an unusual gift from her. Flowers, particularly roses, were more her style, but this particular present represented something more to me. It suggested that we were running out of time. Less than four months later, Chris and Natalie were both gone. The day before Chris embarked on her world tour in January of 1984, I carried Natalie into a church in Maida Vale, near where we were staying at the time. I said a prayer that basically asked for Natalie to be okay. I knew the separation was coming but couldn't accept it. For a while all the songs in the world could not console me; somehow I had to keep it together.

WORKING AT THE FACTORY, 1984–86

The making of the next Kinks studio album, *Word of Mouth*, was full of bad feeling and rifts between me and Dave. My breakup with Chris in the spring of 1984, which was well-publicised, temporarily knocked me off my creative path while I reorganised my personal life. Clive Davis was also concerned that my writing and general studio performance might be affected by the breakup, but the album was still on schedule, and the playing of the band was up to the usual standard. My eldest daughter, Louisa, and her boyfriend moved in with me while I recorded and she sang backup vocals on some songs on the *Return to Waterloo* sound track. Less than a year after *State of Confusion*, *Word of Mouth* emerged as the next and final Kinks album of the Arista deal.

Clive went straight into renegotiating a new deal with very fair terms for the Kinks, but our management, and particularly Dave, wanted to move onto fresh fields. More important, they wanted higher advances so that we didn't have to subsidize our albums by doing long tours. MCA Records must have been dangling a chequebook in front of Dave's "advisers," and without my knowledge, someone started negotiations with the company and its new president, Irving Azoff. My London lawyers were still negotiating with Clive because I saw him as a quintessential driving force in the revival of the Kinks in the United States. My relationship with Clive meant that there was a definite creative empathy between record company and artist, whereas it seemed to me that—without putting them down unduly—MCA just seemed interested in obtaining our "product." This was not their fault. Contracts can spell out the product commitment, commercial conditions, and artist's obligations in the most intimate detail but they cannot specify one crucial ingredient—that is how to create chemistry between the artist and its label.

I met with Clive again in New York, and we talked about the pros and cons and struck what appeared to have been a deal. A week later, during a U.S. tour, I received a message from my confused UK lawyer informing me that Arista had suddenly pulled out of all negotiations. Apparently an article in a trade magazine said that MCA had signed the Kinks. I was disappointed and outraged because I'd never even taken a meeting with MCA at that point. Who had done this? Was it my paranoia, or was it just mischievous publicity-mongering on the side of MCA or speculation on the part of the magazine?

Nevertheless, the damage was done. I was heartbroken, and, by all accounts, so was Clive. We had worked hard and successfully together. It was more than an artist–record company relationship—it was a musical friendship, a marriage between art and business, but now that bond was broken. More than anything else, Clive understood the Kinks. He appreciated my writing—he knew that I wrote for characters and that these characters populated the Kinks' world. Now these characters had to learn to function in a more corporate world, which was not such an understanding place.

Word of Mouth also marked a crucial event—the departure of the original Kinks drummer, Mick Avory. Dave and Mick had continued their quarelling over the years, and it had become at times unbearable to witness. Anyone who cares knows about my spats with Dave, but brothers can have monumental quarrels that can be put down to normal sibling rivalry.

When Mick and Dave went at each other it was brutal; even minders like Tony and Big Bob backed off. Dave also felt that we should part company with our manager, Elliot Abbott. This was another blow to me. Elliot and I had worked really closely together, but Dave didn't seem to see the sense in that. *Return to Waterloo* had proved to be a small success for me as a writer-director, and Elliot had asked me to move to L.A. to focus on making movies—a move I chose not to make at the time and an opportunity I still regret not taking. Elliot was going. Now I was having to part company with my chum Mick Avory.

I would often speculate what the "last gig" would be like; the last concert put on by the original band. We didn't know it at the time, but Mick's last performance as a member of the Kinks in America was in Cedar Rapids in late January 1984. His last date ever with the band was a few months later on March 9, at DeMontfort Hall in Leicester. These were just dates on an itinerary at the time, and we thought nothing of it. If we had thought about what was happening, it would have been too emotional to contemplate.

The departure of Mick Avory and the arrival of drummer Bob Henrit ushered in a new era for the Kinks. Bob brought a new drumming sound; it was less sympathetic, perhaps, with my lyrical vocal style, but it was more aggressive and driving, and our subsequent albums were more powerful and sonically driven than our Arista albums. But somehow I missed the happy errors and "comedy drums" that Mick played, and as a result I felt a lack of poetry in the finished product. The learning curve for me was steep as I gradually got my head around Bob's drumming style. In many ways Bob had a more American sound, which was appropriate for our newly found audience. Dave thrived on Bob's "slamming," his sonically superior sound, which had also been part of my brother's solo albums. In a strange way, having Bob Henrit in the group helped put more of Dave's stamp on it. However, I was still the person who had to write and produce Kinks albums; by now this was even to be specified in our new contract. Even though we had larger recording budgets than we had at Arista, it was harder to make the records live up to corporate expectations, which were later explained to me by Irving Azoff: "Just make the same records that you have always made, and if they sell better than the others we'll be happy." According to music business insiders, the deal with them was already done even though I had not put my signature to, or even seen a contract, so I wanted to quietly go to L.A. to meet the people I would be working with to see if we got along.

THE FIRST TIME I WENT TO THE MCA OFFICES IN L.A., I asked for Irving Azoff at the front desk. But even though he was the new head of the company—the brilliant entrepreneur and manager who'd masterminded the career of the Eagles and other bands—they couldn't find his name on the long list of employees. He was lost in the Rolodex at a major corporation.

This was supposed to be a secret meeting to explore the possibilities of working together. Arista had backed out but there were a few other labels interested in the Kinks too, so I wanted to keep the meeting as low-key as possible. In L.A. music circles, this would prove to be impossible. Irving took me to the Palm restaurant for lunch, where it seemed that everyone and anyone in the record industry was also having lunch. There, other interested corporate "suits" came over to our booth to congratulate Irving on his new position and congratulate me on my success with Arista. Then it was off to the Forum for a Lakers basketball game. We did not sit in an out-of-the-way seat in a secluded corner, but in the front row, where we could be seen by the world.

At least I was temporarily distracted from my predicament by watching Jack Nicholson jump up and down in his court side seat in an excited and animated way as he supported his team.

After the game, Irving and I were walking to the parking lot when a car pulled up beside us. The window rolled down to reveal the smiling face of Tom Ross, one of our agents at Creative Artists Agency. Tom didn't even stop the car, but spoke as he drove past. "Have you guys closed the deal yet?" I knew there was no way out. I longed to be at the down-to-earth Utopia Diner on the Upper West Side of Manhattan, but here I was hanging around Beverly Hills, completely miscast in the role of L.A. Ray. It was a tactical coup for Irving and MCA—all the other labels had either been frightened off or had already lost interest. Now my UK lawyers had to negotiate from a weakened position. MCA sent over Zach Horowitz, who proved to be a formidable negotiator. Observing these negotiations proved to me that American corporate attorneys were light-years ahead of UK solicitors. I watched Zach psych my guys out while my team conceded point after point. It was awesome to watch and almost a privilege to observe what to me was the bizarre and unnerving efficiency of corporate Americana in operation. There were many competent people at MCA—very capable in their own way—but there didn't seem to be anyone there to give the Kinks the focus that we had at Arista. I soon didn't feel like an artist anymore. I was lost—literally—in a state of confusion.

Meanwhile, Elliot had moved from his house in the Hollywood Hills to Tarzana, in the San Fernando Valley. (I later found out that the area was originally founded as a suburb by *Tarzan of the Apes* author Edgar Rice Burroughs, and it was named after his most well-known character. I was a little shocked to discover that in 1919, Tarzana was meant to be a whites-only suburb.) Once when Elliot and I were having a meeting with Ken Jones and my booking agent at CAA, Elliot had to get home and said he had to leave early to beat the L.A. traffic. When he left the room, Jones quipped sarcastically, "Yeah, it's a long drive to Tarzana." I thought Jonesy's comment strange because at rush hour everywhere in greater L.A. is difficult to get to.

It was an off-the-cuff remark, but to me the subtext implied that Elliot might have had enough. The remark stayed in my head, and I often quote it whenever I see a situation coming to an end. It also summed up the journey we made from east (Arista, in New York) to west (MCA, in Los Angeles), in which the freeway took the place of the wagon train. At this time, I visited Elliot at his home in Tarzana to try to make some sense of the whole mess created by the MCA-Arista mix-up. I never got to the bottom of what actually happened. We had made the journey west, but there were so many unanswered questions and so many unresolved issues. Elliot was a good man, but even he was confused. I left him by the pool at his house to go back to my hotel and discovered that it is also a long drive home *from* Tarzana.

As I travelled back from L.A., I thought back to the times in New York when I would bump into Arista employees on Columbus Avenue. I'd see Abbey Konowitch, Dennis Fine, and Richard Palmese standing on a street corner discussing the promotion of a Kinks album with Elliot, who had an apartment a few blocks away from Michael Kleffner's place on West End Avenue. I knew that Clive was always nearby to make a decision or comment about my music. Unforgettable days.

Now the Kinks' career was heading west, at least in a corporate sense. MCA had an office in New York, but all the real decisions were made on the West Coast. As is true of so many idealistic journeys, the opportunities were not as bountiful as expected at the end of the road. The Kinks' wagon train had made it across the great canyons, survived attacks by predators, and endured thirst in the barren waste of the desert only to reach a new corporate nirvana.

> *"It's a long, long way to Paradise isn't it?*
> *In the never-ending search for perfection*
> *And it seems like an eternity, since we first turned the ignition*
> *And took our trip down the highway.*
> *Because I told you lies*
> *It seems a silent never-ending drive.*
> *Now the West Coast is getting near*
> *Soon all our doubts will disappear.*
> *It's a long drive home to Tarzana*
> *And once we're there we will see there's nothing there except the space*
> *Beautiful space . . .*
> *Travelled so far to find this place.*
> *It's a long drive home to Tarzana*
> *That spaced-out community*
> *All freeways lead to Tarzana.*
> *No more ghettoes.*
> *Just open road*
> *That's fine with me."*

The thing is, that as hard as we wanted success, as hard as we worked to get there . . . well, it's like the Gertrude Stein line: once you get there, you find "there is no there there." I bet old Gertie would have understood. It's a long drive home to Tarzana. Even though it is not near the sea, it represented the end of this particular journey.

One of the songs on our first album for MCA summed up my predicament—"Working at the Factory":

"All my life, I've been a workin' man
When I was at school they said that's all you'll ever understand.
No profession, I didn't figure in their plans
So they sent me down the factory to be a workin' man
All I lived for, all I lived for
All I lived for was to get out of the factory
Now I'm here seemingly free, But working at the factory.
Then music came along and gave new life to me
And gave me hope back in 1963
The music came and set me free
From working at the factory. . . .

All my life I've put in a working day
Now it's sign the contract, get production on the way
Take the money, make the music pay
Working at the factory.
All I lived for was to get out of the factory
Never wanted to be like everybody else
But now there are so many like me sitting on the shelf
They sold us a dream that in reality
Was just another factory."

If I had been honest with myself, I would have realised that music never made me free. The moment we had success was the moment we entered the factory. It seemed that freedom is an illusion; the secret is to always try to be free in your head. Like my old song says *"I'm not like everybody else."* No one, whoever they are, can take away your freedom to speak out. If we had been making music for a truly dictatorial label they would have vetted the song and not allowed it to be released. On the other hand, a darker force would have let the song go out but simply not promoted it. Even the great artists of the past needed benefactors. Rembrandt, Michelangelo, Caravaggio, and the rest all relied on financial support from the rich and powerful in order to get their work done. I should have been grateful that MCA offered to take us on; in many ways I was determined to make it work. Perhaps it was time to change from Arista after all. I was down because I'd lost a few workmates and friends on the journey, but it was only a matter of time before Arista became absorbed by a bigger conglomerate, which meant that Clive's time would become even more precious and he would be less available. I decided to turn it around. I said to myself, "You know, it's okay. It's good to move on." There would be some great new opportunities at MCA.

What bothered me even more was my creative relationship with my brother. There were a load of issues to resolve, and the thought of it scared me. Now we had no one to act as mediator except Ken Jones, and Dave's new personal relationship had made it frustrating to get a hold of him. Nevertheless, I kept coming up with more songs. The first MCA album, *Think Visual* (1986), contained some songs that made me proud: "The Video Shop," "How Are You?" and "Lost and Found," for which I directed an epic video that still makes me smile. In it, a black-and-white 35mm period drama (which I also directed and performed in) is projected on a cinema screen while the Kinks provide the music from a soundstage. At the end of the silent movie (filmed in my back garden) the tragic hero holds his leading lady and promises that they will confront the "hurricane and storms" of life and "face the future . . . without fear." Perhaps the video for "Lost and Found" was telling me that I was temporarily lost, but I would find myself again. That would work for the movie but would it actually happen in the real world?

18

AFTER THE FALL

"Ask yourself why you go through it all
When morality kicks in who will catch you when you fall
I'm a sinner waiting at the traveller's rest
Seeking refuge from a storm, and I'm a grateful guest
Then a prophet cries out in high platitude . . .
Even at the gates of heaven I'll be waiting in a queue. . . ."

NEW ORLEANS, JANUARY 7, 2004

The doctor's words sounded like a message of hope. "Let's get you home today, Mr. Davies."

Home, I thought. "Where is that?" For the moment it was New Orleans; I had a titanium rod holding my femur together. There was a risk of infection from the bullet wound, and my ticker was acting up, so I wasn't going anywhere in a hurry. Bob and Jeanne had offered me some space to recuperate in their house.

I was trying to get my few possessions together, but then there was another problem. During checkout, the registrar said the ambulance couldn't take me because someone said my insurance wouldn't cover it. I had no cash, but in any event they would prefer that I pay with a credit card. It was a Saturday, so my insurance man was not available. J.J. jumped into the situation. "Excuse me. We were . . . robbed. All the . . . credit cards were taken. I'll carry him out of here myself if I have to. . . ." She argued the case with such attitude and conviction that the hospital registrar backed off. Within an hour an ambulance crew arrived to carry me out of the hospital.

The ambulance arrived outside Bob and Jeanne's old sprawling colonial-style home, which displayed decaying grandeur alongside Bob's modernistic sculptures in the front garden. Giant slabs were piled on top of one another.

A gigantic swordfish hung from a tree. The woman paramedic gasped.

"I know this house. I used to play around this neighbourhood when I was a kid. I wondered who lived here."

Just at that moment Bob and Jeanne arrived at the front gate to welcome us. Bob, an elegant-looking sixty something, walked with the aid of a cane. Jeanne, a little younger, was pretty, curvy, and opinionated.

The first problem: how to get me up the winding staircase to the top floor. The strapping woman paramedic suggested that she and her partner just carry my wheelchair up the stairs. "Heave-ho. One. . . . two . . . three." Problem solved.

The second problem: they wouldn't get me into the double bed Bob and Jeanne had set up because the paramedics considered it too high. I could fall out of bed during the night and injure myself. Bob rummaged around in the garden and came back with some cinder blocks. He skilfully built a makeshift staircase beside the bed, but the paramedics still considered the bed too high. Then Jeanne suggested that I take the attic sitting room, where her mother used to stay, because it had a low sofa. The paramedics agreed it was suitable, settled me in, and went on their way.

Third problem: after the paramedics left, my temperature started to soar. Jeanne went out for my medication, and Bob stood watch over me. I told him to write down my temperature and take a note of the time. I began to panic. I sensed that Bob was beginning to get scared. He called Dr. Lander, who said it might be advisable to take me back to the emergency room. I prayed that my temperature would go down so that I wouldn't have to return to the hospital. Eventually my body reached an even temperature, but I was sick all night all around Bob and Jeanne's attic flat.

I had a small single sofa, which, when covered by Jeanne's exotically embroidered pillows, resembled a throne suitable for a sultan. The look was exotic, but the reality was that it was totally impractical for a recovering gunshot victim. Nevertheless the sofa gave the place an air of elegance, which would come in handy if ever I received visitors. The simple matter of getting out of bed became my first daily chore. I developed a knack for slipping my good left foot under the injured one to give it support and then sliding myself around and off the couch down to the floor. Once there I could push myself up, supported by my crutches. Then I could make my way through to the kitchen area, which led into the bathroom. Once in the bathroom, the whole exercise of using the toilet while holding my right leg straight posed a new set of problems.

I eventually developed a technique in which my left knee was jammed against the end of the tub while my right (broken) leg jutted out horizontally to the right side, almost like a ballet dancer in the midst of a giant leap. Timing was of the utmost importance. Because of all the medication I was taking, my bodily functions were, to say the least, unpredictable. J.J. volunteered to stay on in another room to look after me because my rooms were too far away from the main house. Her room was further on past the bathroom, and she placed a small cowbell at the side of my bed that I could ring whenever an emergency arose. Rather "unrock" and roll, but at least the cowbell instilled a degree of dignity to the situation, as well as some heavy-metal moments when in desperate need I had to beat it out four to the bar.

Anything to do with mobility became arduous. Movements that normally would be taken for granted became tedious. I would manage to make a cup of tea in the kitchen, and then realise there was no way to transport it to my bedside. Even in New Orleans there is still a chill in the air on January mornings, which made it preferable to eat and drink under the covers of the sofa. The apartment was last used by Jeanne's mother, who, sadly, had died, and in the corner of the kitchen I discovered a walker with wheels and a small Formica top. This enabled me to have some degree of mobility, but I still had to use my crutches, so the only way I could use the walker as a meal cart was to push it around with my body. This process inevitably took up a large amount of time, and by the time I'd finished my morning tea it was almost time to start lunch.

Somehow, this simple existence was of some benefit to me. Until the shooting I had been living in an alternative or parallel universe, where I saw everything in song or lyric form. I viewed every person as a potential character to write about. However, the predicament I now found myself in made me realise that real life does not necessarily have a beginning, middle, and end. It just goes by moment by moment; day after day. This enforced "stop" was of some use. Maybe it was showing me that life must occasionally stop.

Like so many other people I had met in New Orleans, I had been running through, or away from, and at times into, something or someone. Yet people can only run so far before they come back to themselves. The immovable "You" is always there, whether you like it or not—despite all the diversions and obstacles you try to put in the way.

This period gave me the opportunity to think about the habits that I and everybody else inadvertently build up throughout our lives. Once I was given painkillers just so that I could get through a tour. I thought about the extravagant measures doctors go to in order to "fix you up" so that you can get up onstage. I once cut the knuckles on my left hand before two sold-out shows at the Meadowlands in New Jersey. Every time I bent my hand to play a chord, the wound opened and the knucklebones were exposed. Stitching up the wound wouldn't work, because the stitches would come out during my performance. A paramedic came up with a solution. He took some white powder that looked like cocaine out of a bag and filled my knuckle wounds with it. This both stopped the bleeding and killed the pain. In fact it worked so well that he repeated the procedure the following night. I also had a toothache at the time, so he gave me some magic white painkiller to rub in my gums before the show. Then I remembered that a Harley Street back specialist had once prescribed synthetic morphine to alleviate my chronic back pain while I was on tour, and that I had become a zombie in the true meaning of the word—not quite dead, but not really alive. It got me through the tour though, and that's all that mattered to everyone.

Now, because of my injury, I was forced to rest during the day, and at night I actually fell asleep naturally. Perhaps this violent episode made me realise that I had to heal myself of so many things. WWOZ played Dixieland and blues in the mornings. I found myself getting into a pattern again. There *was* life after breakfast, consoling and mocking me at the same time.

"Is there life after breakfast?
Yes there is, after breakfast
So don't live in agony
Is there life after breakfast?
Yes there is, after breakfast.

AMERICANA

Cheer up son, put on the kettle
There's no point in being glum
Make your mind up, try to forget her
Boil the tea and I'll be mum. . . .

Just because all of the plumbing
Isn't all it used to be
Turn the tap, see, a little bit's coming
That must make you feel relieved."

19

SCATTERED

"Sitting alone in my hotel
Looking in the mirror wondering, 'Well,
After all this time you never thought you'd still be out on the road?'"

THE ROAD, NEW YORK AND EUROPE, 1988–89

The Kinks embarked on our first MCA album, *Think Visual*, full of energy and enthusiasm. Richard Palmese had left Arista to join Irving Azoff, so there was more continuity between the company and the artist than I first expected, even though their West Coast location still presented a geographical problem for me. The Kinks made some good records for MCA, but there was one album that nearly killed me. It was called *The Kinks Live: The Road*.

During the tour to promote *Think Visual* we recorded many of the concerts, hoping to amass enough material for a live album that would have an impact similar to that of our 1980 live album, *One for the Road*. I also wanted to give some songs from our first MCA album, released a year earlier, another airing. In many cases these live performances were much more energised than the original studio recordings. I had also written two new songs for the album; an experimental jazz-rock piece called "It" and a new studio track called "The Road." Because the album was "scheduled" before it was actually made, the recording, mixing, and touring schedule was compressed in order to make both the release deadline for the album in May 1988 and the band's upcoming summer European dates. At this time, I was spending more and more time in Ireland, and I was frequently flying back and forth to New York, where I was planning a documentary for Channel 4 television about jazz bass player and composer Charles Mingus. My musical *80 Days*—about Jules Verne—was to open in La Jolla, California, in August 1988, so I was a busy boy, to say the least.

The Road was mixed at a residential studio called Puk, near the city of Randers, Denmark. I felt I could focus more on the mixing in Scandinavia, where I wouldn't get distracted by the other projects that were starting to collide with my record production. The title track was about our days on tour, and I was very pleased with the way it seemed to sum up our life as a band at this point. Postproduction went well, and we got all the tracks mixed to perfection. Overall I felt that this album was better organised than our last live album. More to the point, it was on schedule.

I flew straight from Denmark to New York to cut the record at Masterdisk with eminent engineer Bob Ludwig. He was ready to start mastering when he noticed something as we played the mixed tracks back.

Every time Bob played back the quarter-inch digital AGFA tape it started shedding. The quality of sound was becoming affected as the tape disintegrated. As a result the sound had clicks and drop-outs increasing every time it was played, and Bob was so concerned that he was reluctant to play the tape anymore. After more investigation it was discovered that the condition arose because that batch of AGFA tape was defective. For a time we thought we had lost everything on the record, and then I remembered that as a precaution I had put down a stereo mix onto two tracks of the master tape while it was being mixed, which meant that we had a copy within the master multitrack itself. That tape was still stored at the studio in rural Denmark but after a series of panicky phone calls, the multitrack tapes were flown from Denmark to New York, where Bob rented a multitrack machine from Mitsubishi on which he could play back the safety mixes. The head honchos of Mitsubishi sales and maintenance came down to the cutting room, concerned that there was a problem with the compatibility of the quarter-inch digital tape and their machinery. This proved to be the case, but Bob managed to salvage the mixes from the multitrack before putting them onto another trusted backup format.

The record was ready to be mastered, but because of the mixing issue, the mastering had been delayed by a week. I had to attend to the mastering process over the Thanksgiving weekend. There is an old music-hall song about England with the line "everything stops for tea." Well, in America, I discovered that everything stops for Thanksgiving. Because of his prior commitments, Bob was unable to work, so I had to stay in New York rather than travel to London to visit my mother, who had been taken ill with cancer. There was a debate about whether I should stay in New York to finish the record after Thanksgiving or fly to London to be by my mother's bedside, which in turn would have possibly delayed the release of the record. My return tickets had already been booked prior to the mastering delay, so to clarify the situation, I phoned London and spoke to Mum's doctor. He said that she would be fine for another few weeks and that it would be all right to stay in New York to complete the project. I rearranged all my flights accordingly and told Bob I would be in the studio the day after the Thanksgiving holiday. The next day I received a phone call from London to say that my mother had suddenly died. I spoke to my brother, Dave, who was helping look after Mum with my sister Gwen. When they told me the news I shouted, "Check. It might be a mistake!" Dave simply said there was no mistake; the doctor had pronounced her dead.

I'd had a telephone conversation with Mum a day or so before and was shocked to hear how much she was struggling through her pain. All through her life, I had never seen her so much as take an aspirin, so it must have been humiliating for her to be subjected to hospital treatment and medication. The doctors had allowed her to leave the hospital to stay at my sister's home. According to Gwen, Mum kept talking about "a beautiful lady in a long, flowing dress" who kept coming to reassure her and help relieve her pain. Apparently, just before she passed away, Mum called my sister into her room. Her eyes stared past my sister, as if she were looking at a heavenly vision. "Gwennie, the woman is there again. The one in the blue dress, and she is telling me not to be afraid." Then, according to my sister, my mother's head dropped back and she passed away.

I walked around the Upper West Side of New York in a total daze. I saw Mum on every corner, and eventually I stopped at a church on Amsterdam Avenue to sit inside. Prayers seemed like irrelevant excuses for not being there with her when she died—all because of a wretched delivery schedule. Now, though, the product commitment seemed secondary.

I had to make rapid changes to my schedule so that I could be home for the funeral, but I had a few days to reorganise. During my stay in New York, I had been at Calliope Studios to make some demos for the *80 Days* musical, which I was going to give to Des McAnuff, the artistic director at the La Jolla Playhouse, when I next saw him in L.A. There was one song called "Just Passing Through," which Jules Verne sings to Phileas Fogg—the fictional protagonist of Verne's book *Around the World in Eighty Days*—as they journey through India. I had set up a chorus of chanting fishermen to accompany Verne and Fogg as they sail down the Ganges River. Fogg describes things he sees as the fishermen chant a mantra, but he is oblivious to any significant spiritual meaning behind the chants. Fogg is only looking at the sights, whereas the fishermen chant to enlighten their daily existence until they pass into a better world. Suddenly Verne bursts into the song, exposing Fogg as a stubborn, unfeeling Englishman who is not moved by anything. In the show, Verne has unwittingly created his ultimate monster. A man with no passion or love.

> *"I suspect you must be a man without feeling*
> *You only look without seeing*
> *Always on the move but only passing through."*

I played the demo at the apartment, put myself in the role of Fogg, and became guilt-ridden. I was only doing my job, finalizing our album, but because of that horrible delay caused by the tape machines I had not been able to finish in time to be at my mother's bedside.

I left instructions with the record company, who would master the record without me. Then I went to the airport and flew back to London on the red-eye in time for the funeral the following morning. Before the funeral, I stopped by my mother's apartment and sat in her living room. It was more or less the way she'd left it before being taken to the hospital and released to die in the front room of my sister's house. There were tell-tale signs of concern here and there, such as a pamphlet about living with cancer. An early Christmas present for my daughter Natalie. Cigarettes stubbed out in an ashtray; attempts at writing her life story on the backs of birthday cards—all the clues of a person's acceptance that life is coming to an end.

I wasn't aware of it at the time, but my mind was taking in images of what I saw. Not in a hard, unfeeling, Phileas Fogg way, but in the way a more sensitive person would collect information in order to grieve. It would have been disrespectful to take notes, but the images were ingrained in my memory.

"Like a seed that is sown, all the children are scattered
By a breeze that is blown, now the crops are all scattered
We are torn, we are shattered, and some of us are barmy and battered
And the fields where we gathered are overgrown in weeds and in tatters
Through it all we were scattered.

To the fields we are scattered, from the day we are born
To grow wild and sleep rough, till from the earth we are torn
And a soul that is free, can live on eternally
And the spirit can live on, though it's scattered in the world beyond
And I've been out of my mind, ever since she's been gone.

I look around that empty room, no sight nor sound
She's left so soon, she's out of view
But then I find, those scattered clues she left behind
A photograph with a smiling face, a cigarette stubbed out on the
*   fireplace*
A coffee cup with her lipstick stains, I guess I'll never see her again.

Now my life is all scattered, ever since she's been gone.
I feel older, I feel fatter, I feel the blues coming on
We get bruised, we get battered
But we'll pick up the pieces that scattered
And with emotional glue, we're gonna stick together body and mind.

Ever since she went away, I've been alone to contemplate
Time and space and why worlds move, while sitting in my solitude.
I've watched the stars and wondered why, they're scattered up there
*   in the sky*
And is she up there out of view, on some higher platitude.

I wish I knew, wish I could prove
The reason why this life on earth is scattered like the universe
I'm scattered here and scattered there, bits of me scattered everywhere.

To the fields we are scattered, then from the dust we are born
We survive somewhat battered, to a new life, a new dawn
In the end what will it matter, there'll only be my ashes to scatter
And all the logical answers to a worrying mind
Will be scattered in time, beaten and battered
To the earth you are scattered, you're going home so what
    does it matter
To an atomic mind, scattered here while you travel time."

Then I went into Mum's bedroom. I looked on the wall, and there was a picture I had bought her a few years earlier of an elegant Victorian woman wearing a flowing blue dress. Through that image, I felt I had been with Mum in spirit when she died.

AFTER THE FUNERAL, I FLEW BACK TO LOS ANGELES to meet with Des McAnuff. I told him about my mother's vision of the woman in the blue dress; a story that he found chilling. During the flight over to L.A., I started getting pains in my lower abdomen; I thought it was just nerves or tension due to the stress of my mother's death and finishing the record, so I ignored it. Directly after the meetings in L.A., at the beginning of December, I flew to Berlin to start the tour with the Kinks.

On the long overnight flight from L.A. to Berlin, I started writing a short poem called "Breakfast in Berlin." On arrival in Germany I purchased a German-English dictionary, which I used to start cobbling together a semi-legible lyric: "*Frühstückinnen Berlin* [Breakfast in Berlin] . . . *west of the Wall, East, West, what's the difference . . . left right all the same. In the end nothing matters . . . blah blah blah. Geographically speaking, I'm insane.*" It was a stream-of-consciousness piece involving my mother's generation, who'd lived through the Second World War, combined with a psychodrama about a writer who receives messages in his letter box containing clues about a great event that is about to happen. At the time I put it down to a grieving process combined with tiredness, but the message from the anonymous informant kept telling me that something significant was about to occur. I put this all down to jet lag and decided to abandon the idea for the time being in order to get on with my touring schedule.

During that tour, the pain in my abdomen started to spread to my chest. In Frankfurt they had diagnosed it as an ulcer, and by the time we got to Hamburg the doctor said I should have an ECG when I got back to London. I wasn't quite sure what an ECG entailed, but it sounded daunting. When we played Hanover, I was in such pain that I couldn't sing the last few songs; Dave had to sing "You Really Got Me" and "All Day and All of the Night" while I collapsed in the dressing room. The tour ended up in London, where we played a three-hour set at the Town & Country Club on December 20.

The following morning I went to the doctor for a checkup, and he rushed me straight to a hospital in the West End. Apparently he suspected I had a case of deep vein thrombosis. The consulting cardiologist I saw must have had a gap in his schedule because he wanted to do bypass surgery straightaway, but I felt I couldn't trust his diagnosis. In any event, I wanted to go to Ireland for Christmas. I looked at the doctor—who was so tastefully dressed that wouldn't have seemed out of place in a shop window in Savile Row—and explained that I would think about my options over the holiday. I arrived in Ireland in terrible pain and met the local doctor, who kindly opened his modest office late in order to see me. He said, "I'm a great fan, but if you don't get into the hospital immediately, Mr. Davies, you're going to die." Fortunately, there was a space for me at a hospital in Cork, where I was examined by an excellent cardiologist who had actually seen us play many years earlier. I was then sent to Dublin for surgery, which successfully removed the blockage.

After a short rest, I went straight to New York to prepare for the tour to promote our second MCA album, *The Road*. This was all part of the marketing strategy that had been arranged through an office building in Hollywood. The machinery of the corporate world was at work again, and on a very strict delivery deadline. We cobbled together a quite good promotional video for *The Road* with English editor Peter Shelton on a rented system at an apartment in New York, using footage I'd shot over the years as well as footage shot at the last UK gig.

THE THIRD MCA ALBUM was provisionally called *Breakfast in Berlin*, to tie in with the upcoming fiftieth anniversary of the beginning of the Second World War. Things had changed in Europe since the war, especially with the advent of the EEC, though I remained a Eurosceptic. I wrote a whole film treatment based on the notes I had made on my flight from L.A. to Berlin a year earlier. I envisioned that the songs on the album—such as "Down All the Days (Till 1992)," "War Is Over," and another song called "Now and Then," about how trivial politics really is compared to people's lives—would be used to score the film. How would I present such a highfalutin idea to an American rock-and-roll audience? After discussions with MCA's rapidly changing marketing staff, we came up with the idea that the album should be called *UK Jive* instead of *Breakfast in Berlin* so it would resonate with people who still remembered the British Invasion. In hindsight, I wish I'd stayed with my plan and made it a conceptualised videodisc. This would have been in keeping with the times and would have made the message of the record clearly understood. Then I remembered one of Clive Davis's aphorisms: "If you have a message to send, use Western Union." It wasn't enough to get records on the radio anymore. We had to get into the psyche of the DJs, who were now becoming more insightful about the music they were playing, resulting in them being more opinionated about the lyrical content of a song. In theory this was perfect for the music we were making. If they understood the record, they would play it. I had also started writing a song about my mother, called "Scattered," but the album's release date was too close, and I didn't have time to record the song properly. In any event, the content of "Scattered" seemed too personal.

Making the *UK Jive* album was interrupted by trips to San Diego, where I was writing and workshopping *80 Days*. In a curious way, my Englishness was written through the Phileas Fogg character and all his cohorts in the upper-class Victorian establishment at London's Reform Club. In our version of Verne's novel, Fogg eventually travels to America, arriving in a blaze of publicity at San Francisco. To write this song I had the opportunity to step out of my rock-and-roll persona and write a few tunes from an older, more traditional American Broadway musical perspective. For a regional theatre, La Jolla Playhouse offered an incredible music department, including Danny Troob and English book writer Snoo Wilson; with Des McAnuff as artistic director, we had the pick of Broadway and West Coast theatre talent. I christened us the "high achievers." We certainly had to be in order to get such an ambitious project together in such a short time.

Writing songs for the Brits was relatively straightforward, but writing for the American characters gave me the most fun. An actress called Randy Graff played the part of Nellie Bly, the gung ho journalist who welcomes Fogg to the United States. I thought about all the great musicals I'd seen as a kid; I thought about Sousa marching band music, about cheerleaders and ticker-tape parades. My mum had been an Ethel Merman fan, and Mum's voice sounded not unlike that of the great Broadway actress. I didn't want to write a "welcome to America" song, but I thought I should include something with a "Star-Spangled Banner" feel to it, so I wrote a song incorporating all these elements for Randy to sing as the gutsy female reporter Nellie Bly. The song is called "Here."

> *NELLIE: He's got his deadline timed right to the minute,*
> *He's got a schedule that's so far been on time*
> *He's surely got to be some kind of super being*
> *The kind of hero that this nation loves to find.*
> *He symbolises the spirit of this land*
> *That recognises and praises this kind of superman*
> *He thinks he's seen the world.*
> *REPORTERS: Yeah, Yeah.*
> *NELLIE: He ain't seen nothing yet.*
> *REPORTERS: No, No.*
> *NELLIE: We've got the greatest show*
> *That he will never forget.*
> *We've got the get up and go*
> *We've got the energy here*
> *We've got the scenery here.*

ENSEMBLE: Yes it's time for celebration jubilation.

NELLIE: Let's give him a cheer such a welcome

When he arrives he'll always want to stay here.

[Four women, Daughters of the American Revolution, step forward
    smartly on the welcoming platform]

D.A.R.: From coast to coast, we've got everything we'll put it all on show.

REPORTERS: Yes, Ma'am.

D.A.R.: We got the biggest, brightest, and the best right here in San
    Francisco.

ALL: Energy, energy, vitality, vitality.

NELLIE BLY: I know this man is really something special his
    punctuality must be revered

So do your best to show him something special.

ALL: Show him that we are sincere.

NELLIE: And if you've got a goal

You can achieve it here.

And if you've seen it all

Just wait till you get here.

NELLIE and ENSEMBLE: And when you win that race just listen

To us cheer 'cause we appreciate and

Love a winner here!

NELLIE BLY: We've got the Mississippi, Great Missouri, Salt Lake,
    Utah,

All across the Rockies to the Carolinas back to California

From coast to coast, we've got everything

We'll put it all on show, 'cause we're the biggest, we're the brightest

We're the newest and mightiest.

ALL: We're gonna show you we're the empire of tomorrow.

NELLIE: He's got his timing down right to the second here he comes;

I think I see him now let's show him something really special!

NELLIE and MEN: Let's show this Limey how.

NELLIE BLY: If you've got something to say you've got the freedom
    here . . .

WOMEN: And if you want to play, the recreation's right here.

NELLIE BLY: If you've got something to prove you can achieve it here
And if you want to stay we'll gladly welcome you—here!

My other American song was sung by a love-struck princess as a group of hillbillies took Verne and Fogg across the American Wild West. The hillbillies sang about the landscape while the princess supplied the romantic counterpoint in the song. When I'd first met Chrissie Hynde we discussed how difficult it would be for us to stay together. Working on *80 Days* and writing for Phileas Fogg, whose stiff upper lip was stereotypically British. I began to realise that despite all my success as a rock writer and musician, I was still quite a reserved Englishman underneath. I remember saying to Chris that even though things might not work out for us, I hoped we would both have a place in each other's hearts. Overly romantic and "naff," to say the least, but true. Now I had to write a song that would encapsulate these emotions, so I turned the idea on its head and recast the line for the princess.

PRINCESS: I can't explain
Am I letting my emotions get the better of me?
You're always on my mind
And I want to tell you that I'd willingly follow you.
But if I can't have you,
All I ever want is to have a place in your heart.
But, I wouldn't be so bold
As to expect you to have feelings for me oh no.
I can't admit it to you,
'Cos I know just how much you want to be free.
I wouldn't want to bother you
Because then I would have to admit
How much it's bothering me.
ALL: See the moon up ahead, see the sun behind . . .
ALL: Just past Omaha City soon we're gonna be over the incline.
PRINCESS: You're always on my mind
But I can't tell you that I'd willingly follow you to the end of the world.
ALL: Make the most of nature's great highway

West to east see night turn into day
Move so fast too bad that you can't stay
A place in your heart.

The show got fine reviews when it opened. It almost transferred to Broadway, but as is so often the case, the producers decided not to take *80 Days* on straightaway and then the show was shelved indefinitely. It was simply not ready for the next move and needed another workshop to get in shape. My only consolation was that Randy Graff went on to win a Tony for her performance in the next show she did.

Then it was back to the UK to finish the *UK Jive* album. We shot a short promotional movie called *Million-Pound-Semi-Detached*, based on a song that never made it to the album. It was the era of click tracks, sampled sounds, and special effects on records. During my trips back and forth to La Jolla I had put together a complicated backing track on a sequencer for Dave to play his guitar over. I had foolishly broken my rule of always letting Dave set the tone of the track by letting him play live with drums and bass. Dave started playing his overdub; then, as a sign of protest, he went into a devastatingly brilliant wailing atonal solo that was so loud it spilled through the soundproof walls of the studio. When the track finished, he went on playing in his own sonic stratosphere. When he did eventually stop, he lay down his guitar while it was still feeding back and just walked out of the building. It was an uncoded, unsubtle message intended to remind me that I was still playing in a rock band. I was angry but quietly admired him for making such a musical statement of intent.

In retrospect, it is confusing, because when Dave subsequently recorded his own work, he would often use the same technology I had used on *Million-Pound-Semi*. It would have been more appropriate if we had discussed it over a pint in a pub, but at this time Dave and I only saw each other onstage or in the studio. Needless to say, we didn't use the track on the album; I put the tape away and never played it again. All that survives is a demo I did of the song that appeared on a bonus compilation years later. Another song was called "Aggravation"; this was, thankfully, not only to Dave's liking but also used in our live shows, where it was incorporated into a hip-hop soundscape that used my spoken words to describe the migration of people to the New World after the Second World War. It also incorporated a choreographed dance piece performed by two female dancers.

IN MANY RESPECTS, I HAD THE PERFECT RECORD COMPANY in MCA to promote these albums, but my focus was split by the fact that in the rest of the world these albums were released by a UK company, London Records, led by Roger Ames. After I had returned to New York, before the release of *The Road* album, Roger came to see me at the apartment on the Upper West Side for two reasons. The first was to ask if I would be okay to tour and record after my health scare. The second was to discuss the problems inherent in the different recording cultures in the UK and the United States. Roger summed up the dilemma perfectly.

"The title *The Road* in America conjures up images of the wild rock and roller travelling down the highway, while to people in the UK 'the road' means the provincial M1 motorway from London to Birmingham, that is if you don't encounter road works on the way."

That was the problem. The split deal. Two very different sets of mentalities. Scattered: emotionally, geographically, musically, personally, professionally—in every sense of the word.

After my meeting with Roger, I bumped into an old musician friend at my local bar on 72nd Street and Columbus Avenue. When I told him about my record company dilemma, he shrugged his shoulders. "You can try to serve two masters. You can please some of the people some of the time and the other half of the people some of the time, but when you try to connect with both at once, you're in danger of pissing everybody off." It was a typically unintelligible, semidrunk, bitter remark from him, but his message was spot-on.

The tour to promote *UK Jive* started in America on the ninth of September, 1989—the twenty-fifth anniversary of the first Kinks number one hit, "You Really Got Me." I thought about the origins of *UK Jive*—how I had written the "Breakfast in Berlin" poem on the way to Berlin and channelled lyrics about a mystery messenger who left letter-box clues about a "big thing" that was going to happen. Two months later, in Germany, out of the blue, the Berlin Wall came down. The whole political landscape of Europe would never be the same again. I should have listened to my instincts after all. Then I thought about the wonderful creative journey I had taken, the miracles that we take for granted every day, and the countless ideas that accompany all the souls scattered in the universe.

20

PHOBIA

"Everybody got something hidden
In a darkness deep inside
Everybody got a fatal flaw
Everybody got something to hide
Take a look into my eyes
See the fear and silent cries
Phobia."

ROCK AND ROLL HALL OF FAME

WALDORF ASTORIA, NEW YORK, 1990

The thunder ripped through the sky, heralding the arrival of a rainstorm. When this happens in New York, the sound echoes around the avenues and tall buildings as if the city is at the epicentre of a Cecil B. DeMille biblical epic. The power of nature has a way of pointing us mere humans in unexpected directions. The rain was pelting down, so I was taking shelter in a doorway on 72nd Street when I bumped into Seymour Stein, the founder and president of Sire Records. Like the storm, this meeting had been totally unexpected. Without any small talk, Seymour announced to me that he'd been at a meeting of the Rock and Roll Hall of Fame voting committee and that the Kinks were going to be among the next group of inductees. I was shocked, as I thought our MCA record would be the Kinks' last.

At the time I was concentrating on setting up my documentary on Charles Mingus, entitled *Weird Nightmare*, for Britain's Channel 4. I was actually thinking that I would give the Kinks a rest to focus on the film-making aspect of my career. Nevertheless, I was excited about my band getting the award! Particularly as the news came from Seymour, whom I'd first met when he was over in London with the Ramones in the 1970s. His company, Sire Records, recently had a successful run with Madonna, the Pretenders, and the Talking Heads, among others, but unlike many in his position Seymour was still a song man. The Kinks' induction had not been without controversy. These awards have a tendency to be judged by chart entries, tour grosses, and album sales. I was surprised that the Kinks met these criteria. One journalist later noted that our induction was probably due to our body of work, but deep down I felt that it was for making it back to the big time after the ban. In music business terms it was the equivalent of raising Lazarus from the dead, but little did the world know that I was considering breaking up the band after the MCA commitment was met.

The thunder and rain changed my mind and made me think twice about disbanding the Kinks. Perhaps the world did understand us after all. Then, as the narrator in *The Ten Commandments*, Cecil B. DeMille, would have said, "So it came to pass that the Kinks were to be inducted into the Rock and Roll Hall of Fame at the Waldorf Astoria hotel in New York."

We were only the third British band to be inducted, after the Rolling Stones and the Beatles, and I think as a political compromise they inducted both the Kinks and the Who on the same night. I felt very close to the Who since they opened for the Kinks back in the '60s, and I was looking forward to seeing them at the Rock and Roll Hall of Fame induction ceremony. The Who, or the High Numbers, as they were called then, had supported the Kinks at the Goldhawk Social, a club in London's Shepherd's Bush area right at the beginning of our careers. Then they appeared with us when we played with the Beatles, and then when we topped the bill on our own show. The last time we had played with the Who was at the Kinetic Playground in Chicago on October 31, 1969. The venue burned down a week after we had performed together, so I was a little concerned about what would happen at the Waldorf. Pete Townshend had always credited the Kinks' sound for inspiring the Who and had always praised my songwriting, so it seemed appropriate that the two of us should be inducted at the same time.

AT THIS POINT, OUR ASSOCIATION WITH MCA was just coming to an end, and we had a caretaker-manager arrangement with Kenny Laguna, who had been introduced to me by some mutual friends. Kenny, the producer and manager of Joan Jett and the Blackhearts, was a true rock-and-roll believer who had been a member of Tommy James and the Shondells, of "Mony Mony" fame. He knew and was liked by most people in the business, which he seemed to know inside out, and his accent was unmistakably Long Island Italian. I was, and still am, sceptical about awards ceremonies, and before the induction ceremony began I paced around my suite at the Waldorf Astoria while Kenny sat nervously in an armchair. I looked at Kenny and said to him, "I've got to think of something incredible to say tonight; something that will make everybody remember that the Kinks were in attendance; something that will be quoted; something that will be a definitive statement about the music industry and in keeping with such a great event." Kenny had a glazed look on his face, and after pausing for breath said in a very quiet Long Island accent, "I can't help youse with dat." We both laughed. We knew all along that we were probably not compatible as manager and artist and that it would not likely last, but Kenny had a good sensibility and totally believed in the Kinks. More to the point, Kenny not only sang about blue suede shoes, he actually wore them.

Later on that night, when I did give my acceptance speech at the Waldorf, I remembered seeing some old black-and-white footage of a speech that Winston Churchill had given when he came to America in 1952. Britain's postwar economy was stretched at the time and needed American aid to help rebuild and rearm. Churchill stood in front of the members of Congress and said, "I have not come here to ask you for money," which received copious applause and laughter. Once the applause subsided and once he knew the audience was on his side, he delivered the punch line—". . . to make life more comfortable or easier for us in Britain"—which received even more of a response. Everybody loved Churchill for that statement. I wanted to make a similar sort of impact.

When it was time to give my own speech as the Kinks were inducted, I had nothing on my mind until I walked onstage and saw all those people in the audience. They were there to celebrate rock and roll, the former domain of rebellion, way-out style, and outrageous clothes. These people, however, were dressed in their tuxedos and evening gowns, looking very, very respectable. I looked at the audience and thought of Winston Churchill. "It is fantastic to see that rock 'n' roll has finally become respectable," I said. The audience broke into the same spontaneous, copious applause that had greeted Churchill. Once the applause subsided, I took a deep breath before saying, "What a bummer." This was even more ironic because I was also dressed for the black-tie event. This little quip, although not as eloquent as Churchill's, did have some impact and made the headlines the next day in reports about the event. To me it implied that the industry had become so corporate that it was in danger of losing its street cred. Nevertheless, and despite my somewhat irreverent remark, I was proud to see the members of my original band share the stage with so many great musicians and to be acknowledged by America for being part of a culture it had invented.

As we left the stage, my exit was blocked by two scary-looking people. It's hard to describe why they looked scary, but maybe it was the way they just stood there with no emotion on their faces. I was walking toward them, but they weren't going to move. They both stared at me with large, unblinking eyes. This made me panic slightly because some people might have taken offence to what I had just said on stage. It was not until I got close to them that I recognised them as Allen Klein and Phil Spector. They both reached out and were the first to congratulate me on the Kinks entering the Rock and Roll Hall of Fame. The Kinks had made it back in true biblical fashion. There should have been a roar of thunder, a triumphant musical finale, as we wandered out of the wilderness. The credits had started rolling, but the movie wasn't over yet.

21

STILL SEARCHIN'

"I'm a drifter who has lost his way
And I'm still searching for my dream
A wandering nomad with no home to stay
Just like a gypsy or a refugee
Lookin' at another sign, for another town
Wondering if I'm ever gonna settle down
Or am I gonna keep on searchin' till my dying day?"

WALL OF FIRE, NEW YORK, EUROPE, 1990–94

The hunger was still there. The Kinks were now inductees in the Rock and Roll Hall of Fame. We were still a great touring band. There were still songs that I wanted to write, but I decided that if the Kinks made another record it would have to be managed.

The manager Nigel Thomas had been recommended to me by Freddy Bienstock, my publisher at Carlin Music. Freddy knew a class act when he saw one, and Nigel gave the impression that he was the typical English gent: a mixture of cad and lovable scoundrel from the British *Carry On* comedy film series combined with a cold and calculating MI5 intelligence agent out of a John le Carré novel. He seemed (and probably considered himself) much too aloof and well bred to become involved with rock bands, but he did like the Kinks. He also had managed Joe Cocker and, later, Morrissey, as well as acts he described as "metal rock gods," such as Saxon and Yngwie Malmsteen. Nigel was—and portrayed himself as—nothing more or less than a real aristocrat. He stayed in a manor house at Upper-Swell in the Cotswolds on weekends and lived in an apartment at the Savoy during the week. According to Freddy Bienstock, Nigel was qualified to manage us for that reason alone.

The MCA corporate experience ended in the spring of 1991. Now, amazingly, the Kinks were about to be involved with another giant of the music industry. The old Columbia Records building where I had first been introduced to Clive Davis by Allen Klein had now been absorbed into the Sony Music empire. The dark granite CBS Building on Sixth Avenue in NYC had been given the nickname Black Rock many years earlier. Now it housed probably the largest music company of the 1990s.

The Sony deal was Nigel's idea, and he encouraged us to sign with them. I was particularly sceptical about whether the Kinks would fit into the way Sony did things, but I felt that it could work out if Nigel were running the business end, leaving me to concentrate on the creative aspects, where I felt more comfortable. There were also some pluses to the Sony move. Former Arista promotion man Donnie Ienner was running the company, and Donnie had been part of Clive Davis's Arista promotion team.

I had put together a sample DAT of four songs, one of which was "Scattered," which had been written for the *UK Jive* album but hadn't been included because it wasn't finished in time for the release schedule. Donnie and his team heard these songs, and according to Nigel, it was "Scattered" that persuaded him to sign the Kinks.

By the 1990s, the average record contract, with all its provisions—the artist's obligations and all the other dos and don'ts—was seventy to eighty pages long. Before an artist signs on the dotted line and makes a final commitment to make albums, it can take lawyers sometimes two to three months to negotiate a boilerplate contract. This is done with great thought, consideration, and expense. Marriage is a lot simpler. When two people want to get married, they usually sign the first piece of paper put in front of them.

The Sony contract took quite a while to negotiate, but eventually the deal was closed and we could concentrate on the music. There were some great "stand-alone" songs we had ready for the *Phobia* album, particularly "Still Searching," "Scattered," "Only a Dream," "Drift Away," and an apocalyptic anthem called "Wall of Fire." According to Nigel, Donnie liked what he heard, but it was agreed between them that Sony A&R exec David Kahne would oversee the recording process. David was a good song man and a producer in his own right. I did most of the production in those days but did not consider it an insult or feel compromised in any way by this suggestion because I knew it would make Donnie and the rest of the company more comfortable. The reality was that the album would be recorded in London at Konk, but the company and its A&R department were based in New York, so there would be minimal intrusion.

When principal recording was over it was agreed that the American music engineer Bob Clearmountain would be hired to come over to Konk and remix two or three tracks. Clearmountain had become known as the legendary "Dr. Mix" and would arrive with his effects rack of tricks and gizmos whenever artists needed a fresh pair of ears on key songs, particularly when that track was a potential single.

I arrived at Konk one night after he had already started mixing "Wall of Fire." Usually when I make a record I am very possessive about letting someone else "touch" my band's work, but in watching him I realised he was doing all the right things: putting the snare drum in the right perspective in relation to the vocal; making sure there were enough guitars with the correct amount of power; and, more than anything else, ensuring that the song had that "loud" factor that is so important. He had been responsible for getting that elusive big snare sound that both Bruce Springsteen and I were trying to achieve the time we were both making albums at the Power Station studios in New York many years earlier.

During a break, I recalled my conversation with Bruce about trying to use the overhead mike and asked Bob how he finally ended up getting that big snare sound on *Born in the U.S.A.* I was thinking he'd found a way of adjusting all the overheads to make the sound work. Bob, a slim, poker-faced gentleman, gave my question a certain amount of consideration and seemed to rack his brains for an effect he used many mixes ago. "Nah—we probably ended up adding a white-noise sample." I was disappointed but relieved— it would have taken a magician to have pulled off that sound. Rather than express my disappointment, I asked if he could get the same snare sound on "Wall of Fire." "I already have," Bob said, and I continued to watch him work. His postproduction mixes typified most contemporary rock records of the late 1980s, and it was a pleasure to have him mix a few tracks on the *Phobia* album.

The other upside to the new arrangement with Nigel Thomas was that Nigel and my brother got along well. The only problem was that when it was time to start recording, Dave decided to go live in Los Angeles full-time. This both irritated and frustrated Nigel, as he wanted the record done as soon as possible so that the advances could be paid and the album could be officially commissioned by his company. More importantly, he'd also promised the label delivery within a certain window of time so that Sony could adhere to a release schedule. The pressure was on, but one of the most important members of the band was only available by appointment. I also had the added stress of finishing my Charles Mingus documentary. Things were mounting up in my personal life as well as my professional life, but I carried on relentlessly, dividing my time between both of them. I was on a creative high.

Sony had put some funds into the Mingus film, and that was eventually delivered, but not until the film presented a few dramas of its own. Two key guest appearances in the film were made by Keith Richards and Charlie Watts, who were to perform the Mingus song "Oh Lord Don't Let Them Drop That Atomic Bomb on Me." They were a key piece in the jigsaw puzzle of musicians that I had pieced together into my film. In true Rolling Stones tradition, they were difficult to pin down when it came to their whereabouts. In June 1990 the Rolling Stones were set to play a few nights in Madrid. Hal Willner, the producer of the album my film was documenting, had been told he could record the track in Madrid while Keith was in town. So with only a few hours' notice, we put our small crew together and flew to Spain with documentary filmmaker Jack Hazan as cinematographer.

The track was recorded and filmed at a small studio in the suburbs of Madrid. Keith and Charlie, along with Bobby Keys and his band, turned in a great performance. It was important that we got enough takes to work with in the editing room afterward, but I was told by Keith and Charlie's handlers that there was no time to shoot any further. My instinct told me that the next take would be the master take, and I refused to be denied. (I had also suffered from the intrusion of film crews myself in the past and was aware of the unwritten rule that you never, ever give a film crew an even break, particularly when the filmmaker is a musical contemporary of yours.) I had already anticipated such an incident, so I looked at Jack Hazan and asked, "Did we get that last one, Jack?" Jack shrugged his shoulders. "I'm sorry, but we ran out of film halfway through the take." I explained this to Keith and Charlie, and they agreed to do another take, which indeed turned out to be the master. It was a pity to be so insistent, but if the roles had been reversed I'm sure they would have done the same in order to get the film shot.

I also interviewed Keith and Charlie for the film; I asked the questions and they gave me intelligent answers. Charlie was particularly knowledgeable about Mingus and about jazz in general. We even had time to reminisce about the old days. It reminded me of a time many years earlier when Charlie and I had been sitting with some other musicians in a pub on Archer Street in London's Soho. Charlie said that he had been offered the gig with the Stones but seemed unimpressed. Another musician sitting with us said, "It's not jazz, Charlie, but it's a gig." Charlie nodded approvingly and considered the gig, which the world now knows he took. That was a long time ago.

During the Mingus session I did notice that Keith was wearing a T-shirt with NO PROBLEM written on the front. I should have heeded the warning, because when I got back to New York to insert the footage I was summoned for a meeting with the Stones people, concerning issues over the footage I shot. Eventually the matter was resolved; the film finished in time to be aired as the start of a new jazz series on Channel 4 in the UK.

Then it was full steam ahead to finish the album. On a Mingus-related side note, after the first tour to promote *Phobia*, I produced and financed an improvisational theatre workshop in North London that incorporated performances of the songs from *Phobia* together with new songs written for the workshop. One of the participants was Eric Mingus—the son of Charles Mingus—a fine singer-songwriter in his own right. (I remember that Eric stayed at the Konk Studios in London for a while and, in return for studio time, offered to paint the interior of the building.)

THE *PHOBIA* ALBUM WAS, in the opinion of many, a creative success and possibly the best album we had delivered since the Arista days.

One of the joys of working on the *Phobia* project was having Sue Coe, an English artist based in New York, do the artwork for the album cover. Sue was a motivated person who had attended a prominent art school in London before moving to America to become a well-respected and widely exhibited political artist whose work has been published in numerous newspapers, magazines, and books, including *The New York Times* and *The New Yorker*. I visited Sue and played her a few tracks from the album.

We bonded over our similar opinions over the totalitarianism of the "capitalist corporate" world, which I described in some of the songs as a cultural wasteland on the edge of a precipice. I shared with her my night-mare vision of the executive trying to scale the "Wall of Fire" in order to be top dog. Sue and I stood on the roof of her apartment building on the East Side and envisioned burning skyscrapers with people hanging from windows, eerily imagining a scene similar to 9/11 nearly ten years before the event.

Sue also cared for animals in distress and later that same night she walked into her living room holding what I thought was a white cat, but upon closer inspection I realised it was a giant albino rat that had been passed on to her to care for. She told me that the rat was harmless and that it could hardly walk. She asked me if I wanted to hold it, but I declined the offer.

I didn't realise until halfway through the recording that *Phobia* was a conceptual album; it should've been an expressionist theatre piece about the decline—moral and financial—of the corporate system, personified by a suc-cessful businessman who'd reached the peak of his corporate powers only to realise he was afraid of heights.

I had a vision of a man standing on top of a skyscraper, not unlike Black Rock, which he owned and controlled. Although terrified of heights, he was looking down upon the city. The irony and contradiction of a man with acrophobia having to climb to the top of the corporate world stuck with me.

The nearer the release date for *Phobia*, the more importance Columbia placed on the track "Scattered." I think that because it was not included on the last MCA album there was an issue as to whether the song could be included on the record. It was a relief to know that Nigel would bear the brunt of the negotiations with Donnie and Sony. I'd even met with Bob Clearmountain at a studio just outside Amsterdam to remix the track. Bob performed his magic, which made the song sound even more special. I had been given a generous budget to produce a video for the song, which was shot in the English countryside—a stand-in for Amish country. Dave and I drove through the rural setting in a red Ford Mustang convertible while the local farmers acted out the narrative of the song.

The recording had also brought Dave and me together, at least in a musical sense; in fact, his playing throughout the record was a cut above anything he'd done on the previous three albums. Still, there was the drama of whether or not "Scattered" would be on the album. According to Nigel, Donnie believed in the track so much that he was threatening to pull the record if the song was not included. I saw no problem in including the track and wanted it on the album, and hoped that the rights issue was worked out.

My last encounter with Nigel was acrimonious, to say the least. Late one Friday night in January of 1993, as he drove home to the Cotswolds, Nigel called from his mobile phone and said in no uncertain terms that if I did not agree to release the "Scattered" track as the first single from the *Phobia* album, he and Donnie Ienner would see that there would be no album at all. I explained that I, too, thought it was essential to have the track included, but there must have been a mix-up by Sony business affairs, and I was in no shape to become embroiled in complicated rights issues after spending months in the studio. I slammed down the phone and started to compose a letter that in effect asked for Nigel's resignation. I considered the legal implications, so I was careful about how the letter was worded.

I called up his home the following morning to ask for his fax number only to find out that Nigel had collapsed and died from a massive heart attack earlier that morning. The shock and sadness I felt as a result of his death completely outweighed any ill feeling I might have had over whether or not the album would come out. His obituary stated that in his private life, Nigel had been a philanthropic man who often contributed to charities. He was one of a kind, and I wish that we could have continued to work together longer. The previous April, before his death, Nigel had accompanied Dave and me on a short promotional visit to the States, where we played at an Earth Day concert in Boston. Then we made some promotional appearances, accompanied by Nigel and Columbia Records' top promotion man, Kid Leo, who had been a legendary DJ in Cleveland. Both Nigel and Leo were heavy smokers, and the limo we were travelling in became so full of smoke that I lost my voice for the first radio interview.

Nigel was probably one of the busiest people I had ever met. He did most things single-handedly and rarely delegated. Rumour had it that Nigel wanted to be buried with his mobile phone and a bottle of Armagnac. After his funeral, at a picturesque cemetery in the Cotswolds, I stood by his grave. Then, after most of the mourners had left, I turned to go and was convinced I heard Nigel's mobile phone ring. The reality was that the man who was responsible for our deal with Sony was no longer around to liaise with the record company.

AT THE START, I SENSED SOME CONFUSION about where Sony felt we fit into their roster. We were considered to be classic rock, but it was the early days of the Seattle "grunge" scene—post-Nirvana, the band who had single-handedly turned American rock music on its head.

There was also a lack of understanding in regard to our sense of humour. For example, at one meeting, a title for the unfinished Kinks album was being discussed, and I was asked what the title should be. At the time, every record label was looking for a new band in the style of Nirvana, and as a bad joke I suggested "The Next Nirvana." This comment—which might have brought howls of knowing laughter from Clive Davis and (especially) Bob Feiden—elicited only glazed expressions tinged with confusion, as if we were speaking a different language. It was not the fault of Donnie or Kid Leo or anyone else in particular. The fact was that the music industry had moved into an urban groove, and there was no space for smart-ass behaviour or risk taking—particularly by a Limey from North London. I wondered whether in his enthusiasm to secure a deal with Sony Nigel Thomas had misinterpreted what he thought the Kinks were to deliver. I will never know.

Before his death, Nigel had also been partly responsible for ending another important Kinks relationship—the long-term association with our tour manager and friend Ken Jones. One night Nigel and I had to fly to New York for a crisis meeting about upcoming releases and promotional tours, and I thought Ken should accompany us. Nigel was irritated by this request but instructed the Sony-Columbia travel agents to "take care of the situation." Jonesy had always resented anyone who was above him in a managerial capacity. He had worked well with Elliot Abbott because Elliot was astute enough to recognise Ken's problems with "authority" and finesse his way around the moody roadie from Northern Ireland. Ken was devoted to the band, but it was to an almost excessive degree, which at times frustrated anyone else trying to work for us. Nigel, on the other hand, had no time for such subtle management, which resulted in Jonesy walking away from his job. It came to a head in the following exchange, which took place in the Concorde departure lounge at Heathrow airport. Nigel and I were checking in, and Ken, who was due to fly out the following day, asked what class he would be travelling. Nigel was empathetic and to the point.

"Sony has only budgeted for two Concorde flights. I am afraid, Ken, that you will have to travel regular economy."

The disappointment was visible on Ken's face. "But I can't fly anything less than first class. You've got to help me on this one, Nige."

"Sorry, Ken. That's the ticket assigned to you. That's the way it has to be."

Ken was devastated, but seemed resigned to his fate. To him, not flying with us on the Concorde was bad enough, but not going in first class was a complete humiliation. Perhaps I could have intervened, but I had taken on Nigel to manage the project and was not going to get involved in another spat at this stage. We checked in and had made the flight just in time, and as we entered the gate area I looked around to see Ken walking away with his head downcast. I knew that Ken had sufficient air miles to get an upgrade to any class he wished to fly in. There was also an element of grandstanding going on between Nigel and Ken, so I stayed out of it. I was shocked when a short time later Ken resigned, leaving the band he had worked with for more than twenty years.

Ken went on to work for Kiss and John Entwistle, but he contracted terminal cancer while living in Florida a few years after leaving the Kinks. Near the end, John Entwistle let Ken stay in his house in England. I was in

New York and tried to phone, but Ken was unable to speak coherently at the time so I wrote him a note that I sent by overnight mail. It arrived just in time for Mick Avory to read it to him on his deathbed. Apparently, as Mick read my letter aloud to him, Ken cried, and as the tears were still rolling down his face, he died. One of my most dedicated and stalwart allies was gone. In hindsight, the only consolation I had was that after that Concorde flight Nigel had cruelly denied Ken, British Airways lost Nigel's baggage. This resulted in Nigel behaving in a bad-tempered way throughout the trip, and I watched in horror as on a daily basis he would drink two bottles of wine over dinner followed by half a bottle of the best Armagnac—with the assistance, I might add, of my good self. Nigel was good at cutting deals and was a super tactician in negotiations, but it was clear that patience was not his virtue and that dealing with the hierarchy at Sony was, in his opinion, a tedious and unnecessary affair. All this before the record was finished and released. It did not bode well.

It was clear that the dealings with Sony had to be resolved one way or another, and I was slightly shocked at how little Nigel had kept them in the loop about my artistic aspirations for the album. I was equally surprised to hear what their expectations for the album would be, particularly with regard to touring. Our manager was dead, and our long-serving tour manager had also departed, along with keyboard player Ian Gibbons. We had made a great album, but all the plans for its release were in disarray. I was not prepared or qualified to turn into a do-it-yourself businessman, and the situation itself was not a project any self-respecting manager would gladly embrace.

I had a corporate ally at Sony Columbia who had been an executive at RCA when the Kinks had been signed there. Mel Ilberman was an admired and knowledgeable record executive who was reputedly close to the executives at Sony and was respected by Donnie. He was also someone I could talk to. I found an opportunity to "reach out" to Mel and visit his office at Black Rock, where I suggested in the most polite possible way that the Kinks be released from the remainder of the Columbia deal. I was accompanied by Eugene Harvey, a former manager of Whitney Houston. who came along to the meeting as moral support. We even discussed a scenario where Gene might manage the band, but nothing ever worked out.

Mel said it would be difficult because of the contractual issues and the personalities involved, but he would consider how best it could be achieved politically and amicably. Doing another Sony album would have meant a large advance and would have safeguarded our career for another year or two, but the thought of having to write and produce records for a huge corporation that did not seem to understand the Kinks was too much to go through without management to act as a buffer.

To our surprise we discovered that Sony was agreeable to giving us our freedom and we were able to look elsewhere, which was generous of them.

After the meeting I walked around the West Side. I stopped at my favourite "old man's" bar to play a song on the jukebox, and then headed over to Tower Records and wondered where this would all end. I remembered how I'd enjoyed going into record stores as a kid—if not to buy, then just to look at the exotic names on the singles and albums. "Searchin'" by the Coasters on Atco Records. *Teen Scene* by Chet Atkins on RCA. Dion and the Belmonts, Danny and the Juniors, and Johnny and the Hurricanes. "Honky Tonk" by Bill Doggett. "What'd I Say" by Ray Charles. The Stax label. Chess Records. I thought how thrilled I had been to see the finished 45-rpm record of "You Really Got Me" by the Kinks on Reprise, with my name—Ray Davies—on the label as composer. Now there were more names, more labels, all merging into one another. Corporate takeovers and company mergers were starting to become fashionable. The bottom line was God. Perhaps it always had been.

I remembered a story about a young exec at Columbia who had seen good sales reports on an artist called Robert Johnson and tried to track him down to persuade the bluesman to do a press tour, only to discover that Robert Johnson had died decades earlier. Perhaps, on this occasion, God had done Robert Johnson a favour.

That night I went to the top of a building overlooking Central Park to look at all the skyscrapers. I thought of the character from "Wall of Fire" whom I'd described to Sue Coe, and how in a strange way I had become like that character . . . so high up that I could not hear the cries from the people detached from me down in the streets below. Then a helicopter momentarily hovered above me before speeding off toward the Hudson River as the sky faded to black.

22

OVER MY HEAD

"Waking up, feeling rough
Totally wrecked.
Every day is a day at a time
Step by step."

NEW ORLEANS, JANUARY 2004

The Louisiana winter sunlight appeared to come from every direction through the large angular branches that cast shadows across the avenue. It flickered through the bedroom window across my eyes, as if gently to whisper, "Wake up." The same dancing light moved across the pillow before hitting the face of a beautiful woman lying sound asleep by my side. I peeked over and was surprised to discover that the woman who'd slid into in my bed was Rory. The electric clock ticked over to 8:30 a.m. Then the radio clicked on to WWOZ, and the breakfast-time show played an old King Oliver track. In the bed I made a careful turn from my left side to my right side and was followed by Rory, who snuggled and tucked her body inside mine for one last cuddle before she got up. I was half awake, but she was still talking in her sleep.

Eventually Rory got up and shuffled through her morning procedure of going to the bathroom, yawning as she flushed the toilet, and making her way toward the kitchen. Suddenly there was a knock on the door.

I thought it was unusual to get a visitor so early; this was too early even for the mailman. She yelled out, "It must be a FedEx delivery," and, still bleary-eyed, she casually walked over to the front door and unlocked it without thinking.

She did as she was told and stayed silent as the thief pushed her firmly but silently into the living room with the pistol pointed in the side of her face.

I was still groggy, but heard the intruder's voice say, "Keep your mouth shut, bitch, or I'll kill you both."

I looked over and saw that Rory, who was still wearing her stylish silk pajamas, quivered with fear while the intruder slipped his hand into her bottoms and pulled them down. "Nice ass," the intruder whispered as he slid his hand around to her buttocks. I couldn't believe my eyes. It was the guy who shot me. He moved his gun up to her mouth. I broke out into a cold sweat. I was shaking so much that I knocked the cowbell off the bedside table, which drew the intruder's attention to me as I struggled to get up.

"Leave her alone!" I shouted.

This must have amused the intruder, because he smiled malevolently.

Rory was in shock. I could barely hear her whisper across the room.

"Help me, Ray."

The words had barely come out before the intruder put the gun in her mouth and pulled the trigger. A moment later her body slammed to the floor. She must have died instantly.

The shooter came close to me.

"This time, I'll finish you good."

He pointed the gun at my head and shot me in the eye from point-blank range.

That was the last thing I remembered before I woke up in a sweat, alone in my bed.

MONDAY, JANUARY 12. "I've got to let these dark thoughts out of my head. Today will be my first day of getting better."

After such a rude awakening I was relieved to see that it actually was a bright winter morning. I made a cup of tea, but then realised that I couldn't carry it to the table while I was using my crutches. A whole new mobility regimen had to be learned.

Nine thirty a.m. No police sirens. Unusual for this time of the morning—just a "shouter" across the back alley. Then the pulsing electronic bell at John McDonogh High School rang, signaling the change of classes. The day passed slowly. By then I had perfected a method of making an omelet by hobbling between the stove and my makeshift bed. The hospital called to tell me that they could not supply aftercare, as I am not a Louisiana resident, but thankfully the lovely staff nurse I met at the hospital came over to check my medication and suggested an outside physician who could take over until my insurance came through. The process seemed overly complicated, but the issues connected with insurance were paramount. I had also received some criticism in the local press for chasing the mugger. This raised the issue of what tourists should do if confronted by a robber with a gun. I think some of the police and the mayor were embarrassed because the city relies on tourism so much. For the most part, muggings go unreported in the press, except that in my case I actually fought back and made news. I put this all to one side while I decided how to fill my day.

Partly for company, and partly to relieve my boredom, I left the TV on the TCM channel all day with the sound turned down. My appointed doctor arrived just as Orson Welles's seedy character in *Touch of Evil* appeared on the screen. For a moment, the doctor and Orson Welles seemed to blend into one person. My doctor, whom I will call Dr. O'Malley, was a tall, overweight, red-haired gentleman with sweat pouring from his brow. He was only in his late sixties, but still had a youthful glint in his eyes. He was dressed in a grey suit, complete with crumpled pants and a few stains down his shirt, as though he'd spilled his gumbo during lunch. He sat down beside me, still sweating and out of breath, and went through the usual Q-and-A routine that culminated with questions about my medical insurance. As he spoke in his thick New Orleans accent, my attention was drawn to the thickness of his deep red hair, which appeared to stand up strong and high on his head. He looked up from his notebook to stare at me.

"Are you really a rock star? I've never treated a rock star before . . . . Hey, man, it's great to hang out with you." Normally I would have found an excuse to rush straight out the door, but as I was physically compromised we both knew I was a captive in this situation and completely at his mercy, so I pretended to listen with rapt attention. As we talked I became more reassured by his down-to-earth gruffness, and what he lacked in charm he more than made up with his know-how—and his stories were good.

"New Orleans is a small town. . . . You were treated by Dr. So and So? Son of a bitch, but a great doc. . . . Yep, word gets around in this town." O'Malley had little bedside manner; he was rather more direct, which was good for me right then. He reached into his pocket for his cell phone and called several other doctors about various issues. His voice bellowed out, "Hey, you know the English rock singer who got shot the other week? Well, I'm with him right now . . . yeah, he needs this and that . . . blah, blah . . . oh, and by the way, I'm not sure if this guy is insured, so go easy on the bills for the time being, you know what I mean? I'm sure he's good for it, but hey . . . I'm your buddy, right?"

Sensitivity was not a major issue with Dr. O'Malley—sensitivity is a trait that must become numbed in the mortality trade—and without missing an emotional beat he flicked over to call waiting, where he began talking about another patient. "Sorry, but I have to take this call. I've got to give somebody some bad news . . . yeah . . . I agree . . . I suggest we ditch the life support." Later he explained that the other patient had been a sailor at Pearl Harbor "the day the Japs bombed it." Now, after all that, late in life, the poor old guy was in a coma and had to have both legs amputated. O'Malley agreed with the family that the best thing to do would to be to let the guy go out with some dignity. My pretty middle-aged nurse returned just as we were discussing the unbelievably difficult job O'Malley had to do. He paused to reflect and then resumed his professional demeanour. Perhaps it was just his job, after all.

"Now, I want this beautiful nurse to change your dressing. I know she can't wait to get her hands on your body, can you, babe?" Both the nurse and I felt embarrassed. O'Malley needed a copy of my insurance policy, so I gave him what I had, and he said he would send someone around later to get me to fill out a questionnaire. He and the nurse left as my physical therapist arrived. Tony—a happy-faced Filipino—went to great lengths to explain how much he could help me, and promised to bring me some special tea bags his friend sent him from London. Tony told me that he had friends in Greenwich, South London, and that, unbelievably, he had a friend who was in the same emergency room at the same time as I was. O'Malley was right—this was a small town.

Tony also needed to see insurance forms (I swore that from that day on I would take them everywhere I went). Then he looked around the kitchen and examined the bathroom, proclaiming that the toilet was the wrong height. Midway through our conversation, his eyes stared past me at the TV, which was now showing yet another James Bond film—maybe it was the same one that had been playing when I was in the hospital. Sean Connery was being thrown around by some heavies. Perhaps Tony was thinking about all the physical therapy work he could have gotten after a fight like that.

WEDNESDAY, JANUARY 14, 10:00 A.M. My insurance man called from the UK to give me an update on my situation. The U.S. division of their company would pick up all my medical bills. I explained that I was starting to have nightmares about the shooter breaking into the house to finish me off, but the agent stopped me in my tracks. They would not pay for a stress counselor or a hotel. He said he would argue about food reimbursement, but I was not to travel for four to six weeks until the doctors agreed I was fit enough to be mobile and free from the risk of infection or blood clots. This presented me with a problem, because I had agreed to do an upcoming benefit for Philip Glass at Carnegie Hall, which now looked to be in jeopardy. I asked about expenses: "I have no money; everything was taken. Cards, cash, everything." I didn't want to ask my friends, because I was staying in their house, after all. The insurance agent said he would speak to my office about getting some money sent by Western Union.

FRIDAY, JANUARY 16. Tony the therapist came by and showed me how to walk up and down the stairs on my crutches. "Make sure you don't try this on your own yet. These are early days." I was very tentative, but it gave me confidence.

Later in the afternoon I was surprised by Alex Chilton who stopped by unannounced. I knew that he had a reputation as being reclusive but by now we had become quite good friends, possibly because we shared the experience of having been in bands since we were barely in our teens. He asked me about some of my Kinks records, but he was surprisingly shy about revealing much in connection with his own music. He was from Memphis and sang the lead vocal in the Box Tops hit "The Letter" before going on to have a second career with the band Big Star. We also shared the same booking agent,

Frank Riley. Frank had reputedly rediscovered Alex after he saw him washing up crockery in a restaurant in New Orleans, a story that was confirmed by Alex. After his "rebirth," Alex saved enough money to buy a house in New Orleans and took great pride in telling me what a good deal it was. He also shared confidential details about some of the mutual acquaintances we had in New Orleans and warned me to be careful of certain characters.

Alex was very dismissive about recording "The Letter."

"We just got into a session one day, and the song had been written by a contract writer, the same guy who composed the song 'Always on My Mind,'" Alex said. "Then we ran through the song a few times, and that was it."

Alex made no further attempts to embellish the story, and I didn't push it. This was a conversation, not an interview, and I respected that. We then discussed the pros and cons of being in bands. Alex knew a lot about his demons and confided that he was a recovering alcoholic. We chatted on about music, everything from the Eurovision Song Contest (which he loved but didn't quite understand) to gospel (which he knew a lot about). At about 5:30, a message came up the stairs that Dr. O'Malley would stop by to see me after work, on his way to a Hornets basketball game. By the time he reached my rooms, on the top floor, he was so out of breath that he had to sit down for five minutes to recover before we could discuss my problems. He was a big man and terribly out of shape for someone in his late sixties. We talked about stress and the current situation I was in.

"I feel your pain," he said, somewhat surprisingly. "Not physical pain, but the emotional pain you seem to be in."

"Apart from medical stuff, you appear to be in shock and traumatised. You also seem to be in need of a friend; someone you can go out to a bar and hang with."

I looked over at Alex, who just sat there, disconnected. Dr. O'Malley looked at his watch. "Well, I've finished work now, so I'll have a drink with you." Then he asked me if I had any beer in the fridge. "I don't, actually, but even if I did, do you think I should?" I was trying to be a good patient, but he said it would be okay. He sent Alex out to the local store for a six-pack.

While Alex was running his errand, O'Malley took down some more personal details about me and filled in a few forms. He phoned the orthopedic specialist to discuss my case and occasionally put his mobile on speaker-phone so that I could hear what the specialist was saying, as if to emphasise a certain point here and there. He looked at me in a reassuring way as he ended the call.

"It's okay. That call was off the meter. Don't want you to think all doctors are money-grabbers."

We talked a little about growing older, dating younger women, and what all that entailed. I told the doc that I had suffered from spinal problems most of my life, so that even as a teenager I felt like an old man.

"Even when I was at school I was considered to be on a geriatric level in terms of my back after an injury sustained playing football had aggravated a congenital condition," I laughed. "Back pain is usually attributed to age, isn't it? Hell, I was probably one gene away from being the Elephant Man, even though from a layman's point of view I appeared to be quite normal." I smiled at him. "When you're in my situation, and you've had mobility issues most of your life, getting older doesn't seem to be much of a difficulty."

The doctor smiled back as he replied flamboyantly, "Touché, monsieur."

SATURDAY, JANUARY 17. Thunderstorms raged all morning and afternoon, giving the house, which was surrounded by rich foliage, an almost tropical feel. I could hear the palm trees rustling through the gauze curtains. The air was warm and damp, but I was as depressed as hell. My sister called from England. I became upset when I explained about my accident to her. She said my family was all very worried. Then an aide arrived to examine the dressing on my leg. She panicked when she saw that my right ankle and calf were swollen, and she called her supervising doctor on his cell phone. He was worried that it might be phlebitis or a blood clot. If it didn't go down I would have to go straight to the emergency room. I phoned Dr. O'Malley, who came over right away, arriving with his stethoscope around his neck. He thanked me for getting him out of the house on a weekend. He looked at my leg and told me not to worry. Then we began to chat again and he went on to tell me about his own background, his Irish-Catholic upbringing in the Northeast. How he came to the South and ended up in New Orleans. Married. Then he asked me what rock and roll was. I was confused about what to say, but tried to explain that it's about the backbeat. We talked for a while about nothing in particular, but I got the feeling he was just assessing how I was dealing with the emotional side of things. Then he again told me not to worry about my leg and left.

Alex dropped by to leave his Martin acoustic guitar for me, "just in case you get inspired to write or need to pass some time." Before he left, Alex played a few songs of his own on the guitar and explained how difficult it was for him to find reliable musicians. "Most of them don't want to rehearse, and they demand top dollar for playing even a small bar. Then they cancel at the last minute because they have been offered a run of dates that clash with the date they promised to do for you, but if you cancel them, why, all hell breaks loose and you have to pay their fee anyway. So that's why I take along charts of all my songs just in case one of those SOBs lets me down."

I'd never seen Alex get so riled up before, but I could relate to a lot of what he said even if I did not agree with it all. We both agreed that's why we enjoyed playing in bands as opposed to using pickup musicians. For a moment I thought of offering him a drink, but then I realised he had told me he had an alcohol problem. Suddenly Alex reached inside to finally offer up something deep. "Playing songs is ageless; the songs never seem to get old. You can sing a song that you wrote twenty or thirty years ago, and it's like the first time you've played it. It makes you feel young, but the reality is, you're getting older, things are changing inside . . . . somehow performing music cheats age, but the fascination only lasts as long as the song."

He was right, and there was nothing more to say. We were like two old cowboys trying to put the world to rights. As Alex and I talked, the TCM channel began playing an old black-and-white western. We both sat and looked at the TV even though the sound was turned down. We didn't need to speak anymore. The images said it all.

I thought back to the greatest times I had had with my band while the movie played silently.

23

STORYTELLER

"I'll tell you the story to pass on to the end
As told to me so long ago by my good friend
As we huddled 'round the log fire we laughed the whole night long
As he told me a tale passed on to him by a wandering vagabond.
My friend told me the story,
But I'll pass it on to you
It was passed on through the centuries and he swore that it was true."

SOLO, 1994–98

The opening sequence of the George Stevens western *Shane* shows the cowboy hero riding alone across the prairie. He appears to be simply following his instincts, going where destiny leads him over unknown and unchartered territory, uncertain yet confident that the journey will end up somewhere worthwhile. In much the same way, the sudden realisation that it was possible for me to do some dates without the Kinks filled me with a lot of insecurity but also a sense of freedom. There were no boundaries or confines. No rules—because as far as I knew, no one from my generation of musicians had ever attempted anything as bold, brave, or as stupid as what I was about to embark upon.

In the spring of 1994, I took the Kinks into the Konk Studios in London to film and record our own unplugged versions of most of the significant songs in our catalogue. The audio portion, an album titled *To the Bone*, was first released in the UK in October 1994 by an up-and-coming indie distributor called Grapevine and was later sold to Guardian Records, an independent arm of EMI America, but the video portion was never distributed. In 1994, my "unauthorised autobiography," *X-Ray*, was also released. I did some book readings, which were well attended in all the bookshops. I found that it was possible to promote two projects at the same time, which was liberating, to say the least. I then organised a few events at which I both read from the book and played certain Kinks songs where appropriate. I even wrote new songs to accompany some sections of narrative and was amazed to discover that people wanted more.

Storyteller evolved from these book readings to promote my *X-Ray* autobiography. I already felt that I was detaching myself and needed a break from the band and its entourage for a while. I started working with guitarist Pete Mathison, who came recommended by the owner of the guitar repair shop next to Konk. Pete was an accomplished "jobbing" musician who specialised in country and blues, and working with a new sideman allowed me to approach my work in a fresh way. If nothing else, it gave my head some clear creative space. I still hadn't decided to stop playing with the Kinks, and in fact there were some tour dates scheduled in the States later that summer. The band was to play a series of "soft" summer gigs that could be easily sold out. Prior to those Kinks dates, I played a few more "tryout" solo dates in tiny venues around London, but to my surprise, my agent was reluctant to book these dates for me and I ended up having to use a promoter who specialised in cabaret bookings. Perhaps my agent's theory was "Why should we promote Ray as a solo performer in a three-hundred-seater when the Kinks could play to fifteen-hundred-plus people for a larger fee?" I think my agent and possibly my band thought that these shows were an indulgence and I would grow tired of playing them, particularly as there was hardly any money involved. The *X-Ray* shows were far from cabaret, though—they represented a total shift in my performance style.

The first night I performed the solo show was in a small theatre in Kent. I stamped my feet so hard to compensate for the lack of a rhythm section that my legs and feet became bruised, and I couldn't walk properly for days afterward. Then an unexpected thing happened. Word of mouth started to spread, and as a result the audiences and venues got larger. I had accidentally created something that our fans wanted. Not only that, people were coming to the *X-Ray* shows who would not have normally come to a Kinks show. I had accidentally found a new audience, even a new demographic. These were younger and older people who had heard of the Kinks but who might not have bought tickets to see them play at a concert. These people might not even go to rock concerts regularly, but they found these acoustic-based events more palatable and easier to sit through. The show was significant in one other crucial area: it had low or almost no production costs. It simply required a small PA system and no stage personnel except for one backline person. It was four men in a van—a complete contrast to the Kinks, who required a complete stage crew with sound and lighting technicians and extra transport to carry the equipment. For the first time in my career, I actually picked up the fee and paid my musician and tour manager directly. I even carried my own receipt book. I only did this for the first few dates before leaving that side of things to my tour manager. It was all very small-time, but very liberating just the same.

The media became supporters of the show, and my agent was eventually won over. In the summer of 1995 he got me a prestigious booking at the Edinburgh Festival Fringe, which was a coup in itself, as it was and still is the foremost "legitimate" fringe art and theatrical festival in the UK and rarely featured rock or pop music. The festival took place in August, and during my first two-week run, the *X-Ray* show received encouraging and at times rave reviews. Someone described my show as a breakthrough, a new kind of stand-up comedy, a mixture of theatre and a concert. Other more clichéd accolades included "unplugged" and "unmissable."

THE MORNING AFTER MY LAST EDINBURGH SHOW I drove down to London and straight on to Heathrow, where the Kinks took the Concorde to New York and then made a connection on to Cleveland. The wait for the connecting flight at Kennedy Airport was longer than the Concorde journey from London, but we eventually caught the flight to Ohio and headed for what turned out to be the final Kinks concert in the United States. It was September 2, 1995—the inaugural concert for the opening of the Rock and Roll Hall of Fame at the Cleveland Stadium in Ohio. Since we had been inducted at the Waldorf hotel in 1990, the Hall of Fame Foundation had settled on building the museum itself in Cleveland, Ohio, partly because of the city's connection with Alan Freed, the man many people had credited as one of the first DJs to play rock music on the radio in the 1950s.

We arrived at the stadium straight from the airport barely in time to do a sound check. The show was to be broadcast live on HBO, and Cleveland Stadium would be full of seventy-thousand-plus fans. To my surprise, the Kinks were the only completely UK-based, UK-born-and-bred band on the show; the Rolling Stones and the Who were notable absentees. There may have been some individual members of British bands at the event, but from what I would recall, the Kinks were the only ones to play as a whole unit. In a strange way we felt vindicated by the fact that we were the only British band flying the flag. All those years spent rebuilding our career in the States after the four-year ban had truly paid off. It was an acceptance that really hit home that night in Cleveland, when Jon Bon Jovi announced the Kinks. What made the event even more gratifying was the fact that Donnie Ienner and some other Columbia executives were there to witness our performance.

However, we had flown over in such haste that our backline roadie had forgotten to bring any guitar plectrums. As we hit the stage I shouted to my absent-minded roadie for my plectrum, but he just shrugged his shoulders in an apologetic way. The crowd was already boiling over with excited cheering, and there I was shouting for something as basic as a guitar plectrum. Suddenly, as if from nowhere, an unknown individual thrust a plectrum in my face. It had the name Chuck Berry written on it. I still do not know to this day whether it came from the great man, who was also at the Cleveland Stadium that night, but I was moved by the possibility that one of my childhood heroes—one of the people responsible for inspiring me to play the guitar—had offered his own plectrum for me to use at my last U.S. concert with the Kinks.

As this plectrum crisis was resolving, I realised that Dave and the others were in the process of being pushed onto the large stage. I knew that the longer we took to go on, the wilder the audience would become, so in order to maximise the impact I called out to Dave and the others to walk on more slowly than they would normally. By the time we strolled onstage the audience was at their peak. I was dressed in my now legendary Union Jack suit and did a little dance, like a prizefighter skipping around while psyching out his opponent. Then Dave exploded into one of our old hits, and the show was on its way. We only did two songs, but we had completely stolen the show.

Our fans knew it, our doubters (and there were still a few) knew it, and, more than anything else, the TV audience knew it. All those years of hard grind, starting with those comeback shows at the Fillmore East, had been worth it. This was the real victory. We had conquered America. James Brown saw our show and invited me onstage to join him in "Sex Machine" when he went on. He even sent one of his pretty dancers up to my dressing room to ask if I would participate, but by then I was exhausted and politely declined. I was genuinely worn out by the travelling and the event itself, but looking back I wish I had accepted the offer to do a song with the hardest working man in show business.

THERE WERE OTHER OFFERS FOR KINKS CONCERTS coming in at this time, but my *X-Ray* show was beginning to take priority. I didn't get any withdrawal from not playing with the Kinks, because *X-Ray* was a show that told the story of the Kinks, and in many respects it alleviated any separation anxiety I may have felt at that time. I fooled myself into thinking that I didn't need the band. I could still talk about my songs and reminisce about our exploits. It was as though the group was still onstage with me. I was, in fact, no longer with the band. But doing the show softened the blow. *X-Ray* was often up to three hours in length and had turned into quite a trendsetting event.

In 1995, I had played a series of larger theatres, and there was enough demand to take the show off-Broadway, to a small theatre in lower Manhattan called the Westbeth, on Bank Street. At the suggestion of my old friend Ned Sherrin, I had engaged Deke Arlon to manage the project. Jimmy Nederlander and Ron Delsener copromoted, and after a short rehearsal period, we began the run of shows on February 12, 1996, at the Westbeth. Everyone involved was excited about the show, which was now entitled *20th Century Man*, but I couldn't help thinking that all the production participants considered it to be a bit of a lark and they would soon be able to book me at larger venues with the Kinks. Again, we defied all expectations. *The New York Times* gave the show a fantastic review, and business was so good that we added an extra week to the run. This was all a new and exciting experience for me. Audiences returned, and some hard-core fans saw the show almost on a nightly basis; I varied the performance slightly most nights to accommodate that audience.

I was approached by VH1, who wanted to have the show recorded and shown on their network as the inaugural episode in a new series. They would then send out tapes of my show to other artists and encourage them to perform their own versions of my show. After some discussions, the title *Storyteller* emerged, and I was to be given credit as creator and inspiration for the series, and as an extra inducement, they offered me an opportunity to develop another series for them. However all these negotiations were verbal and needless to say nothing materialised other than a deal for my *Storyteller* show. It transpired that my show inspired a series that ran for many years and is still in reruns. It is a bit bittersweet because even though I was given a small credit for inspiring the series, that was all the acknowledgment I received, but no one can deny that my show set the standard and was the basis for all the shows that followed.

After the Westbeth run and the success of my *Storyteller* TV special, I started touring performing arts centres and small venues across America. One notable run was in Chicago, where the show was extended. We ended up playing there for three weeks. We even took the show to Japan, where it played to an audience of two thousand people, which for a largely spoken-word concert was a fantastic achievement. For the Japanese shows we had special translations printed out, and throughout the show I would hear the sound of pages politely turning en masse whenever I reached the end of a section. But it was in America that *Storyteller* was in continued demand. This was partly due to the success of the TV series I had inspired. By then it seemed like every artist of note had participated in their own version of the show, and I could not help feeling quietly proud of the fact that my show, which had started out as a book reading, helped inspire and launch a massive TV series.

The following year was spent touring with the *Storyteller* project, which had almost made it to Broadway. During this time, I recorded the live show, which was released by EMI, and returned for a further run at the Edinburgh festival. My musical of *Come Dancing* was workshopped at the National Theatre as I began to plan my first solo studio album. On a professional level things never seemed better, but throughout this time my marriage was finally coming to an end and my wife wanted to move back to Ireland and wanted to take my daughter with her.

BRINGING UP BABY, IRELAND, 1998

"I was walking on the coast road when the harbour
   came in view
It was there I saw the hilltop that I used to walk with you.
We'd sing of the old country now it's such a lonesome climb,
Our world faded once when you were mine.
Why is true love so difficult to find?
With you were here to see it with me one more time."

T he house was not visible from the road; it seemed to be surrounded with greenery, bushes, trees, and hedges, almost as if it had been deliberately hidden away, like a gem waiting to be discovered. Sometimes people don't pick the houses, the houses pick them. The sun came out especially for us on the day we looked at the house for the first time. Pam, the real-estate agent, was waiting at the bottom of the drive by the road, sitting on her bicycle, looking out at a river. It was quite a windy day, but the foliage around the house protected it from the gales that would often sweep across the southern coast of Ireland. The sunlight blasted in through the windows as we walked around the house, and I noticed that in every room there were fireplaces for burning solid fuel to keep out the bitter cold of winter.

There is always dampness in the air in County Cork. But the people not only learn to live with the discomfort, they create through it. That's part of the culture, part of the melancholy . . . sipping whiskey, scribbling notes by a coal fire in the land of poets and scholars. Sadness and joy exist side by side in rugged lush green fields of hope surrounded by a sea of tears. Grim-lipped laughter sends a message of cautious optimism tinged with the smile of bitter expectation that folly sometimes brings. It might be cold and damp but I know that the fire would keep them warm.

We decided immediately that this would be the house where my ex-wife would live and my child would grow up. I took Eva, who was then three years old, up to the room that would become her bedroom. This would be where the child would grow first into a teenager and then into a young woman. The two of us looked out the window at a bridge that crossed the river. In the far distance we saw the Irish Sea glimmering on the horizon. I glanced down and looked into Eva's eyes, which seemed fixed on the bridge just visible past the sloping garden of the house and the road that led up to it. It was as though we both had questions. What future lay ahead? I knew instinctively that the child's eyes held the truth; the future lay before her. I was full of acceptance that soon she would be leaving Surrey and the comfort of the English countryside for the wilder, more rugged terrain of southern Ireland.

I was determined to keep up contact with her. My ties with Ireland would soon be broken, except for my visits with Eva. Hopefully, I would still be able to watch her grow, albeit from afar and in my song that showed her progress into a young woman. The view from the window showed her life spread out before her.

"Little baby standing at the window crying,
Mama I don't wanna go out there
There's so many wild girls in here.
It's a cotton-wool world,
One of these days your gonna look back on this time
At Barbie dolls who always smile,
Old teddy bears stood up in a line
Micky Mouse Club generation it's your time.

Papa what are we becoming?
Do I have to go along with all this calculation?
Help me, where's the medication
Sometimes your gonna look back on this day
To change your life in a positive way
Headlines cry out, bring a national attention
Little girl saved by rock-and-roll intervention.

Oooohh can it be
Every day is a new revelation
Growing up is tough when you're ever so impatient
Baby standing in the window
Wondering where does every day go
Moments snap like a photograph
Baby your growing up so fast
Cartoon e-mail mobile phones, boys come around says she's leaving home
You're sad for a while then you start to glow, you gotta rock and roll
    playing on the car radio.

But ooohh can it be, baby boomers look at your kids
They throw away nearly everything you wanna give
Reject you now but surprise you one day
Bringing up baby's always been that way

Daddy don't you feel blue now,
I am looking after you now
Look at me
See how much I've grown
I won't leave you here all alone
One day I'm gonna raise my kids
Bringing up baby just like you did
Coming back here with all good intentions
Giving you rock-and-roll intervention.
Bringing up baby's never been any other way."

I imagined my daughter growing up in this wild, windswept place; going to school, to college, and to the local dance hall. I was looking for a way of retaining some connection between us, so I started a song that basically said that if I never saw her again, one day she would hear music that would remind her of me. The song "Otis Riffs" emerged because I'd always been inspired by the rhythm section in the Otis Redding band, particularly Al Jackson on the drums and guitarist Steve Cropper. Whenever Eva visited me in England, I tried to play her as much of my favourite music as I could so she would recognise what had inspired me, including those Otis riffs.

Once, on a trip to New York, I had travelled out of Shannon Airport, in the west of Ireland, where I'd started the song "Green Carnation," which describes how Oscar Wilde would often wear a green carnation in his buttonhole to show his Irish roots. The song itself was about my conflicting relationship with Ireland—the brilliance of the humour displayed by its literary bards in stark contrast to the rowdy Irishmen whom I'd seen in the airport, drinking heavily before they got on the flight to New York. The song delves into the contradictions of Irishness: the good, the bad, the ugly, the indifferent—but always lyrical, musical, and up for the *craic*. Often a brutally sharp yet delicate wit would be combined with unruly, intoxicated genius, especially in personalities like Brendan Behan, John B. Keane, and quite possibly dear old Oscar himself. I had often witnessed verbal brawls by impassioned poets in the bars around town and gazed in wonderment at their brilliant wordplay and violent linguistics—and felt relief at the lack of bloodshed when the pubs finally closed for the night. In Ireland, I would have gone home, lit a fire, and then watched the flames light up the room. Now, in New Orleans, there was just a clammy heat. I could feel it but couldn't see it. The darkness was all around me with those zombies and demons with pointy ears always nearby.

24

THE VOODOO WALK

"When the heat stops you sleeping at night
And the dead leaves rustle around
And the calmness keeps you awake
And you pace around the room

That's the zombie in you manifesting itself
And you can cry out loud and nobody can help
And it's a one-way sign to the gates of hell
And there's no way back
No, there's no way back
Ain't no wonder you can't sleep at night.

You just heard the voodoo call
So you pace around, do the zombie crawl
And you shuffle around in your prison cell
Doing the voodoo walk, dancing with yourself."

NEW ORLEANS, FEBRUARY 2004, NIGHT

This time I was awake. Or was I? Another night had passed, but my dreams were still merging with reality. By now I was pretty mobile on my crutches, so I made my way along the short corridor to look at the view doing what I was beginning to refer to as my voodoo walk. The large oak trees on some of the avenues in New Orleans sprawl skyward in haphazard directions, resembling something growing out of the head of Medusa—yet another ominous example of the sinister quality this whole place can exude. Even on a bright day the large, twisting branches can shut out the sunlight, yet when the light shoots through them it spreads a blanket of almost laser-like

281

optimism. When night falls it creates a mysterious underworld that has the French Quarter at its epicentre.

The very things that had attracted me to New Orleans in the first place—the music, the mystery, history, and folklore—had turned around and bitten me hard. My weird dreams and "spooked out" feelings intensified as I continued my recovery, so I spoke to a guy who frequented a nearby voodoo shop. He more or less confirmed what I had suspected: that the "voodoo" makes you realise that you have haunted places inside you. It's up to you or your subconscious just how many of those places you want to discover. In the end, though, you do the voodoo to yourself. I reacted to his assessment with a certain amount of skepticism, but perhaps my experiences over the previous months had been my haunted places giving me a warning—the shooting simply brought all these issues to a head.

Later that morning I had an appointment at the hospital. On the cab ride there, my elderly driver reflected about his experiences growing up in the Marigny. When I explained that it was the district where I was shot, he shook his head.

"I'd never live there now," he said.

"The violence all began in 1965, with Hurricane Betsy, when the whole of the Marigny got flooded. So many families moved out, and many workers came into New Orleans from the farms and poorer parts of Louisiana and brought violence with them. Then the drug culture took over, and one thing led to another."

He went on to say how different things were in his day.

"The original inhabitants of the Marigny had a handle on the city. They understood the dynamic. On the other hand, the new workers from the farms did not. It's not like other parts of America down here. The real problem will come when the Hispanic gangs come looking to take over. That's when something will erupt."

I listened to the driver without making any comment, because I was in no mood for a quarrel. At the end of the ride I pointed out that the man who shot me was not actually from the city but was, according to the police, a career criminal from Atlanta. The driver nodded. "Well, he wasn't a local, at least." As if it would have made any difference to me.

My hospital visits continued, and each day ticked away slowly while I waited for clearance to go back to London. On my next checkup at the hospital I was shown the X-ray of my leg. I was shocked to see the size of what the doctors described as "metalwork" in my right femur. My physician said that in addition to my regular physiotherapy, he would allow me to do light exercise at the New Orleans Athletic Club to try to keep my upper body in condition so I would be fit for my return journey. So still on my crutches, I went about my tentative workout in the gym. The New Orleans Athletic Club was a throwback to a more genteel southern style, with gentlemen's (and ladies') steam rooms, spacious changing areas, a swimming pool, saunas, and a luxurious cocktail bar. I imagined wealthy southern merchants smoking cigars in this semi-decadent grandeur while white-gloved waiters served drinks. I was brought back to reality by remembering the image of the X-ray showing my leg literally bolted together with a titanium rod. It made me think about the last Kinks album, *To the Bone*, and what a great album cover my X-ray would have made.

Recording that last, unplugged, live version of our catalogue in 1994 was, for the Kinks, one of the most liberating periods for us artistically. We chose the tracks and recorded them live at Konk, where they were also mixed. The playing was relaxed, as were the sessions themselves. Dave and I could even exchange a laugh or two, something that had been missing on our recent tours with the band. The reason it worked was because we were in our creative "home" at Konk, where there were no expectations from any record company; we just enjoyed the music and pleased ourselves. It made me realise how important a musical unit is and what great support I had received on our American adventure over the years from bassists Pete Quaife, John Dalton, and Jim Rodford, keyboardists John "the Baptist" Gosling and Ian Gibbons, and drummers Mick Avory and Bob Henrit. Then there was my brother, Dave, the irrepressibly original guitarist and vocalist who'd been with me through thick and thin since childhood. Always a thorn in my side, but close to my heart.

The last Kinks show anywhere in the world would be at the Norwegian Wood festival in Oslo on June 15, 1996. Though at the time we didn't know it would be the last date, there was a feeling of finality among the participants, as some of the songs took on an emotional edge. If it had been planned or announced it would have been too emotional, and the actual show would never have matched up to the significance of the event itself. It was just another gig.

HAUNTED PLACES

"Those terrified faces in haunted places
Jump from the shadows with poisoned arrows."

The success of *Storyteller* and the subsequent record of my solo show had launched me on a new career path, but the road, particularly for a solo artist, is an even more haunted, lonely place without the band. I had spent more and more time in America, but the characters within the songs were "stateless" exiles looking for a place to take refuge. Then finally, in New Orleans, the whole American dream had turned into a nightmare. I'd nearly died; now I was on the road to recovery in the physical sense, but the shock of the incident had sent me into a deep trauma. While I recovered from the physical wounds, all my past emotional demons came alive to sabotage all my triumphs.

In the real world, there was a tour of Europe for me to do as soon as I could walk on a stage, but I was not sure if I was ready; it was unclear whether I had the confidence ever to be able to play again. The tour had been set up before I had left the UK. Now these dates were in danger of being cancelled, but I knew that if it was humanly possible, the right medical help would get me onstage. As in the past, somehow, with the help of medical technology, the show would go on with the aid of that "quick fix" mentality I'd experienced all my life as a touring musician. The ruthless mind-set of the touring business was: "Get the people back on the road, get them functioning, get them up and running, as long as they fulfil their commitments. Then let them deal with the physical and emotional debris later. Pamper them; give them all the drugs they need (legal or otherwise) just to get through. Once the tour is over they can be dropped, then left alone to look after their own wreckage."

Over the years this attitude had probably contributed to my current situation, but now I was looking to change all that and make a fresh start. I had
seen numerous other singers and performers end up as casualties, but I was
determined not to be one of them. Till then I would have to obey the doctors
and take the medication. I would come through it, after all. Rock singers are
invincible. Aren't they? Without a tour entourage, I had to get better and
learn to fend for myself. I took the bold step of going to get my own medication rather than ask someone else.

A CAB BEEPED ITS HORN and waited with its engine running outside the
front gate of Bob and Jeanne's house. I made my way down the drive as fast
as I could on my crutches so the driver wouldn't leave. Eventually I got in
and asked the driver to take me to the nearest Winn-Dixie drive-through
pharmacy. The driver turned around to stare me in the eyes. He looked like
a beached whale, with rolls of fat hanging over onto the passenger seat; his
voice was deep, mischievous, and sonorous. He could see that I was nervous
and vulnerable looking.

"I can take you the safe, long way, and that will cost fifty dollars round-
trip, or I can take you the quick, cheap way—through the projects, where we
might get shot at."

There was no choice.

"I'll take the long, scenic route. That'll be fine."

The driver seemed disappointed, even though I promised I'd give him
a big tip.

"That's a shame, because I carry my own gun in the glove compartment
in case we come up against something."

"Why would you do that and risk getting shot at?" I asked. Then he took
out the revolver and showed it to me.

"Because I enjoy it."

WHEN I ARRIVED BACK AT THE HOUSE with medication from the pharmacy, I scurried through the front door on my crutches and climbed the

stairs to my room as fast as I could, but not before taking a beer from the fridge to wash down a painkiller.

As evening fell, I listened to WWOZ as it played some slow, hypnotic, mournful tuba-led jazz. I wrote in my notebook:

> *"The soul is an undercurrent—like a river running through the*
> *senses—in between conversations and superficial moods.*
> *The spirit-soul has almost an alternative plot to the real and conscious*
> *world. It has another flow to it.*
> *Stay close to your dreams throughout life and eventually the two will*
> *flow together."*

That night I dreamed a song. In my dream my wounds were healed as I walked down the street on a bright summer's day. If I believed in it enough it would become a reality. I'd be ready to play again. I'd go onstage in a wheelchair if I had to. The show would go on, even if I might be falling apart inside.

25

A STREET CALLED HOPE

"I'm walking down a street called hope
I'm gonna find some satisfaction in my soul.
I'm leaving that street called fear;
Blow that negativity right outta here.

No rush, no push, no worry
I am not in too much hurry.
No panic driving me, no more fake anxiety haunting me,
Don't want to walk into trouble do we?

No more speedin' down that dark highway
I'm on that street called hope
And it's taking me there one way, some day . . .
I'll find my home."

After a few weeks recuperating at Bob and Jeanne's, my last stay in New Orleans was at an apartment in the Tréme. By now I was becoming quite a local celebrity—"the English guy who got shot and survived." One day during the festival season I was invited to a cocktail party at my neighbour's house. She was unfamiliar with my name or my music, but she knew my initials were R.D., so she called me by the first name that came into her head, Mr. Reece Daniels. "Hey, meet Mr. Reece Daniels; apparently he's a big-shot rock star." "Hey, Reece, would you like a drink?"

After a while I gave up trying to explain that my name was Ray Davies, but it didn't matter—I was accepted, and the initials R.D. or Mr. Reece were good enough for me.

As my recovery wound down, I was determined to continue my discussions with the music department at John McDonogh. I attended and videotaped some band rehearsals at the school, where my crutches and gunshot wound seemed to give me special "cool" credentials with the students. I wrote several short stories that would form the basis of a musical outline for the piece I was developing for the school. After discussing it with the school principal, I concluded that the project could not get started until I had finished mixing and then promoting the album *Other People's Lives* when it was released.

Meanwhile, there was some business to conclude with the local police department. One morning I had a meeting with an assistant district attorney at a coffee shop on Esplanade Avenue. He was accompanied by a bodyguard because he said he was concerned that he might get attacked or shot at by some criminals he had helped convict. This did not make me feel at ease, but he was doing his best to befriend me.

His pleasant manner didn't change but all of a sudden he got serious.

"On the afternoon of January 4, 2004 . . ."

I felt like I was in a bad scene from *Dragnet*.

The attorney launched into a question.

"What kind of sentence would you like this man to have?"

"I just want the man who shot and robbed me to go to jail and serve what would be a normal sentence. I just want justice to be done."

He shook his head. "That's easier said than done." What did he mean? I was already not feeling too good about my situation since some people who worked on my case insinuated in the press that I had been in the wrong to protect myself, J.J., and our property when I chased the mugger who'd stolen our stuff—I saw it as defending our lives. I was flabbergasted to find others questioning my actions.

I finished the meeting and said I would be available in the future to give evidence in court, provided I wasn't in England working.

That was a plus for my case according to the assistant D.A. He indicated to me that some victims were reluctant to give evidence in court because they feared recrimination from the criminals. This case was different, though, as I was eager to go to court. They had caught and arrested the driver, who was related to the alleged shooter. They were offering the driver a plea bargain so that he'd help them with the case against the shooter, which would enable them to issue a warrant for the shooter—who might have to be extradited from another state. That concerned me. I didn't want my case strung out for years. On top of this I was still pretty shaken up by the events. I needed to get back to London to fulfil my obligations there as well as continue my recovery.

I stayed in constant communication with the local police department about my mugging. Ironically and somewhat mysteriously, a court hearing had been scheduled for a time when I had been planning to be in England to receive my CBE. I had no legal representation in the States at this time, although the DA's office was in touch with my solicitor in London from time to time. But I felt that the DA was very vague about court appearances and the legal process in general. Yet it was a sort of organised chaos—there was some method to the disorganised manner in which they worked the legal system.

I wanted justice but I felt alone and confused and suspicious . . . and maybe a bit paranoid due to what I had just gone through. As time went on I even tried to keep my travel plans a secret in case a court hearing would be announced for a day when I would be out of town. I don't know if there was a connection or not. It was probably a coincidence but it made me feel bad. However, more than once when I was abroad, I would be given only a few days' notice, and if I was not there in court it meant that the case would eventually get dropped because I would be deemed a "no-show"—and who was I to tell the court when to hear cases.

Eventually, my case would be thrown out after I could not attend a hearing in 2007. I don't know the official legal reasons but I do not feel I received justice. I chose to stay in the studio in London to mix tracks for my new album and fulfil my recording commitments over returning to New Orleans.

THERE WERE SOME UP MOMENTS when I was visiting New Orleans for the last time in 2004. I was still hobbling around the French Quarter on my crutches one afternoon when David Bowie called me on my mobile to invite me to his show that night, which I attended with a few friends. Our bands had been on tour together in the 1960s, when as David Jones he'd played saxophone in a group called the Manish Boys. We'd been in contact via email recently so I thought it would be considered rude not to go to his concert even though I must have looked very un–rock and roll on my crutches. Afterward I chatted with David, who looked slightly drained by the exhausting tour he was on. It was good to talk to another Brit at this time, even though he seemed visibly shocked to see me having to use crutches.

The last time I had seen David Bowie was a few years earlier, when we had performed together at a Tibet House benefit at Carnegie Hall. At that time we were unsure how to approach singing a duet of "Waterloo Sunset." Eventually, we'd decided that the best way to get through the song was to impersonate one another, which we did in a chameleon-style vocal parody. We'd both "hammed it up" onstage at Carnegie, but now, after his show in New Orleans, one of us was drained from hard touring and the other was using crutches to hobble around. What a difference just a few years make in the life of a rock and roller.

After his show in New Orleans, David introduced me to Trent Reznor of Nine Inch Nails, and when I explained that I was due to start mixing the remaining tracks on my album, Trent offered his studio for me to mix in. A few days later he showed me around the facility, which was ironically called Nothing Studios; in studio terms, it actually had everything that a mixing engineer needed.

As he gave me the tour, I found him to be a very clean-cut, astute, organised, and accommodating fellow with a good business head on his shoulders—befitting his music, which I found equally astute, well organised, and businesslike. At the time, his hair was cut in the popular swivelled-to-one-side look. The curious thing was that nearly everybody who worked at his studio had the same haircut, as if it were some sort of uniform that his employees were to wear. I found everyone at Nothing Studios to be really helpful, so much so that I considered mixing some tracks there, although I thought twice about getting the same haircut. I had some multitrack tapes flown over from London so that I could mix some tracks for my album while I recovered and waited for a court hearing. Later, a mix-down engineer named Phil Bodger came over from London to assist me. One thing that struck me about New Orleans was the lack of good studios to choose from. I would have expected that, being a city known for its music, the place would have had many more establishments at which musicians could record their music. I concluded that New Orleans is all about great live music; the recording is secondary to the experience, but if the tape is running for posterity, it can only be a bonus. I was fortunate to meet Trent, who allowed me to use his well-equipped studio. After mixing a couple of tracks there, I was cleared to travel, so I decided to cut my losses and go back to England to finish mixing the record at Konk in London.

While I was packing up my things at the apartment for the last time, Alex Chilton stopped by. He sat down with me in the living room and asked me to write some songs for an album he wanted to make. Not just one song—he wanted me to write the whole album. I was kind of flattered by this because he had great credentials of his own. He gave me one of his Big Star albums to take with me, and I said I would give it some thought.

As Alex left to cycle home, I looked out the window. I saw a neighbour trimming leaves off a fence, tidying up his modest backyard. Why had I given all that up? I could have been in North London, tidying up my backyard on a day off if I hadn't toured so much. Why did I continue to keep going? It was America that made me continue. Maybe I should have changed my path long ago, learned another career, found an alternative—but something kept driving me on. The songs.

That man trimming the leaves on that working-class street in New Orleans seemed to have everything worked out. Compared to him I was still a confused human being; a drifter who had nowhere to stop. I wanted to be content—trim the fence, mow the lawn. I had that once and lost it. Something inside me had to get back to conquer America, but it was stopped by a mugger's bullet. It was a symbolic moment, but just the same, I couldn't worry about things I had no control over. If I dwelled on it, it would bring me down.

Then the man stopped trimming the leaves because his wife started shouting for him to help her with the laundry. A terrible quarrel started, and the situation kicked off into something violent. The man pushed his wife away as he got into his car and drove off in a huff. On his way out of the driveway he nearly collided with an oncoming truck. Maybe my problems were not so bad compared to other people's lives.

THE DAY BEFORE MY FLIGHT BACK TO THE UK, Bob Tannen took me for a final drive around the city. After we ate some lunch at a Creole place, Bob drove me to see the pump stations and pointed out the levees that New Orleans was so dependent on. Bob and Jeanne were still active in the "save the wetlands" campaign in the South. Most of these wetlands are either reclaimed, like much of the Mississippi delta, or below sea level, like New Orleans, which is in constant danger of flooding. The pump stations looked to be in a state of ill repair, and the levees needed stabilizing. Bob was concerned about what would happen to the city if at any time undue stress were put on these defences in an emergency. There was simply no contingency plan in place in the event that the unthinkable happened. "If those levees go, it could be catastrophic. Still, we have to live with it." Bob had tried to meet with President Bush with some other lobbyists when Bush had visited New Orleans during his reelection campaign. One of the subjects on Bob's associates' agenda had been the need for more federal help to sustain the cities' infrastructure. I'd watched Bush give his speech on local TV, but was saddened to hear that he'd taken a helicopter and left town before Bob and his campaigning friends had a chance to speak to him.

On the day I left, the insurance company finally "delivered" in a spectacularly ostentatious manner. They picked me up in a stretch limo, complete with a TV and cocktail bar, from my humble apartment. On the ride to the airport, I pondered the good as well as the bad times I'd had in the city. I'd had so many ambitions when I first arrived: I still wanted to return to start a music program for the kids at John McDonogh High School at some point. I also wanted to help Bob and Jeanne raise funds for the local marching band,

and assist them with their arts projects. Until then I would take life a day at a time. For better or worse, my adventures in Americana had made me a wiser person as well as giving me the will to put myself back on track again. I asked the limo driver to take a short detour past the street where I'd been shot.

These experiences would not stop me from seeing the funny side, but just the same, I never forget a face and one day, if I return, vengeance will indeed be mine. Meanwhile, I'd celebrate my origins rather than hide them. The incident in New Orleans had given me a limp, that if not treated could turn into a permanent voodoo walk. The next time though, if I saw that zombie on the street he wouldn't spook me out as much. I'd recognise him when I saw him coming and even rewrite an old song to sing called "You Really Shot Me." Then as he did his dance on the street corner, I'd smack the zombie over the head with my Fender Telecaster and I'd kick him in the balls as he crumpled to the ground. Then I'd strap one of Dave's amplifiers to his head, turn the volume up to eleven, and hit a power chord so loud that it would blow the bastard's brains out. Then as he squirmed around in the gutter vomiting puss all over his baseball cap, I would shout defiantly into his grovelling, puke-ridden face, "Now don't do that again! D'ya hear me? In the future don't fuck with a Kink or else."

ROCK 'N' ROLL COWBOYS

As the car took the scenic route it made its way out of the picturesque French Quarter and into the more generic suburbs that are typical of any American city, I remembered the ending of *Shane*, in which Alan Ladd, as the hero, keels over as if he had been shot. Just when you think he is going to fall off the horse, the stallion rears up, and Shane looks back and seems to wave before heading for the mountains, where the movie ends.

In another classic western, two aging gunfighters are about to meet their end. I remember falling asleep in a hotel somewhere while watching that movie and thinking to myself, "I relate to these characters." One of them had been mortally wounded in his last gunfight, and the dialogue goes something like: "We are from another time . . . . It's the best way to go . . . . We weren't meant to grow old somewhere . . . . We knew a bullet was waiting for us." In my real world I fell asleep before the end of the film, but the scene played on in my subconscious. The movie became one of many that have put me to sleep over the years. The next sunrise, I had to travel to my next gig. Sometimes at the end of a long tour, I think about the last scene of that movie.

"Rock 'n' roll cowboys where do you go now
From the final shoot-out at the O.K. Corral?
Do you give up the chase like an old retiree
Or do you stare in the face of new adversaries?
Night falls, the coyote calls underneath a full moon
Hey you all, it's the final call at the last-chance saloon.
Your time passed, now everyone asks for your version of history.
Did you live in a dream or did you live in reality?

Rock 'n' roll cowboys on the old wagon train
You had your time that can't come again.
You rode the prairie and you always stood proud
So tall in the saddle and your head was not bowed.
We need great new leaders to speak to the crowd
And show us a better place than we are now.

Pity the good guys are not around in our hour of need
In these most uncertain times of money, corruption, and villainy
But we just can't sit like good old boys
Trading stories and living in old memories.

Do we live in a dream
Or do we live in reality?"
See the sun, the day has come, and the night is just a memory
Do you live in a dream or do you live in reality?"

Like the old Wild West, the rock tour was a simple affair. You knew who the bad guys were, and the good guys always wore backstage passes. If a band blazed a trail that started in New York and Boston, you knew that in a few weeks they would get bushwhacked in Baltimore or break up in Oregon. Those who survived the journey west would return as changed men with different viewpoints. The old-style tour had its own survival kit . . . its own list of casualties. In the world of the pioneers of post-'60s rock, a new adventure was always waiting at the next stop on the journey. After dying a death in front of a tiny crowd in Springfield, Illinois, you'd have a chance to redeem yourself in front of a sellout crowd in Chicago. Each gig was a chance to start anew after a disaster the night before. The trails were endless, and it's a long drive home to Tarzana. By the time you reached Arizona, you still had three weeks to go. You reached California only to be told by your record company that your album had lost its bullet in *Billboard*, meaning that it's time to start the tour all over again.

EPILOGUE

SECURITY

"Just a drifter who's far from home
Given up everything that I once owned
Now I'm ten a penny in a world that promises no guarantees,
I crossed the border didn't hesitate,
Left behind all my friends and now my conscience aches,
Now I'm one of many trying to get a break with a new identity,
Security.
I'm always followed by that shadow man,
When the sunshines he's close at hand,
Reminding me of just who I am . . .
Security.
Though I'm a stranger in a foreign land,
When I'm standing by my shadow man,
He keeps reminding me of just who I am . . .
'Cos I've got this feelin' when I'm freewheeling
That I'll never settle down
As the train passes town after town
Day turns to night and still the engine sounds
To me it sounds like security."

Songs are like friends who comfort you so you don't feel alone. Believe in them hard enough and they come true. I wanted to say good-bye to my shadow man, even though the song was in my head and could bring him to life at any moment.

I was to be wheelchair-assisted at the airport on my trip home. My ostentatious limo pulled up at the drop-off at Louis Armstrong, where an airport worker was waiting to wheel me to check in. Unbelievably, Travis Davis was standing there at the terminal, waiting for me at the curb. He opened the door of the limo and popped his head in. He looked as suave as ever. "I couldn't let you leave without wishing you bon voyage."

Travis helped me out and told the airport worker "It's okay, man. I'll take over from here. I'll take him through check-in, and then you can take over at security." The worker pocketed Travis's tip and followed along behind.

I was extremely flattered that Travis had actually bothered to come to see me off, and a bit taken aback because I had really only ever encountered him at night, in clubs or in bars because he must have slept in late. He helped me through to the check-in and waited while I got my seat assignment; then we had a quick cup of coffee.

I noticed that Travis was carrying a small black case.

"What's in the case, man?"

Travis looked a little sheepish.

"Ah, that's my horn. I'm thinking of taking up the trumpet again. There's no money in the bar business. I need to get some gigs."

"I think that's a great idea, Travis."

I needed to know the answer to something that had been bothering me for years.

"Why did you change your name all those years ago?" I asked him. "'Travis' sounds more like a country singer's name than a jazz trumpeter's."

"Well, when you play the trumpet and your name is Gabriel, it sometimes gets embarrassing at gigs. You know musicians. They can be merciless."

I could see that he was getting embarrassed, so I stopped enquiring. Then he continued talking about my situation as he started to slowly wheel me down the concourse toward security.

He asked what all my recent dramas had been about and whether I would ever return to New Orleans. I said that I would like to do the project with the school marching band but I actually didn't know if I would return. He warned me about coming back to testify in court. It might get tricky if the criminal were extradited.

"These people have been known to take reprisals. They come back to town just to kill witnesses." Travis said that he still believed it was some inside setup.

I shrugged my shoulders. "I don't believe so; it was just an accident in the wrong place at the wrong time—that sort of thing."

Travis squinted his eyes as he shook his head.

"No. These people have a way of behaving down here. Still, you're safe now; you're almost on the plane."

We sat and watched a bunch of arriving tourists walk though to baggage claim. They were already wearing their Mardi Gras beads, even though it wasn't Mardi Gras. Then Travis gave me a long, serious look but seemed to be focusing on his own life. Talking about himself.

"Maybe that's why my own relationships never worked out. They got in the way of my work."

Travis seemed to be momentarily lost in memories of his own world. Then the smile came back as if he'd reached a conclusion.

"You know, Raymondo, some singers are like actors. They're no good without the right lines. You, my boy, need songs to exist. Without the lines to express the way you feel, you just run away."

I took slight exception to what he had said, but I knew he was on the right track. Nevertheless I tried a smart-ass reply.

"Nah—I'm not running away. I have to be back in London to collect my CBE from the queen. I'm gonna take my daughter Eva to Buckingham Palace."

Travis gave a wry smile.

"So it was all about Eva, then?"

I looked at him and thought hard as I pondered over the relationships I had lost as a result of years of travelling. That's what Eva represented to Travis. All those lost relationships.

"All about Eva?" I replied. "I guess it always was."

As we moved towards the security area, where I was to be handed over and then escorted to the gate, I continued talking. I wanted it to be man-to-man, but as the words came out I still sounded like a fan.

"You know, Travis, you seem to have popped up at every crucial point in my life. You gave me inspiration at the start when I needed it. If you had been our big brother, maybe Dave and I would have gotten along better."

Travis whispered back, "That's okay, Ray. See you down the road. I'll hand you over to security now."

I continued speaking without acknowledging what he had said.

"I always wanted to tell you that . . . it's strange, but I feel as though you have been my guardian angel."

I looked over my shoulder for a response, but Travis was already gone; in his place was the airport escort. I looked around the airport, but Travis had disappeared in the crowd.

As I was wheeled through security I heard the distant sound of a trumpet coming through the airport PA system. For a moment I thought it was Travis playing a tune to send me on my way, but when the track moved on, a voice came on that I recognised as being Louis Armstrong singing "Do You Know What It Means to Miss New Orleans?"

I sat on the plane as it taxied along the runway and concluded that another problem had been solved. Nearly everyone I'd met in the city said "N'awlins," rolling the words "New" and "Orleans" together. Louis Armstrong was born in New Orleans, and when he was singing the song he pronounced it the way I would have said it: "New Orleens." If anyone knew the right way to pronounce it, Satchmo did. On the other hand, maybe it rhymed better. The song made him sing it that way.

Weeks later, on Saint Patrick's Day, I took Eva to Buckingham Palace, where I received my "gong" from the queen. As she put the medal over my head, Her Majesty said something like ". . . so many songs." I wanted her to add something about the nasty chap who shot me, but I suppose that would have lowered the tone of the occasion.

OVER THE FOLLOWING MONTHS I continued my recovery before going back in the studio to finish mixing my record *Other People's Lives*.

The very last track I mixed for the album was called "The Getaway (Lonesome Train)." Hearing it played back in my studio in North London, I remembered that on one of the last weekends I spent in New Orleans I'd gone down to Bay Saint Louis, Mississippi, which was humourously referred to as the Redneck Riviera. There I watched a freight train roll endlessly through the landscape and across the river and realised how transient my life had been; that I'd never really settled anywhere despite the good intentions of the people I'd stayed with and the homes I had. I always seemed to be on my way to somewhere else. No wonder I couldn't hold down a relationship—there was always another record and a tour to promote that record, which meant another set of plans to change . . . and my life would have to be put on hold yet again; I was still not ready to end my journey. In a strange way, that mugger's bullet was trying to tell me to take stock of my life. New Orleans had taught me another lesson. Always trust your dreams and stay in touch with the spirit world. We can't make music without it.

I thought about two of my uncles who worked on the railroads in London, and how the rolling sounds of the trains passing near where I lived as a child had always stayed with me. The railroad must have been the inspiration for classic songs like "Long Lost John," "Rock Island Line," and "Smokestack Lightning." It was certainly the inspiration for my own "Last of the Steam-Powered Trains." There have always been trains in my life . . . always rolling with the promise that they could be taking me somewhere else, giving me that optimistically secure feeling of knowing we are always moving on to something better. But, as my song "The Getaway" says at the end, it can be a "lonesome train" if you don't get it right. Still, I live in hope that one day I'll get it right. That someday . . . I'll find my way home.

INDEX

Numbers beginning with *P* denote pages containing photographs and captions.

LYRIC CREDITS

All Song Lyrics Reproduced by Permission of Davray Music Ltd. /
Sony/ATV Music Ltd, London, W1F 9LD

Words and music by Raymond Douglas Davies © Raymond Douglas Davies

2: "The Real World" (2007)

4, 35: "Empty Room" (ca. 2000)

7–8: "Next-Door Neighbour"
(recorded 2002, released 2006)

12–13: "Expectations"
(recorded 1983, released 1985)

18–19: "The Tourist"
(recorded 2003, released 2005)

20: "The Getaway (Lonesome Train)"
(recorded 2002, released 2006)

77, 83, 87: "Thanksgiving Day" (recorded
2003–5, released 2005)

97, 103: "Celluloid Heroes" (1972)

125: "Sleepwalker"
(recorded 1976, released 1977)

137, 138, 139: "A Rock 'n' Roll Fantasy"
(1978)

148: "Misfits"
(recorded 1977, released 1978)

157, 173, 174: "Better Things" (1981)

160: "Low Budget" (1979)

165: "Catch Me Now I'm Falling" (1979)

182, 229: "After the Fall"
(recorded 2002, released 2006)

190: "Things Are Gonna Change
(The Morning After)"
(recorded 2002, released 2006)

191, 194–95: "Morphine Song" (2007)

208: "State of Confusion" (1983)

220: "Animal" (1996)

227: "Working at the Factory" (1986)

232–33: "Is There Life After Breakfast?"
(recorded 2003–4, released 2006)

234: "The Road" (1987)

237: "Just Passing Through" (1987)

238–39: "Scattered"
(recorded 1990, released 1993)

242–44: "Here," from musical 80 Days,
1988

244–45: "A Place in Your Heart," from
musical 80 Days, 1988

248: "Phobia"
(recorded 1991, released 1993)

252: "Still Searchin' "
(recorded 1990, released 1993)

271: "Storyteller" (1998)

277: "One More Time" (2007)

281: "The Voodoo Walk" (2008)

UNRELEASED

21: "The Art of Movin' On"

22–23: "Wings of Fantasy"

26, 37–38: "The Great Highway"

33: "Back in the Day"

68: "The Big Weird"

82: "Honest"

140, 147, 179–80: "The Big Guy"

278–79: "Bringing Up Baby"

287: "A Street Called Hope"

296: "Security"

UNTITLED: 29, 42, 50, 90–92, 226,
263, 284, 294

PICTURE CREDITS

[Numbers refer to insert pages]

1T: Courtesy Ray Davies; 1B: © Michael Ochs Archives/Getty Images

2T: © Pictorial Press Ltd/Alamy; 2B: © Donaldson Collection/Michael Ochs Archives/
Getty Images

3: © Dick Barnatt/Redferns/Getty Images

4T: © NBC / Getty Images; 4B: © Lisa J. Kristal

5TL: Courtesy Ray Davies; 5TR: Courtesy Ian Gibbons; 5B: Courtesy Ray Davies

6T: © Ebet Roberts; 6B: © Claude Gassian

7: © Mark Duncan/AP Photo

8T: © Skip Bolen/WireImage/Getty Images; 8B: © Peter Simpson/AP Photo